The Sack of Rome

THE SACK OF
ROME

E.R.Chamberlin

B.T. Batsford Ltd
London

First published 1979
Copyright E.R. Chamberlin 1979

Filmset in 10 on 12 pt. 'Monophoto' Imprint by
Servis Filmsetting Ltd, Manchester

Printed by
Redwood Burn Ltd, Trowbridge and Esher
for the Publisher B.T. Batsford Ltd,
4 Fitzhardinge Street, London W1H 0AH

ISBN 0 7134 1645 9

Contents

Acknowledgments

The Author and Publishers are grateful to the following for permission to reproduce the illustrations in this book: Anderson-Giraudon, fig. 13; Bibliothèque Nationale, Paris, fig. 6; Giraudon, figs 4 and 5; Internat. Bilder-Agentur, Zurich, figs 8 and 11; Lauros-Giraudon, fig. 16 (painting in the Louvre, Paris); the Mansell Collection, figs 1, 2, 3, 7, 9, 12, 14 and 15; the Radio Times Hulton Picture Library, fig. 10.

List of Illustrations

PROLOGUE

Breakthrough

Shortly after dawn on Sunday, 5 May 1527 early-risers in Rome became aware of a cold, flickering light that seemed to be moving up the steep side of Monte Mario, the hill that raised its green, rounded bulk across the river just outside the north-western limits of the city. Those watchers who were interested enough, or apprehensive enough, to follow the course of this curious light noticed that it disappeared shortly before reaching the crest of the hill, reappeared on the other side descending towards the valley, disappeared again and reappeared on the side of the Janiculum Hill. There it changed its form from a long, sinuous river to a stationary but growing mass. By this time, the fully risen sun disclosed the source of the light to the keen-eyed. What the watchers had seen were the rays of the sun reaching across the shadowed bowl of Rome to be reflected from the steel helmets and breastplates of a very large armed force that was making its way outside the city walls from the northern to the western gates of the city.

By mid-morning, the force had ceased its steady, cautious movement and was established at two main points, the rearguard on Monte Mario and the headquarters on the Janiculum itself. Traditionally, the Janiculum was Rome's weak spot, the point from which an enemy commander would most prefer to launch an attack even though it meant crossing the Tiber to get at the heart of the city. The force that was now establishing itself was, indubitably, an enemy force. In theory, it was the mailed arm of the Holy Roman Emperor, His Imperial Majesty Charles V, Lord of Europe and, according to Christian theory, of all the world, who happened to be at war with His Holiness Clement VII, Bishop of Rome and, according to Christian theory, Vicar of Christ over all the world. In fact, the imperial army consisted of some 22,000 men of three races and two religions whose only common goal – the destruction of the city before them – was shared not through thirst for military glory nor through religious fanaticism but through the simple knowledge that if they did not succeed in capturing Rome then, very shortly, most of them would be dead of starvation. The leader of the army was an exiled French nobleman, Charles, Duke of Bourbon, commonly held to be a renegade and traitor to his king. His thoughts at this stage are not recorded, but it may be assumed that they were as

9

desperate as those of the most desperate of his ragged followers, for whether he
succeeded or failed in capturing Rome he had arrived at the end of his journey.

Within the city, the morning brought excitement and fear but not, as yet,
outright panic. For most, the idea that Rome could share the fate of lesser cities
was, quite literally, unthinkable. Again and again over the centuries hostile
armies had assembled under the massive brown walls and made their ritual
gestures of hatred and threat. Some had even entered the city but, invariably,
bribery, judicious assassination or the skilful playing-off of enemy against
enemy dispersed the threat. The army at present encamped outside the walls
was unusually large; but unusual, too, was its state of dilapidation. The
garrison on the walls confirmed what had been reported over many weeks: this
imperial army was composed of tattered men on the brink of exhaustion, many
of them actually starving. Admittedly, there were only 8,000 professional
soldiers in the pay of the city – nowhere near sufficient to man the immensely
long circuit of walls. But a snug, well-found city could hold out indefinitely
provided that the enemy had no cannon. And this enemy was as short on
cannon as they were short on everything else: they did not even possess siege
equipment. The garrison watched while this tatterdemalion army rooted about
among the vineyards, pulling up stakes and lashing them together to make very
rickety ladders. It was exceedingly trying for the owners of the vineyards, in
particular for Cardinal Francesco Armellino whose large and luxuriant orchard
ran right up to where the city wall skirted the base of the Janiculum; but
damaged or destroyed vineyards were to be expected as the result of the passage
of even a friendly army. This, it seemed, was the worst that was to be expected,
confirming the high hopes of Rome's commander-in-chief, Renzo da Ceri,
who, only a few days before, had loftily rejected the offer of substantial
reinforcements from his allies in the League. Later on the Sunday afternoon he
contemptuously rejected the ritual demand for ransom brought by the enemy's
herald.

Not all the citizens shared Renzo's confidence. The canny or fortunate ones
had long since fled the city, taking with them their jewellery and plate and silks
and brocades. But there were not many of these. His Holiness, Rome's spiritual
father and very earthly lord, had apparently disliked the vote of no confidence
implied by the first trickle away of wealthy refugees and had promptly issued
his edict that no other citizen should leave the city except for very good reason.
Their movement thereby abruptly halted, the wealthy made what shift they
could to prepare for the future in a city which seemed to be under siege even
while the enemy was a good week's march away. Some of the smaller burghers –
those embarrassed with the possession of bulky bullion or gold-plate but with
no really safe place to store it – adopted the most primitive of all means and
simply dug a hole in which to bury their belongings. That buried treasure was
to buy the lives of some. Others – the stupid or the plain greedy or the
unfortunate – would surrender their lives to keep the secret of their treasure's
locality; and it would remain buried for centuries, to be brought to light at last
by the spades of casual diggers.

The poor took what comfort they could from the promise of Divine protection as enunciated by their Holy Father. In any case, there was, for them, no alternative. The great men of the city – the nobles and the cardinals and the rich merchants – withdrew into their palaces. A generation ago the great buildings of the city would have been primarily fortresses. But as the golden sun of the Renaissance had mounted in the Roman sky, so crude needs of defence had given way gradually to aesthetics. There were over fifty palaces now in the heart of the city. In the May sunshine they gleamed and glowed, crisp new buildings that expressed in stone the joyous confidence of this new age. Even now there was no particular urge to turn homes again into fortresses. The ordinary domestic machinery could take care of any sudden influx, for the major-domos were accustomed to cater for a household of a hundred or more members.

Throughout the Sunday the tension increased. In her well-supplied, well-garrisoned palace on the Corso the Lady Isabella d'Este decided that, though there was really no need for alarm, a few precautions were in order. All that week her son, Federigo, Marquis of Mantua, had been urging her to leave Rome and to return home to the safety of Mantua. But she was a strong-willed woman and refused to do any such thing until her mission in Rome was accomplished. On the other hand, she did not feel that her courage would be diminished if tempered with prudence: a messenger was accordingly sent hastening to Charles, Duke of Bourbon, with the request that he should place her palace under his direct protection, should the worst happen. She could not share the prevailing Roman view of Charles of Bourbon as a species of ravening Antichrist, for he was, after all, her nephew. Only a few months ago, indeed, he had turned up at her palace in Mantua after his escape from France, hollow-cheeked, staring-eyed, glad to claim his Italian kinship. She had held out a hand to the wretched young man then and it was only reasonable that she should turn to him for assurance now, particularly as one of his staff officers was her other son, Ferrante. Such tangled loyalties were commonplace and Lady Isabella had no doubts about her ability to survive unscathed any unpleasantness that might befall Rome over the next day or so. Her precautions taken, she turned to the business of restoring order and calm in the palace. Nearly 3,000 people – mostly ladies of the better sort – had taken advantage of her hospitably open door and crowded in, and the domestic chaos and hysteria offended Isabella Gonzaga far more than any theoretical threat from the troops commanded by her respectful nephew.

In the palace of his rich friend Alessandro del Bene, the goldsmith Benvenuto Cellini surveyed his preparations with his customary profound self-satisfaction. Del Bene had prevailed upon Cellini, a fellow Florentine, to exercise his talents as a soldier in fortifying the palace and, for a handsome consideration, Cellini had graciously consented to do so. Over the previous week he had set energetically about recruiting a bodyguard and now, on this Sunday morning, fifty young bravoes swaggered round del Bene's palace, eating and drinking generously at his expense. Satisfied that his friend's palace was well and truly protected, Cellini took himself off to the western walls of the city. The Tiber bridges presented their normal appearance: no preparations had been made to demolish them, and that this elementary precaution had not been taken told again of Renzo da Ceri's confidence – or stupidity. Cellini was openly and loudly contemptuous of Rome's military protector and lost no opportunity to bait his bodyguard.

In the beautiful palace called the Cancelleria, not far from the Florentine quarter, the sixteen-year-old Marcello Alberini was settling down with the remnants of his family, looking to the immediate future with excitement rather than fear. The palace was now the property of the Vatican and the Alberini family had no particular right to be there, but Marcello's father had pulled a few strings among his relatives attached to the papal court. He had no fear of the imperial invaders: on the contrary, he welcomed them, for he was fiercely anti-clerical and regarded those ragged marauders outside the walls as angels of vengeance bearing the fiery brands that would cleanse the city of papal iniquity. But fiery brands were apt to be indiscriminate and a sensible man took what precautions were available. His sixteen-year-old son was the last survivor of the family, for plague had taken off a boy and two girls the previous year, and Giovanni Battista Alberini therefore compounded with his conscience and sought shelter for the boy under a priestly roof.

From the flat drum of the vast circular tomb now known as the Castello Sant' Angelo the Castellan Antonio Santa Croce looked across the brown roofs of Rome towards the vast builders' yard that was the basilica of St Peter. It was traditionally from that direction that danger would come from an attacking enemy. From his vantage point he could see the city walls, distant perhaps half a mile from him, and beyond them the slope of the Janiculum whose spring-green grass was now trampled over by the milling mass of soldiery. The range was great, but not too great for the bronze cannon that poked their snouts out of the embrasures of the battlements. Cannon was an ideal weapon against massed infantry and the infantry of this particular army, Santa Croce noted gratefully, was massing itself in an altogether obliging manner. Admittedly, they had little choice: without artillery the enemy general had no alternative but to try and overwhelm the garrison at one point by sheer numbers. But even if they did break through, the favoured inhabitants of Sant' Angelo had nothing whatever to fear except, perhaps, boredom. The castle habitually held basic rations to enable it to hold out for at least three years: beneath Santa Croce's feet, deep in the stone heart of the castle, enormous jars held nearly 200 tons of grain, 5,000 gallons of oil, 1,000 gallons of wine. In its thousand years as a castle, Sant' Angelo never yet had been taken by direct assault. If His Holiness should decide that the Vatican Palace was perhaps just a little too vulnerable in these troubled times then The Angel was ready to spread his wings over the Vicar of Christ until such time as His Imperial Majesty came to his senses and called off the hounds.

About ten minutes' brisk walk from Sant' Angelo, in an upper room of the Vatican Palace, Paolo Giovio, Bishop of Novara, was waiting with an impatience that was almost visible on his smooth, courtier's face. He, for one, was under no illusions as to what was about to happen to Rome and common sense dictated that he should follow the more prudent members of the papal court and seek the solid safety of Sant' Angelo. But the historian's itch to record, to remain at the centre of affairs at a moment of high drama, kept him in the gorgeous, but suddenly very fragile-seeming, halls of the Vatican until such time as His Holiness might decide to vacate them for safer quarters.

Making a decision, however, was something which His Holiness was just unable to do. Indeed, it was precisely that inability which had created this entire deplorable situation. To die for a principle was one thing, thought Paolo Giovio (even though he could never be accused of risking his skin for a principle), but to die as the result of a colossal mistake – that was another matter entirely. And Giovio was detached enough and informed enough to know that if Rome should indeed fall to the invader, then it would be by a mistake, one of the greatest in history; it would be the sack and massacre that nobody intended. He took no part in the anxious debate that had arisen yet again between His Holiness and his earnest advisers. Giovio regarded his duty as that of recording, not influencing, for influencing meant choosing sides and choosing sides was dangerous. Certainly there was no lack of advisers, each passionately advising some positive course of action. The only problem was to choose between them and that, Paolo Giovio decided, was what Giulio de' Medici could never do, even though he now wore the triple crown as a direct confidant of the Almighty. What else could one expect from a descendant of Florentine merchants? 'Wait and see': that was the true motto of Florence and that was exactly what His Holiness was doing now. 'Wait and see' whether the enemy commander outside would change his mind, remembering that this was the sacred city of Christendom. 'Wait and see' whether the religious differences among the enemy's rank and file might yet lead to dissension. 'Wait and see' whether a messenger from the Emperor might not even at this eleventh hour be galloping headlong down the peninsula, bearing His Majesty's appalled apologies and stern orders to his troops. 'Wait and see' if almost anything might happen that would absolve Giulio de' Medici from making an irrevocable decision. The days of strain were showing on his dark, handsome face: the slight cast in the eye seemed more pronounced. No, he would not withdraw to Sant' Angelo. Not now. Not today. Tomorrow, perhaps, if the situation became worse. Willy-nilly, the court had to remain with him, separated from safety by half a mile of narrow streets that could in moments become a death trap.

From where Paolo Giovio stood it was possible to see the massive drum of Sant' Angelo, mellow-brown, bathed in the evening sunlight, and the long, snaking walkway built on top of the city wall that connected Palace and Castle for a favoured few. The view to the right was blocked partly by other buildings, by the Vatican and by the rising mass of the new St Peter's so it was not possible to see beyond the city wall. But it was possible to hear only too plainly – hear the blare of trumpets and sudden, spontaneously concerted savage yells: hear, above all, the mounting hysteria from the crowds gathering in the streets outside, the citizens of Rome waiting for guidance from their father and lord in whose hands lay life and death for the city.

The aimless conference at last broke up. His Holiness retired to his private apartments and the nightmare of his own thoughts. The rest of his council scattered throughout the palace, some of them to debate afresh, some of them to seek comfort in their God, some of them to record the events leading up to what they felt, instinctively, was an approaching climacteric of history. Few of them were to find refuge in sleep and those who did were wakened by a distinctive sound, the great bell of the Capitol clanging its harsh warning into the mild spring night, the voice of a Rome that had at last come to its own decision, calling the citizens to defend the wall and fight for their lives. At midnight the sonorous clanging was answered by the roar of drums from the army outside the walls. At dawn, a heavy mist arose from the Tiber and drifted up the Janiculum, hiding defenders from attackers – and masking the great guns of the Castello Sant' Angelo.

Section One

THE ACTORS

Chapter I

Crown Imperial

'I speak German to my horse, French to my ministers and Spanish to my God.'
So enunciated the Emperor Charles V, neatly encapsulating apparently
conflicting truths as was his ability. He was a young man, just 27 years old at
that moment when, unknown to him, his troops were about to destroy the
mother city of Europe in his name. But he had known power for ten years, so
that it clung to him now as an accustomed garment, and it needed a young man
to bear the unique burden that genetic chance had thrown upon him. He was
Burgundian by birth, Spaniard by inheritance, German by descent; lord of the
world, in theory, master of Europe, in sober fact – though master only as long as
he could hold the trembling balance in his hands; first of the modern statesmen,
manipulating men and events in the cause of political theory, and last of the
feudal knights, prepared to risk everything – power, crown, life itself – in an act
of personal combat. Physically unprepossessing with his grotesque jaw and the
perpetually half-open mouth that made his speech an indistinct mumble, he yet
had an un-self-conscious majesty that made the style of 'Caesar' sit naturally
upon him.

Caesar. A thousand years had passed since the wretched, ironically named,
little Romulus Augustulus had relinquished his feeble hold on the imperial
sceptre and so brought to a formal, legal end the undivided majesty of the
Roman Empire in the West. But during the long centuries of darkness that had
followed, men had looked back upon that stupendous political structure as
upon a golden age, contrasting its stability and peace with the anarchy of a
continent divided against itself. Therefore, when, on Christmas Day in the
year 800, the great barbarian king Charlemagne took the crown of empire from
the hands of the Pope, it was seen almost as an act of divine intervention, a
bridge between a glorious past and a hopeful future that would carry the
peoples of Europe across the dark chasm of their own day. Neither Holy, nor
Roman, nor an Empire – such was to be the standard jibe, and it was true
enough, but completely missed the essential point. For over a thousand years
Europeans believed that such an organisation existed or thought it ought to
exist, and acted accordingly. Charles of Habsburg, Duke of Burgundy, owed
his towering place in history to such an unshaken belief.

He was born, in the year 1500, into domestic tragedy. His mother, who was to go down in history under the name of Joanna the Mad, was heiress to the huge, newly combined Spanish kingdom of Aragon and Castile. His father, who drove his mother mad, was the good-looking young man known as Phillip the Handsome, son of the Emperor Maximilian, and heir, in his own right, to the dukedom of Burgundy. Joanna, unfortunately for her, was totally in love with her totally faithless, dissolute husband. He, for his part, simply saw himself saddled for dynastic reasons with a dumpy, sallow, querulous woman who was already prone to use her dazzling inheritance to enforce his love and faithfulness. She failed in that. He did his dynastic duty by her as the existence of their six children proved, but he found his pleasures elsewhere and literally drove his wife to madness with jealousy and grief and despair.

Restlessly, husband and wife moved around Europe, Phillip in pursuit of pleasure and political profit, Joanna in pursuit of Phillip. Each of their children was born in a different locality, some of them hundreds of miles apart. Eleanor, the first-born, who was to be Charles' favourite sister, saw the light in Brussels. Charles arrived two years later in Ghent: Isabella a year later in Malines. In 1502 the couple made the long journey to Spain and there the following year Ferdinand was born in Alcala. In 1506 they were back in Brussels for the birth of Marie. In 1507 Joanna, recently widowed, gave birth to her last child in Spain, and succumbed to the dark clouds of madness.

Phillip the Handsome might have been indifferent to his wife's physical charms but he was very susceptible indeed to the charms of her inheritance. Their first visit to Spain in 1502 had ended badly, for Joanna's mother Isabella was still alive and the prospect of Phillip's occupying her throne was dismally distant, and the sprightly young Burgundian found the stiff, gloomy ceremonial of the Spanish court altogether too much to bear. He took himself off to the gaieties of France, leaving a very thoughtful mother-in-law and a heavily pregnant wife to bewail her fate and deliver herself of their third child, the future Archduke Ferdinand. However, the formidable Isabella died not long afterwards and Phillip hastened back to Spain to throw himself into a protracted and devious struggle with a worthy opponent, Joanna's father, the foxy Ferdinand King of Aragon, whose hold on the great kingdom of Castile had weakened with the death of his wife, Castile's queen. Over the next two years Joanna's father and husband fought for control of Castile, using her own inheritance as weapon one against the other. Her husband won at last, but scarcely had he celebrated his victory when death took him off.

He died of a fever, and throughout his illness could have asked for no more devoted a nurse than the wife whom he had betrayed as a matter of course. Though she was now in the sixth month of her pregnancy, Joanna remained with him day and night, scarcely eating or sleeping. Madness must already have been mounting in her cloudy brain as day flowed into night and it became ever more certain that her husband's death was imminent. When that death came she said nothing. She did not burst into tears, or rage, or pray. She seemed almost indifferent when they took the corpse away and buried it in fitting splendour. But at that the balance of her mind turned and she ordered that the body be disinterred and brought to her apartment.

From this point onwards, the relationship of Charles' mother to the corpse of his father belongs as much to legend as to history, as successive writers, seizing on the genuinely macabre details, elaborated them yet further into a Gothic horror story. According to one source, the corpse 'was laid upon a bed of state in a splendid dress, and having heard from some monk a legendary tale of a king who revived after he had been dead for fourteen years, she kept her eyes almost constantly upon the body, waiting for the happy moment of its return to life'. Was Joanna really as mad as that at this early stage? It seems improbable. But even those of her actions which were prompted by sane enough motives took on the compulsiveness of paranoia. She apparently feared substitution and again and again ordered the coffin to be opened to set her mind at rest, although it was quite impossible to identify the lime-encrusted, indistinguishable mass inside as the mortal remains of Phillip the Handsome. Flickering through her darkening brain came the memory of a sexual jealousy that had only too just and sane a cause: it drove her now to madness. The sight of any other woman approaching the corpse threw Joanna into a paroxysm of action. Screaming, clawing at the serving women who entered to clean the chamber or even at her ladies-in-waiting who approached her to condole, or at social peers whom, under other circumstances, she would have called friends, Queen Joanna of Castile drove them away from the body and drove herself deeper into madness. When the time came for her delivery she refused to be attended even by a midwife and delivered her child herself. It was a girl, Katherine: a girl who was doomed to stay within the ambit of her mother's madness, serving dumbly and unselfishly until the big brother she had never seen – Charles, Duke of Burgundy – came to Spain ten years later to take up his inheritance and alleviate his sister's servitude.

Charles was seven years old when his father died and his mother retreated into the labyrinth of her own mind. His parents were nothing more to him than distant names and resonant styles. Rather like cuckoos, they had left their children to grow up in whatever land they had been born in, and Charles spent his childhood in the Netherlands. Malines, some fourteen miles from Brussels, was his home and his Aunt Margaret, the firm, tough-minded compassionate daughter of the Emperor Maximilian, was the only mother he knew. Under her intelligent guidance he learned what it was to be a duke of Burgundy.

Burgundy was as much an idea as a place. It had been born centuries earlier when the great Empire of Charlemagne was split between his three grandsons. One took the vast section in the west that was to become France; one took the eastern section that, in time, was to be Germany; and the third took the amorphous section in-between. Over the following centuries it was to change its name and shape again and again, now contracting to an area around Dijon, now expanding south, deep into Italy, and north, into the Low Countries. Theoretically, its dukes were vassals of the king of France; in practice, their vast power and wealth and arrogance made of their land a separate kingdom, allying itself or warring against the king in France as they chose. At the time of Charles' birth the dukedom was just past its apogee. In the previous century a succession of extraordinary dukes with extraordinary soubriquets – the Bold, the Good, the Rash – had created a glittering, seemingly indestructible unit, all jewelled without, all steel within. But an even greater King of France, Louis XI, the man they called The Spider, had woven his web around the structure and entrapped and destroyed the last of the great dukes, engulfing a huge section of the dukedom into the body of France.

But though the political power of Burgundy was diminished, the cultural richness still blazed, dimming even the blaze of Paris. Burgundy was unique in Europe, the product perhaps of its ambivalent position between two great racial blocs. All the lurid contrasts that marked the Europe of the day – the extreme poverty at the door of extreme luxury; sickening cruelty side by side with dedicated charity; explosive and continual violence as counterpoint to high intellectual endeavour: all these contrasts found their most finished form in this amorphous land. In Burgundy, above all, was worked out that concept which saw the ruler of the state as the personification of the state and therefore as something greater than mortal man. The ceremonies that customarily attended the duke's table, his toilet, his bedchamber were quite deliberately and explicitly founded upon religious ceremony. Thus, at table his cup-bearer was likened to the priest who elevated the chalice in the church. As at the altar, the napkin which dried the duke's hands was kissed as it passed from courtier to courtier; the torches which lit his way to table were kissed, so were the handles of the knives placed before him. His progress through the crowds was as solemn as the progress of a priest bearing the Host. After certain festivities in Arras a shocked Frenchman remarked: 'If God were to descend from heaven I doubt if they could do him more honour than was had by the duke.' Another said caustically 'It seemed as though they had God himself by the feet'.

This gorgeous figure was the centre of perhaps the most splendid, most luxurious court in Europe, a court which would not be matched until the High Renaissance in Italy. The richly dressed men, moving in their siff punctilio, clad in ankle-length robes whose enormous sleeves almost swept the floor, and the brilliantly dressed women with their towering, fantastic head-dresses proclaimed their specialness by their costume and, in so doing, seem curiously unreal to posterity, for all the world like lay-figures taking part in an endless, self-conscious pageant. And so, in a sense, they were, for the etiquette of the court prescribed almost every activity hour by hour. The duke alone could change the pattern of ceremonial and his courtiers followed his fashions with a slavish attention to detail: should he cut his hair short, then immediately male courtiers hastened to get themselves shorn. If he shortened his robe, then within hours scores of male shanks would become visible.

Throughout the fifteenth century the court of Burgundy was a cultivated and intellectual centre overshadowing the court of the King of France. Clothing, armour, musical instruments, architecture, furnishing poured from the workshops of Europe's foremost designers. Ultimately, all this prodigal display and expenditure was paid for by the humdrum means of trade, for Burgundy lay on the cross-roads of Europe. But the Burgundian nobles, despite their outward appearance as dragooned and sycophantic courtiers, still remained faithful to the older, cruder, Germanic tradition which held that the greatest happiness was to be found on the battlefield. Like the great feasts that characterised the court, the mock battles of Burgundy (the tournaments), became spectacular, immensely costly charades which more closely resembled theatre than war. But they could also be the most ferocious in Europe, one of the last survivals of the brutal medieval custom of trial by combat. Burgundy, all silk and gold without, remained, to the end, all steel within.

This was the atmosphere in which the young Charles was brought up. Some of the glory was dimmed. For instance, when Charles was summoned as a vassal to attend the coronation of François I, the youthful new King of France, it was thought prudent to send a representative there. But the wealth and culture remained, although the centre of gravity had shifted now to the rich commercial cities of the Low Countries. That was why the Archduchess Margaret had chosen Malines as the seat for herself and her young nephew, building a palace there that was as splendid as any Burgundian palace had to be, but that reflected, too, something of her sobriety and restraint despite its rococo style.

Charles was born a Fleming and grew up a Fleming: that would hamper him in his relations with Spain, his mother's homeland, and it would also account, perhaps, for the ponderous and puritanical element in his nature. His tutor was a Fleming, Adrian of Utrecht, who in the veiled and distant future was to be made pope when his pupil became emperor, to the rage of the Romans and to Adrian's own distress. Adrian was an austere, old-fashioned, honourably limited man who could see little in the glittering new Renaissance except snares of the devil. He instilled in his charge the qualities that he himself valued, so that the naturally solemn, reserved boy developed into a solemn, conservative youth and finally into a solemn emperor who was as conservative in personal habits as he was boldly experimental in political ones.

It is curiously difficult to get a perspective view of the personality of Charles of Habsburg, either in his youth or indeed at any time during his long and vigorous life. During thirty years and more of continuous, high-level political activity he was naturally the attention of all Europe. Endless reports were produced by ambassadors who, professionally accustomed to observing the most minute convolutions of human character, were concerned to provide their governments with a precise guide to his motivations. Painters and sculptors again and again reproduced his features: he was the subject, above all, for one of the greatest portrait painters of all time, the Venetian Titian. But the end product of all this minute observation and dissection and recording is a curious ambiguity. The tens of thousands of words written about him, or emanating from him, somehow never quite coalesce to provide the picture of a human personality. It is as though one were peering through the heavily grimed windows of some dusty lawyer's office, just able to discern that there is indeed a figure inside, engaged in some important activity, but not able to discern exactly what or why. The most dramatic illustration of this ambiguity is the cloud that hangs over him regarding his mother's madness. Did he, as soon as he came to power, put a mad woman away out of a sense of shame, or did he put

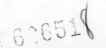

a sane woman away with the deliberate intention of finally driving her mad for political reasons? Either could be deduced from his actions.

The ambiguity is all the more tantalising when compared with the vividness of the portraits of the other two young men who were his contemporaries and rivals, his 'royal cousins' Henry VIII of England and François I of France. And, by a final ironic quirk of fate, these two young men were to enter history as popular figures though, on any consideration, they were his moral and intellectual inferiors. Thus Henry, one of the most savage monarchs ever to sit upon the English throne, emerges in three dimensions under the spurious style of Bluff King Hal; and the essentially shallow François, taught by personal desire and a doting mother to equate his own comfort with the good of the nation, is metamorphosised into a golden Prince of the Renaissance whose greatest vice, perhaps, was that of philandering. Even Pope Clement VII, the man who triggered off the disaster of Rome through a fatal combination of weakness and stubborness, and who, at the end, put the glorification of family as his ultimate goal, achieves a certain melancholy dignity. Charles, however, at best survives in history as a lawyer's hero, a kind of animated textbook on constitutional history, while folklore casts him simply as a foil to Martin Luther.

The future emperor emerged out of the obscurity of childhood in 1516, the year of the death of his grandfather Ferdinand of Aragon. Ferdinand had done all he could do to ensure that the grandson he had never seen – the grandson he regarded simply as a young Fleming manipulated by Flemings – should never gain the Spanish crown. He had taken a young wife, but, ironically, his too energetic and exhausting attempts to provide himself with an heir helped to place the crown on Charles' head.

At that point, without having raised a finger, the sixteen-year-old boy became one of the great monarchs not merely of Europe but of the world, bestriding the continent and the ocean, undisputed heir to an empire that was potentially greater even than that the Caesars had known. Genetic chance had given him firm and legal footholds in Spain and in Italy, in France, Germany, Austria, the Netherlands and in the vast and mysterious lands of the new world beyond the Atlantic. Ferdinand had been not only king of Aragon but also monarch of the great Spanish kingdom on the Italian mainland, the so-called Kingdom of the Two Sicilies, which included Naples and swept almost up to the gates of Rome. Charles' mother Joanna was still alive, still clinging stubbornly to the title of Queen of Castile but, trapped by her madness in her castle of Tordesillas, she was wholly outside the realm of practical politics. Charles took the title of King of Castile, so alienating the Castilians and providing the grounds for that black mystery regarding his mother. His other grandfather, the Emperor Maximilian, was still alive. Theoretically, the Emperor's was an elective office but when the time came, Charles' German blood would stand him in good stead. And through his Spanish heritage he would be able to claim the lands discovered by Columbus just twenty years before and which the Conquistadores now were opening up.

Charles, at the age of sixteen, seems a particularly unlikely heir for so dazzling an inheritance. Despite diligent attention to his studies, he was only a mediocre scholar. In his liking for violent action as recreation – in particular the violent action of tournaments and the chase – he was proving himself a true Burgundian. He was also proving himself a true Burgundian by succumbing, even at this early age, to that dreariest of the seven deadly sins – gluttony – which was to be his life-long scourge. Conrad Meit's beautiful portrait bust of the young monarch, sculpted about this time, shows what could almost be an imbecile with the long, hanging jaw, open mouth, and staring but sidelong glance. This was the youth who was now faced with the problem that besets all rulers – in particular rulers who seek to control a multi-racial, multi-lingual kingdom. Where would he set his court and how could he avoid being manipulated by his adversaries?

Charles' sovereignty took the form of two sections separated by the vast, not particularly friendly country of France. In Castile, his regent was that extraordinary old man, Cardinal Ximenes, who had been appointed by Charles's grandfather, Ferdinand when it had became obvious to him that Joanna was incapable of government and that the crown of Castile must therefore go to a Flemish lad hundreds of miles away. Ximenes, Archbishop of Toledo, was one of the very rare breed of ecclesiastics who managed to preserve his asceticism and austerity and honour uncorrupted by high office. At an age when most other men were sinking gratefully into slippered ease, he took over the task of holding together Isabella the Catholic's grand design of making Spain one, fighting off external enemies and suppressing justly but quite mercilessly the sudden greedy resurgence of the nobles who, as in every land at every transference of authority, sought to profit by temporary uncertainty. But now Ximenes had yet another burden placed upon his ageing shoulders. The Flemish councillors of young Charles proclaimed him King of Aragon and Castile quite illegally, without waiting for the appointment to go through the cumbersome processes of the Spanish *cortes*. Ximenes defended the concept of the law behind the law: he too, as a Spaniard, was insulted and enraged by the northerners' crass action; but, as a statesman, he realised the inevitability of the fact and so was prepared to accept the technical illegality. But neither as a Spaniard nor as a statesman was he prepared to accept the rapacious flood of Flemings who appeared in Spain, harbinger of the greater flood, eager to sell offices and titles and engage in plain theft on behalf of the King of Spain who was, in fact, still a Fleming, still the Duke of Burgundy. Ximenes began the cruel business of walking a tight-rope over the abyss of conflicting motives.

In Brussels, the Burgundian court prepared to exploit the Spanish goldmine. Adrian of Utrecht was sent travelling south, clutching his own letters patent as Regent of Castile, and left to work out some kind of compromise with the other Regent of Castile, his austere, battle-toughened fellow ecclesiastic Ximenes. The Sieur de Chièvres, Charles' Chancellor, who had presided over the boy's development into a ruler, was an able enough and, within his own lights, an honest enough man. But it was, perhaps, asking too much of a Fleming to expect him to have any feeling of a common cause with a Latin race hundreds of miles distant. A greater man than Chièvres might have raised his eyes out of the swill-tub and looked towards a wider horizon. But Chièvres was competent, not great, and he regarded the heady potential of fusion between Burgundian and Spanish interests, as did most of his fellow Flemings, hard-headed merchants, simply as an opportunity to make a lot of money out of a legal fiction. By the sale of Spanish offices, Chièvres earned more than five times his annual salary.

And Charles? It is difficult to see to what extent he was merely the passive instrument of other men's greed, or was carrying out a considered if immature policy. Certainly he was not altogether a puppet for it was he who, at the age of scarcely seventeen, personally forbade the love-match between his elder sister Eleanor and the Count Palatine Frederick and gave her instead to the King of Portugal. Here, the boy was already looking forward to the problems of the man and doing his best to secure his foothold in Spain by protecting his flank. And, ultimately, it must have been his decision which at last set the court moving on its slow process to Spain. For to Spain it went at last, despite the protests and passive resistance of those Flemings who realised that their grip on the fountain of privileges could only be weakened if the court were transferred to Spain.

Charles left his birthplace to take up his great heritage in September 1517, nearly two years after the death of Ferdinand. The court journeyed by sea, forty of the great northern ships feeling their way around the misty Atlantic coasts down to the Bay of Biscay. There Charles disembarked and, together with his sister Eleanor, set out for Tordesillas and what may have been the most traumatic moment of his life, the meeting with his mother whom he could scarcely remember, for he had not seen her since he was seven years old.

The visit of Charles, King of Aragon and Castile, to his mother Joanna, Queen of Aragon and Castile, had more to it than an act of filial piety. For the problem of who ruled the great heritage of Ferdinand and Isabella had by no means been clearly resolved. Afterwards, the story circulated that when a guard in the castle of Tordesillas had approached Joanna with the words, 'Madam, your son the King has arrived', she had struck back like a cobra: 'I – I am Queen. My son is only a prince.' If the story is true, then Joanna was very far inded from being mad, Charles was equally as far from being legal king, and an impossible situation was being created, for Joanna did nothing to discharge her royal obligations while clinging stubbornly to her royal title.

The meeting took place on a bleak November afternoon. It was already after dusk when Charles and his sister entered the castle and approached their mother's quarters. That fact is known for certain, for the chronicler, Laurent Vital, who had accompanied Charles from Flanders, was present with him at this emotion-laden moment. Vital, it seems, was carrying a torch and as the door of the Queen's chamber opened, he attempted to slip through after Charles, ostensibly to bring a light into the darkened room, in reality to satisfy a most lively curiosity regarding its inmate. Charles blocked the move, however, and brusquely dismissed the man – another indication of the prince behind the puppet. What took place in the gloomy chamber, lit only by the flaring light of the torch that Charles had taken from Vital, can only be conjecture. Was the ten-year-old Katherine present? It seems likely, for she was Joanna's only constant companion. Certainly she stirred the pity of Charles and Eleanor; for the child appeared waif-like, dressed 'like a nun', in dreary clothes, in dramatic contrast to her nineteen-year-old sister Eleanor who was already displaying her taste for rich, not to say gaudy, colours. Either that same evening, or sometime during the following day, Charles and Eleanor took their little sister away, intending nothing more than to introduce her to a way of life more appropriate to her years. But their mother's distress was so extreme, her protests so violent, that they came to a compromise: Katherine would have to go back to the castle, but she would be given her own establishment, consisting of young women who would bring a little colour into her life, and who would act, in part, as buffer between the defenceless child and her deranged mother.

Deranged? So the Castilian *cortes* thought, if reluctantly, and so, in due course, did the Aragonese. Both at last formally recognised Charles as king – but conjointly with his mother and only so long as her madness lasted. A less scrupulous man would have recognised that decision as a warrant to lock up his mother for the rest of her life, mad or sane. Before the long years took their toll and finally snapped the cord of sanity, Joanna indeed protested of treatment deliberately designed to unhinge her mind. The protests themselves may well have been signs of her derangement, but for thirty-seven years Charles lived with the knowledge that his legal right to the throne of Spain was contingent upon his mother's crucifixion. Ironically, she alone of the children of Ferdinand and Isabella lived out the full span of her years, dying at the age of seventy-six in the year 1555, a few months before Charles voluntarily divested himself of the imperial power.

Charles had interviews with two other people scheduled after that first meeting with his mother: one with the Regent Ximenes, the other with the brother he had never seen, the Archduke Ferdinand. He never did meet the Regent to whom he owed so much, which was a profound relief to the Sieur de Chièvres and the rest of the Flemings around him. Vividly aware that their control over the still malleable youth would be challenged and heavily modified by the formidable old man, Charles' Flemish advisers had done all they could to postpone his meeting with Ximenes and, in preparation for it, to erode Ximenes' reputation by the insidious means available to courtiers on the spot. So effective were they that Charles, too, became reluctant to face the man who had held Castile in trust for him, and contented himself with a cold little letter of thanks and dismissal. If the two had met, then the still dormant element of greatness that lay in Charles might have recognised the greatness of Ximenes and immediately responded to it. But the old man died before the meeting could take place, taking with him to the tomb a classical object-lesson of the ingratitude of princes.

The meeting with Ferdinand passed off warmly enough, despite the fact that they could scarcely speak each other's language. Charles' fifteen-year-old brother was an attractive young man: open-hearted, easy to talk to, and very curious indeed about this elder brother who had appeared with all the panoply of power from out of the northern mists. But, again, it was far more than family piety that brought the two young men together in earnest discussion.

Ferdinand, for all his charm, presented a threat. The younger brother of any king presented a threat to the ruler by his very existence, but Ferdinand, in addition, possessed one great qualification to rule Spain which his brother did not, and never would, possess: he was as Spanish as Charles was Flemish, for he had spent all his young life in Spain. Their grandfather, the old king Ferdinand of Aragon, had regarded the boy as the natural heir to the Spanish throne: he was popular with the people and highly acceptable to the *cortes*. The dangerous suggestion had even been made that he should rule Spain as viceroy on his brother's behalf. That particular suggestion had been firmly scotched, but there remained the only too obvious danger that young Ferdinand would present a natural rallying point for a people resenting the incursion of a mob of rapacious foreigners licenced to plunder the country merely because of an accident of birth.

The outcome of the long talks between Charles and his brother was that young Ferdinand went off to discreet and comfortable exile – first to fill Charles' vacant place in the home of their Aunt Margaret in the Netherlands, and later to occupy a throne of his own as King of Hungary. He was to prove a loyal ally of his brother throughout his life.

And now, with Ximenes dead and Ferdinand out of the country, the vacuum of power was filled entirely by Flemings. Looking back, it must have seemed incredible to Charles that he survived the three or four years following his assumption of the crowns of Castile and Aragon. It was not only that he and his court were foreigners, and resented as such; he personally had no intention of remaining permanently in Spain and was already planning to exercise remote control from the outside if necessary. Nothing more clearly shows the degree of Flemish greed, and shortsighted indifference to Spanish feelings than that Charles' mentor, Chièvres, took over the premier see of Spain, the Archbishopric of Toledo – and took it over not simply for himself but for his sixteen-year-old son who was not even in Spain but still living comfortably in the Netherlands.

Inevitably, the Spaniards arose in rebellion, a group of them even rallying round the wretched Queen Joanna, claiming that she was not mad but simply ill-used. The rebellion spread throughout the country like a canker, for it was not simply a revolt of natives against foreign occupiers, but a confused re-ordering of forces that were no longer tribal but could not yet regard themselves as national. Anything could have developed, and it was at this highly dangerous moment that Charles decided to leave the country, rather like a captain abandoning his ship in a tempest to go and prospect for buried treasure.

In January 1519 the Emperor Maximilian died. He was Charles' paternal grandfather but the office was elective, not hereditary. Although the crown had long been in the possession of the Habsburgs, a formidable new rival had appeared on the European horizon, the brilliant young King of France who was just six months older than Charles; François I of the house of Valois. He too made his bid for the crown of Empire and so brought in the second element of the charge that was to explode in Rome seven years later.

Chapter II

Crown Royal

If the cold and rigid personality of the Emperor Charles V can, ultimately, be attributed to a lack of mother-love, then, undoubtedly, an excess of it shaped the too-warm, too-impulsive personality of his great rival François. For François' mother Louise is the classic example of the all-devouring Mother, the woman who has ceased to make – if she ever has made – any real distinction between her own personality and that of her child and who, seemingly sacrificing herself endlessly on that child's behalf is, in fact, sacrificing at the altar of her own ego. With any other person, or in almost any other period or place, Louise's attitude would simply have produced a spoiled and frivolous darling, incapable of either great good or great harm. But custom, in particular Gallic custom, was already predisposed to make a god out of a king. Louise's engulfing, wholly uncritical adulation of her son exaggerated that tendency, so that François, not, at bottom, a bad or an ungenerous man, came naturally to equate the good of the state with the good of his own personal daily affairs.

It is a peculiarity of Louise's story that she seems to have aroused more rage, and got a far worse press after her death than during her lifetime. Some of the charges made against her during her lifetime were produced for ignoble reasons by people who had an obvious axe to grind, or were intent on avenging some injury. But some of the most damaging accusations are made by writers with enough intellect, and far removed enough in time, to have a sense of perspective. Thus Louis-Marie Prudhomme, with eighteenth-century elegance, refers to her as 'this miserable prostitute: sensual, cold, avaricious', and in the nineteenth century the great historian Michelet, after summing up her beloved son as 'part swine, part ape', dismisses her as coarse, sensual, harsh, violent, avaricious and vindictive. It was, perhaps, Louise's misfortune that not only was she widowed when very young, but that also she retained her good looks and frank liking for men into a mature age, providing titillating titbits that made better reading than the solid accomplishments with which she should be credited. It was, after all, this same 'miserable prostitute' who, as Great Regent, kept France together, while her son was languishing in a Spanish prison.

Louise's own *Journal* scarcely helps to correct the bias, undoubted witness for the defence though it is. It bears too much evidence of editing and hindsight, being written years after the events it describes, and gives, indeed, little or nothing of her own personal opinions and motives – except where they touch on her son François. He is the sole and constant hero of the drama of her life. She chronicles the very day of his conception and the hour of his birth and minutely details the manner in which the Almighty guided him steadily to the throne of France by killing off all the babies and young children who stood between him and this high goal. The reader is repelled by the satisfaction with which she records those deaths in the journal, even as edited. A cold and calculating woman, ever alive to the main chance – such is the picture that emerges from her own hand in that semi-autobiographical fragment.

And yet she was not wholly to blame, for she, too, was as much moulded by her circumstances as her son was moulded. As a child she was that most unenviable of figures, the poor relation brought up among the rich. She was orphaned at the age of seven and was brought up among strangers at the court of the king of France. No great household of the day was exactly distinguished for family love, but it must have been a profound and enduring shock for little Louise of Savoy to be uprooted from her familiar little universe and set down in a vast, cold, indifferent court to survive as best she might. Things scarcely improved when she was married off, at the age of sixteen, to a man nineteen years her senior. Her husband, Charles of Angoulême, though of the royal blood, was at least two removes from the throne: Louise had the tantalisation of being so close and yet, for all practical purposes, light years away from the ultimate source of power. She presented Charles with a daughter and then a son, whereupon her husband died of a cold and left her, at the age of nineteen, to make her own way in life and to provide for her two small children.

'François, by God's grace King of France and my own gentle emperor, had his first experience of the world's light at Cognac about ten o'clock of the afternoon in 1494, on the 12th of September.' So she recorded her son's birth. No such loving record was made of the birth of her firstborn, the little girl Marguerite who was to develop into the most entrancing blue-stocking of her day. It was François around whom the world revolved, François, 'my lord, my king, my Caesar' as she habitually described him; the boy whom, doubtless, she loved as any mother loves a son but whom, too, she saw as the means whereby she, Louise of Savoy, might yet attain the power and authority she thought was her right. Insecurity in childhood has blighted the life of many a human being. It merely tempered the steel of Louise's adult personality, making her fiercely determined to lose no opportunity to make a foundation for herself that neither fortune nor hostility could destroy. One of the elements of the Sack of Rome came into being in the mind and heart of a lonely, frightened, seven-year-old girl crying herself to sleep in a strange bed.

As it happened, François was born in the very year of the first, triumphant, French invasion of Italy. That was the year when the baby's second-cousin, the gnome-like King Charles VIII, took it into his astonishingly ugly head to go on Crusade and, en route, reconquer his forefather's possessions in Italy. A huge army followed the stunted, misshapen little man down the peninsula, an army before which the endlessly brawling Italians melted. They raised the fleur-de-lys in Naples, and proclaimed Charles King of Naples and the Two Sicilies, but within a year that triumphant army was hastening back with its tail between its legs, sniped at, harried, grateful to get back across the Alps reasonably intact, all the proud conquests melting like a dream. The army brought back more than the Italian diseases which sapped its strength: it brought to French nostrils the scent of Italy, to French minds the glamour of the dawning Renaissance, stirring up for the northern country the ancient, beautiful, fatal lure of the south.

Four years later, when little François was himself just four, his mother had the satisfaction of noting his next tottering step towards the still distant throne when Charles VIII, with typical clumsiness, smashed his head on a low doorway and died in agony, stretched out in a latrine. François' cousin, the Duke of Orléans, became King as Louis XII, and François himself moved up one, becoming Dauphin, heir to the throne. But then, as in some regal game of snakes and ladders, Louise had the chagrin of seeing her son slip back one place when King Louis divorced his virtuous, barren, sickly wife and married his predecessor's widow, Anne of Brittany. In the complex feudal structure of the day Anne was a very powerful person indeed for she was Duchess of Brittany in her own right and the man who secured her hand also secured – though with certain very important reservations – control of a vast tract of land. But Anne was more than an heiress: she was also a very strong-minded woman and she had taken a very strong and definite dislike to the pushing Louise. Both women had their eyes fixed on the same goal, the throne of France, but while Louise possessed a strong and vigorous male child who would adequately fill that throne some day, Anne produced nothing but a series of still-born children and one sickly girl. With each birth Louise held her breath; with each death she revived and noted the fact thankfully in her diary, as on that occasion when yet another of Anne's baby boys died shortly after birth: 'He could not retard the exaltation of my own Caesar for he did not live.'

Anne did not have to possess particularly sensitive antennae to pick up the waves of hatred and triumph that Louise transmitted and the mutual contempt and dislike of the women increased with their proximity. But it was otherwise with the king. He delighted in the sturdy little François and his graceful fey sister and before he married Anne, many times he invited the children and their mother to court. Even Louise, ever hungry for prestige, ever on the look-out for a slight, was satisfied by her reception. 'And as for the children, he could not show them enough favour,' the courtier Saint-Gelas noted. 'For had he been the father he could not have made more of them. And assuredly there were few children to match them in any walk of life.' Saint-Gelas was a partisan of Louise's but he did not exaggerate: they certainly were delightful children and the ageing Louis would not have been human had he not somewhat wistfully compared these laughing, radiant creatures with the sickly infants that his wife presented to him.

The little family visits came to an end with the king's marriage for he had problems enough without creating domestic discords by having two female rivals under one roof. But he was an honourable man, recognising his duty towards his kingdom when it became ever more apparent that his wife was unlikely to present him with a Dauphin. When François was sixteen he was formally recognised as heir and summoned to the royal court at Blois. Louise was torn. Ever since he had been a baby in his cradle she had stubbornly, savagely fought off all attempts to remove him from her control, but this royal summons was another matter. At Blois François would be shaped to the crown so that when, in the fullness of time, he assumed it, the act would seem the most natural and inevitable thing in the world instead of simply a legal transmission of power So she wept a little but assented and off to court young François went, leaving his mother and seventeen-year-old sister to comfort each other in the family palace at Romorantin. At Blois François learned to swim in the treacherous shoals of a royal court, learned to survive among people whose weapons were smiles, who moved always indirectly, manipulating at least one remove from their victim. He experienced his first love affair at the age of fifteen – an affair to be demurely worked up into a novel by his sister years later. He collected his first dose of pox, gathered around him as in a miniature court the ambitious young men of his day, bully-boys and genuine friends and sycophants, some of whom would follow him in the great military adventures that lay ahead, some of whom he would betray, some of whom would betray him.

The royal court at this period was a curious mixture, presenting the appearance of a dull seed out of which an exotic flower was growing. Louis ran his vast country like a business man, personally keeping track of state and domestic expenditure. He and his queen were frugal to the point of being parsimonious. The king of France dressed plainly – shabbily, almost; his preferred food was indistinguishable from that of a peasant's. When Cesare Borgia visited him, bringing him the much-needed anullment of his first marriage, he openly mocked the vulgar splendour which the Italian princeling thought fit to display on a state visit. The inevitable friend reported to him how the meanest of his subjects mocked him for his meanness: he merely smiled rather thinly and replied: 'I prefer that they should laugh at my meanness than weep for their poverty.' Regarding the antics of the strapping youth whom he now recognised as heir, he remarked glumly: 'This great lout will be the ruin of us all,' so enthusiastically had young François dipped his hands into the treasury. Many and anxious must have been the bedroom conferences about François between the saturnine, rather worn king and the dumpy, not very attractive woman whom he also happened to love. Anne disliked the son more, if possible, than she disliked the mother. Her reasons were by no means ignoble or selfish. She had very good grounds for suspecting that François had designs on her daughter, the invalid, gentle Claude, and the swaggering, insensitive, boastful boy was the very last husband she wanted for her vulnerable child.

Portraits of François in his old age show a face far more prepossessing than that of his youth. Time was to subtly transform arrogant confidence into wryness, intelligence into self-knowledge. Even Clouet's superb portrait of the young man shows a face that verges on caricature, with its immensely long nose, lascivious mouth and sly eyes that regard the world sideways. But in real life the dynamism of his personality, his exuberant good health and good humour gave him that charm and radiance with which all princes were supposed to be blessed. Hunting, whoring and jousting, these were his three delights and he excelled in them. From puberty onwards he threw himself into the series of sexual adventures which seem, in retrospect, one of the hallmarks of French royalty, virtually a toleration of polygamy in which the wives were labelled mistresses and fought among themselves for the cherished style 'maitresse en titre'. His very first adventure supplied his sister Marguerite with material for a poignant little tale which she used years later when writing her series of witty novelettes, the *Heptameron*.

The story as Marguerite tells it has the fifteen-year-old François pursuing a girl of the people, who stubbornly clings to her virtue despite every attempt from François to make her part from it. Intrigue, threat, outright bribery, all measures failed, for the girl wanted to marry a young man in François's own household and, despairing at last of the struggle, he gave in and allowed them to marry, even helping them financially. The story, admittedly, is edited by Marguerite, ever anxious to show her worshipped brother in the best possible light. But she was also an honest editor and would not have drastically tampered with the truth: the tale shows a generous and attractive enough human being, one prepared to go to very great lengths to satisfy his dominant passion but also capable of ruefully admitting himself beaten and retiring with dignity. It was not a bad portrait of François.

The young man was not wholly sensual, wholly given over to the pleasures of chase and table and bed. He was still in his teens when he received an accolade from no less a person than Baldassare Castiglione, the gentle Italian whose book *The Courtier* established the standard of polite behaviour in Europe for over three hundred years. In the book Castiglione made one of his speakers remark that the French were quite indifferent to scholarship and culture generally, the only nobility they recognised being that of arms: 'To them it is a great affront to call anyone a scholar.' 'That may have been true', another member of the circle replies. 'But if a kind fate wills, as it is hoped, that my Lord of Angoulême (François) should succeed to the crown, it is my opinion that just as France is now resplendent and glorious in the matter of arms, so shall you then behold a most brilliant flowering of the art of letters.'

King Louis indulged the young man, allowing him his head in everything – except the one thing he really wanted: to be permitted to take part in the great enterprise of Italy. Louis, in his turn, had led a great army down the peninsula. For nearly two years French arms had triumphed until, ominously, they had clashed with that other great power with a foothold in Italy – Spain. Though again the great banner of the fleur-de-lys was in retreat, this was a glorious arena, the only place worthy of a young French nobleman hungry for honour. Most of the young men with whom François had grown up had been blooded in the Italian wars: even his cousin, Charles, Duke of Bourbon, had commanded his own force in Lombardy, though only four years older than François. But King Louis refused to let the heir to the throne risk his neck in battle and, perforce, François had to content himself with the mock battles of tournaments and jousts.

Louis was justified in keeping François at home. In January 1514 his wife died after prolonged mental and physical suffering, a woman still young in years, for she was not yet forty, but worn out in body, as much by those desperate attempts to give birth to a male heir as by any disease. Louis went into extravagant mourning, calling upon his attendants to prepare his tomb by the side of his wife's for he would join her within the year. His prophecy was very nearly correct but it was certainly not grief that was to send him to an early grave.

There was now, it seemed, no possible impediment between François and the throne. He hastened to make his position even more secure, displaying the coldly acquisitive mind that lay behind his silks and velvets and laughter. Against his mother's wishes he married the unhappy Claude, the late queen's daughter, and so secured for himself the dukedom of Brittany. The wedding was a dreary ceremony for the court was still in mourning. Poor crippled Claude, an unattractive figure at best, was not improved upon on her wedding day by being obliged to wear full black. Louise did not deign to attend her beloved son's wedding, simply noting the event in her diary without comment. The act, for her, amounted to outright condemnation. François himself impatiently hastened through the ceremony, then abandoned his bride for a brisk course of hunting and carousing. He was secure at last: nothing could take the crown of France from his eager grasp when the time came for the worn-out Louis to join his wife.

Or could it? To the delightful mockery of the salacious, to Louise's rage and François' consternation, Louis married again 'although he was old and decrepit', as Louise said with stinging contempt. The king, was in fact, just fifty-two; but it was a well-used fifty-two, whereas his bride was barely seventeen and eager and urgent with it. She was Mary, the sprightly, golden-haired, blue-eyed sister of Henry VIII of England, acclaimed as the most beautiful princess of her day and now thrown away on the ageing King of France as part of her brother's endless jockeying for European power. Louis married her for political reasons, but loved her for his own, turning his careful, frugal régime upside down to accommodate and entertain the girl. Instead of dining quietly at night, he dined now at mid-day, grievously upsetting his digestion for the sake of a pretty girl. Normally he went to bed at six p.m. but this did not suit Mary at all and the round-eyed courtiers now saw their once solemn king shuffling and creaking around in a travesty of ballroom gaiety.

The courtiers saw something else. François, with his antennae so sensitive to amorous adventure, evidently decided to compensate himself by cuckolding his king. It would not have been a difficult task. The besotted Louis was quite unsuspicious, and Mary, her dynastic duty done, saw no particular reason why she should remain faithful to the slippered pantaloon her brother's ministers had wished upon her. François's courtship proceeded well – until news came of it to Louise's incredulous ears. For the first and only time in her life she subjected her son to a searing lecture. Was he really fool enough to trade a throne for an hour's sport in bed? Did he not know what Mary was after? If he did succeed in impregnating her with a male child, he would create his own rival, for Mary's bastard would naturally be Dauphin. Ambition was just stronger than love of pleasure, and François hurriedly backed away from those particular perilous pastures.

He did not have long to wait for his reward. On January 1, 1515, just three months after his marriage, Louis XII, King of France, died and François I, King of France, succeeded. Beside herself with joy Louise noted: 'On the first day of January I lost my husband; on the first day of January my son became King of France.' The long journey was over: the endless nights of prayer and planning had wrought the ultimate triumph. 'My son, my king, my Caesar' was at last on that pinnacle that destiny had reserved for him – providing, of course, that Mary was not pregnant. That seemed highly unlikely to anyone who had known the late king. But custom decreed that the king's widow should become the 'white queen' for six weeks, immured in her chamber until nature itself provided the answer as to whether or not she carried an heir. There was a rumour that she intended to cheat, to smuggle in a baby and pass it off as her own and so secure herself as Queen Mother at least. Louise half-believed the rumour and took the necessary precautions; but they were not needed. Mary now was free to marry the man she loved, the burly red-haired Charles Brandon, Duke of Suffolk, who had accompanied her to France. When therefore François approached her with the ritual question as to whether she were pregnant or whether he might now regard himself as King, she replied promptly that she knew of no reason why he should not. Even now, it seemed, he hankered after the pretty English girl, and was fully prepared to dispose of his own faithful, unappetising wife if need be. But having married to please her brother, Mary said firmly, she was now going to marry to please herself. And she did, passing out of French history with a proud but apprehensive Brandon whose task it now was to explain to his volatile and suspicious king how he had come to marry a Tudor princess.

François stepped into a role that was tailor-made for him. The three previous kings of France might have been estimable men but, undeniably, they had lacked glamour. This was a young man's world and the nineteen-year-old François with his passion for splendid clothes, his laughter, his gallantry, was the perfect expression of the confident new age. The crowds loved him: they delighted in his prodigality, his extravagance and the graceful manner with which he scattered around the gold and silver extracted from their pockets. His coronation in Rheims on January 25 was a vast, theatrical occasion with the venerable cathedral appearing like a richly bedecked stage. That was an occasion which his fifteen-year-old vassall, Charles, Duke of Burgundy, did not attend, but to which, nevertheless, he thought it prudent to send a representative. And afterwards the *joyeuse entrée* into Paris was the most brilliant which even that city had ever seen: over a thousand nobles took part, each dressed in priceless damasks and silks and velvets, glittering with cloth of gold and gems and precious metals, and providing an exotic setting for the auburn-haired young man who, in silver velvet and mounted upon a grey-clad charger, epitomised the state itself. In Italy, the sun of the Renaissance was already high in the heavens; here, in France, it was only now rising above the horizon.

For seven months after his coronation, François threw himself into the delightful business of being king. In the background, his mother planned and schemed and speculated and budgeted, closeted with financiers and administrators, patiently building and maintaining the machinery that allowed her Caesar to move in splendour, untrammelled by nagging details. Endless balls and fêtes; endless journeyings between one great castle and another; tournaments, joustings, banquets, love affairs, music – so the delightful days passed. But François never forgot his high goal, the purpose that had been with him ever since he had realised the nature of his destiny. The humdrum business of running the country could be safely left to his mother and her advisers. His task was the glamorous one of conquest – specifically, the conquest of his forefathers' possessions in Italy.

The principal of dynastic claim has all but vanished from civilisation today. Nothing more clearly separates the twentieth century from almost all its predecessors than that it has discarded the idea that an accident of birth justifies the transference of vast tracts of lands, together with perhaps millions of inhabitants, to a totally alien power merely because that power can prove a genetic link with the original conqueror. Even in François' day the suspicion was growing that, in practical politics, genealogy was subordinate to geography. François' 'royal cousin' and glittering rival, young Henry of England, might on occasion style himself 'King of France' but all parties involved recognised it for the ploy that it was. Nevertheless, the principle was still a dynamic of political life and could not have been better demonstrated than by the endless French claims on Italian principalities. Over three centuries earlier, François' ancestors had conquered Naples – but had been driven out in their turn by the Spaniards. It was a classic, constant pattern only too familiar to the Neapolitans. Greeks, Lombards, Romans, Saracens, Normans – all had sought to impose their will on the great southern city over the centuries; each had disappeared in time, though leaving their cultural impress upon the city. The French, however, were not disposed to be philosophical about their loss. They wanted Naples back, by conquest or conspiracy, and for a generation they threw Italy into a turmoil before at last admitting defeat.

François' claim on Naples was, at least, based upon the arbitrary but unarguable fact of conquest by his ancestors. His claim to Milan was almost bizarrely theoretical. Just over a century earlier Giangaleazzo Visconti, the then Duke of Milan, had married his daughter Valentina to the Duke of Orleans, and a clause of her marriage contract had arranged for Milan to go to her descendants, should the male Visconti line ever fail. The insertion of the clause was purely a lawyer's device to tie up all loose ends for there seemed no reason whatsoever why the male Visconti line should fail. Valentina had two brothers, one of whom became Duke of Milan in his turn, and the Dukedom was still in the family when she died. Even when the line, at length, did fail, there was no vacuum for power, for the ducal throne was promptly claimed by the adventurer Sforza in the name of his wife Bianca Visconti. The brilliant dynasty that Sforza founded seemed absolutely secure, for it was, after all, an Italian family ruling in an Italian city. But its rule was also illegal. Like a time-bomb, Valentina's marriage contract lay for over a century in a lawyer's office in France, awaiting the propitious moment when it would be activated. That moment came in 1494, the year of François' birth, during the triumphant first French invasion of Italy. Milan was lost and won and lost again and now, in the summer of 1515, François swore that this would be the first of the jewels he would restore to the crown of France. By early autumn he had kept his oath.

François was just twenty. Energetic, intelligent and courageous though he undoubtedly was, he was nevertheless an inexperienced boy placed in a position of absolute power by genetic chance and kept there by a thrusting, scheming mother. Apart from tournaments where his actions were anxiously monitored by heralds, his only experience of warfare had been an inconclusive campaign against the English, which had ended in a battle scornfully entitled 'Battle of the Spurs' by the invaders, so precipitate was the French withdrawal. Yet this spoilt inexperienced boy, with little more than a theoretical idea of warfare, achieved in weeks what grizzled commanders failed to achieve in years.

Aware of that medieval tendency to personalise the State in terms of the king, posterity is inclined to be cynical of such prowess, to assume that such an astonishing military feat was the work of the king's generals, for which he took the credit. Such a cynical view of a romantic story would be justified if it had been an Italian victory in the name of an Italian prince, for the Italians had long since emancipated themselves from the mystique of monarchy. There was no place for any ambiguous, two-way relationship in any Italian state. In the republics, the military commanders were kept under very close control; in the principates, the commander was working to an even closer brief, for the prince himself was usually the best general of them all. Campaigns succeeded or failed purely according to logic with no nonsense about noble last-ditch stands. The French 'sword-nobles', on the contrary, were still influenced by their primitive past where the tribal leader automatically sought the place of greatest danger and automatically received the utmost in loyal support, leader and led interacting with each other at a purely instinctual level to produce a powerful symbiotic bond.

Something like this must have happened in the French high command during the first exciting months of the campaign for Naples, as generous young men reacted to the catalyst of their young king. Most of them were in their twenties. One of the oldest was the legendary Chevalier de Bayard, then just 39 years old. Bayard is invariably introduced in the histories of his day with the phrase 'chevalier sans peur et sans reproche', and the ungenerous historian, reflecting that such a style seems altogether too much of a good thing, is tempted to search around for warts and human failings. They are exceedingly difficult to find: Bayard really does seem to have been a gay, courageous, honourable Christian knight, 'sans peur et sans reproche'. His inclusion in the gay company that swooped across the Alps in the summer of 1515 is altogether symbolic of the French approach to war: the knights of François' army have entered European legend, dashing, vibrant figures in their own right, contrasting with the workaday soldiers of Charles, the future emperor, and his Italian allies.

Bayard's name was a trumpet call, but the key figure in the army was François' cousin Charles, Duke of Bourbon, then twenty-six years old, one of the great magnates of France, a territorial lord scarcely less powerful than the independent Duke of Burgundy, and one, moreover, just a heartbeat away from the throne. The House of Bourbon shared a common stock with the Valois and was destined, in fact, to succeed it before the century was out. Charles of Bourbon's Italian ancestry showed in his thin, intelligent face and in his restless, nervous energy. He and François got on well, considering their strongly contrasting characters, the one full of laughter and gaiety, the other sober, almost sombre, a man who put duty always before pleasure, and who, ironically, was to go down in history as the greatest traitor and renegade of his day.

François was sensible enough to recognise Bourbon's sterling qualities and appointed him Constable – the effective commander-in-chief of the military forces of the kingdom. But rather more to the King's taste was the swashbuckling young hero Robert de la Marck, who referred to himself as the Young Adventurer in his own vivid chronicle of the times and was, indeed, to be known formally by that engaging title. Robert de la Marck, Lord of Fleurange was a hearty, good-looking blond young man, three years older than his king. The story was told how, at the tender age of ten, he had insisted on riding in full pomp and ceremony to the court of King Louis and there had offered his sword, begging to be allowed to accompany the king in the forthcoming Italian campaign. Much amused and rather touched, Louis as solemnly accepted the offer but, gently pointing out that the ten-year-old boy was 'not quite tall enough yet', asked him to join the suit of the seven-year-old François. The two lads grew up together, delighting above all to test each other's mettle on the tournament field till the Young Adventurer went off to fight real battles, leaving François restless at home. Now, in this summer of 1515, they were again riding side by side in armour, bound together for the real world of war. But even in the hurly-burly of campaigns, the Young Adventurer somehow found time to keep a journal of sorts, providing a lively picture of the first Italian campaign.

Cast in a similar mould as the Young Adventurer was the Gascon, Guillaume de Bonnivet, a great carouser, fighter and womaniser – as was to be expected of a Gascon. He lost his heart to François' beautiful, accomplished sister Marguerite, was astonished by the chastity she maintained, even though married to the dullest of husbands, and made a spirited attempt to rape her. She fought back with even greater spirit, leaving her mark so clearly upon him that he was obliged to pretend indisposition while his wounds healed. François created him Admiral of France, and admired his progress in boudoir and battlefield alike.

Marguerite's own husband, the Duke of Alençon, was part of the gay company though overshadowed by his brilliant peers. A dull, stupid, lacklustre man, he had been chosen simply as a dynastic partner and, in addition, suffered the misfortune of having a ghost for a rival. For, apart from her brother, Marguerite had only one real love in her life; the gentle, enigmatic Gaston de Foix, known by the French as the Dove but by the Italians as the Thunderbolt, who had been killed at Novara during the last disastrous French campaign in Italy. Gaston's brother, Odet de Foix, Count of Lautrec was in the present army, a marshal, though only in his early twenties. Lautrec possessed a beautiful sister just in her teens – a seemingly irrelevant fact which was to have a profound effect upon all that company, and especially upon Italy and upon Rome.

Stiffened by the addition of such greybeards as Trivulzio and La Pallice who had fought for the late king, François' army moved off from Lyons in July, bright with banners, brilliant with jewels and precious metals, dressed for war as for some courtly game. This was one of the last of the great feudal forays in which war was seen as an extension not of politics but of sport. Beyond the Alps, waiting grimly for this colourful company, were the Swiss, dour, workaday soldiers armed with that unromantic workaday weapon, the pike, that had already torn one French army to pieces. Behind the Swiss were the Italians, subtle, supple men who regarded war as an unsatisfactory alternative to intellectual manipulations and far preferred a victory obtained through corruption to one achieved through force. Fortunately for François, they were divided among themselves. Indeed, that foreigners could descend into Italy, waving dusty claims to this or that city, was due simply to the fact that the Italians hated each other slightly more than they hated foreigners and would ally themselves with the Grand Turk himself to gain an advantage over their neighbours. Lastly, somewhere in the background, pursuing their own enigmatic goals, were the Spaniards. Of all those engaged in the Italian arena these were the most complex, the most self-contradictory: fanatical Catholics who set about the destruction of the Holy City of Catholicism; primitive tribal warriors who used the most sophisticated techniques of modern warfare; Latins who leagued with Teutons in order to destroy Latins. Spain, in the paradoxical manner of the day, best summed up the paradox that was Italy.

François stepped upon the international stage with a brilliant exploit that thrilled all Europe, aroused the bitter envy of Henry, King of England, and caused Charles, King of Aragon and Castile, to raise his eyebrows in surprise and speculation. The Swiss held the two major passes of the Alps, the Mont Cenis and the Mont Genèvre. All informed opinion held that it was quite impossible for an army to cross the Alpine barrier at these two points. François achieved the crossing. Friendly mountaineers picked out a possible route for the army: the pioneers went ahead with Roman panache, blasting a crude roadway, bridging chasms with structures that looked terrifyingly flimsy but remained standing long enough to allow the passage of the army. They had the famous French artillery with them, that had opened up Italy to their predecessors twenty years before – huge, ponderous pieces that had to be dragged and pushed and, on occasions, boldly carried. François complained of the difficulty of wearing armour under these conditions. Even now the knights would not divest themselves of the sacrosanct armour that distinguished their class and the heavily armoured men were forced to travel gingerly on foot. 'Madame, we are in the strangest country that any of this country has ever seen', François wrote to his mother, struggling to describe the barren, savage Alpine scenery through which they were passing. But he comforted himself with the reflection that they would take the enemy by surprise.

He was right. Even before the main body of the army had thankfully gained the Piedmontese plain, a raiding force under the Chevalier Bayard gained a resounding triumph – nothing less than the capture of Prospero Colonna, the Italian commander-in-chief. He had scoffed at reports that the French army were coming through the Alps. 'Have they wings, then?' he had demanded and had boasted how he would hold that famous army 'like pigeons in a cage' before they could deploy their full strength. He was actually at dinner in the little town of Villafranca when the French raiders burst in on him. Bayard tried to comfort the disconsolate Italian. 'Seigneur Prospero, it is the fortune of war – to lose once and to win next time.'

François' gallant army marched across the plain towards Milan, the enemy retreating steadily. Turin fell into French hands, then Novara. But at Marignano the invaders halted, for even François, athirst for 'glory' though he was, would have preferred to avoid an outright clash with the army that protected Milan. The Lord of Milan may have been an ineffective young Italian, Massimiliano Sforza, but the soldiers who kept him in power were Swiss.

Four centuries of neutrality and settled government have given the Swiss an air of somewhat dull respectability in modern European eyes. But in the sixteenth century they appeared to the civilised nations of Europe like so many disciplined savages. Intensely patriotic, fanatically courageous, capable of the very noblest self-sacrifice, they were also distinguished by 'an appalling ferocity, a cynical contempt and pitiless disregard for the rights of others and a deliberate and cold-blooded cruelty'. It was these Alpine herdsmen who broke the long ascendancy of the mounted man, that rich nobleman who could afford heavy armour and a strong horse to carry him. The Swiss reply to this glittering panoply of war was almost laughably simple, consisting as it did of a long shaft of wood tipped with a steel point, the whole measuring some 19 feet from butt to tip: the pike. Its success depended upon one vital ingredient, the pikeman's utter faith in his neighbour. As long as one man held, all held, creating an actual hedge of glittering steel points that projected far beyond the vulnerable flesh that wielded it, a hedge that was unbreakable by the most determined cavalry charge.

The men who wielded the pikes were virtually defenceless at close quarters: a cap and leather jerkin was the most they wore as defence, and many fought barefoot. But this vulnerability gave a Swiss battle force the second of its great characteristics: manoeuverability. Observers again and again commented on the eerie nature of a Swiss advance. Silently, swiftly, with the great pike shafts held upright so that the whole mass looked like a moving wood, the army flowed like some natural force over hills and down valleys, swinging into action to the mournful lowing of the Alpine horns. Backing up the pikemen were the halberdiers, each armed with that terrible weapon which could hack, stab or clutch, a weapon so ponderous that, when two halberdiers encountered each other, mortal injury was almost invariably the outcome for one. And at the end of the battle, those of the defeated enemy who could not run away were butchered on the spot, for the Swiss neither took prisoners nor, in their turn, expected quarter.

Such were the professional killers whom young François faced on the afternoon of Thursday, September 13, 1515. They were mercenaries and he had tried to bribe them and had succeeded, or so he thought, when a substantial number of them had taken their bag of gold, for why should a mercenary fight to the death? But in Milan was Matthias Schinner, the Cardinal of Sion, who hated the French with a fierce and enduring hatred. The Young Adventurer described how Schinner summoned his fellow-countrymen by the beating of a drum and then, mounting a chair, exhorted them to battle 'like a fox who preaches to fowls'. These were singularly ferocious fowls, however, and at the end of the harangue, with Schinner screaming that he wanted to wash his hands and feet in French blood, tribal solidarity triumphed over pure venality and the Swiss marched out to battle, each under the banner of his canton – Uri and Schwyz, Zug, Lucerne, Basle, Schaffhausen, Unterwalden.

The armies clashed at four in the afternoon. Charles of Bourbon saved the French from a bloody and total defeat as he had been sceptical of the success of bribery and kept his vanguard on the alert, holding the first fierce shock long enough to permit the king to come thundering up with the main body of the army. Pikemen were pitted against pikemen, for Bourbon had protected the precious artillery with solid ranks of landsknechts, German professionals who had adopted the same tactics as their cousins of the mountains. Now was demonstrated that sheer brutal test of strength known as the 'shock of pike'. At close quarters, the pikemen could only heave at each other, thousands of men combining in a human tide so that it seemed as though two natural forces were contending, rather than two ranks of humans. The halberdiers on both sides came into their own, jostling for position, for balance. The man who missed his stroke under these conditions was a dead man for he would not have time to recover before the enemy's halberd skewered or hacked him down.

The plain became simply a killing ground, for there was neither time nor space for tactics. The autumn sun fell, a brilliant moon arose, and still the killing went on. There was no front line, no reserves, just a struggling, mingled, heaving mass of men, veiled in dust from all but the nearest neighbour whether he be comrade or enemy. About midnight sheer exhaustion brought peace. Men collapsed where they were. 'The two armies were within a stone's throw of each other and there was neither ditch nor hedge between them. Thus they remained all night without moving and those who were mounted sat on their horses, with only such food and drink as they had with them. And it is the firm belief that no man slept during all that night.' François asked for a drink and someone brought him a helmet filled with water, but it was so full of mud and blood that it made him ill. He had been on horseback for twenty-eight hours, fully armed and with nothing to eat or drink, he later wrote to his mother and it was probably true. His men had only praise for his courage and instinctive skill.

With daybreak the battle recommenced. It seemed as though the Swiss found it quite impossible to believe that the fighting formation which had stood them so well for over two generations was useless under modern conditions. For François possessed what his predecessors had never possessed: dependable artillery which could be loaded and fired at great speed and in such an order as to keep up a continuous hail of fire. Again and again the Switzers charged with lunatic courage, but pikemen supported by artillery could not fail to get the better of unsupported pikemen, be they never so brave. Even so, the battle continued till nearly mid-day when the arrival of François' Venetian allies clearly and irrevocably tilted the scales in his favour.

Some 16,000 men fell at Marignano, that curtain-raiser to the Italian tragedy, 16,000 men, of whom nearly all were non-Italians. The Swiss left perhaps 10,000 comrades on the field but the French and their German mercenaries, too, suffered heavily. The grizzled old Maréchal Trivulzio, who had known many a battle in his time, thought that Marignano 'was not a fight between men but between ferocious giants'. The Swiss pikemen, most dreaded of European soldiers, had been defeated beyond any shadow of doubt by the young King of France in his double début on the stage of war and on the stage of Italy. The Milanese garrison made a token resistance but then surrendered; and Massimiliano Sforza, descendant of that great soldier Francesco Sforza who had seized the duchy of Milan just seventy years before, went into exile rejoicing at his freedom: 'Thank God that I am free from the brutality of the Swiss, from the aggressions of the Emperor and from Spanish perfidy', he wrote cheerfully to his aunt Isabella d'Este from his safe refuge in France.

And now briefly François knew the heady delights of success, of being courted by the powerful, of being deferred to as arbiter of Europe's fate. These next few years were to be happy, golden years: a time in which he enjoyed to the full the sweets of power, unshadowed by failure or by the drab political need to adapt, to compromise. The Pope courted him: the affable Medici Pope Leo X, plump, cultured, jolly, infinitely devious. He and François met in Bologna a few weeks after Marignano and no one could have guessed from Leo's charming, hospitable manner that he had spent years dedicated to kicking the French out of Italy. He offered François a priceless reliquary that had, in fact, belonged to the unfortunate Sforza; rather unsportingly, François asked for the Laocoon instead. Charmingly, Leo agreed that the papal collection should be bereft of its chief pride – but gave private instructions that a copy was to be made. Isabella d'Este courted the young French king, overlooking, as was her wont, the fact that he had just deprived her nephew of a dukedom. She sent her son Federigo hastening to join the King to learn what he could and pick up what he could. The Italian cities that were still free to choose their destiny hastened to send congratulatory embassies to the court of France. In Spain, King Charles heard the news and grew yet more thoughtful; in England, the blustering Hal refused to believe that such glory could fall to his rival.

François left Italy in January 1516, four months after the battle that had made him a European figure. In France, he took up again the role of golden youth, moving affably between one pleasure and another, basking in the love of his mother and sister – 'a single heart in three bodies', as Marguerite put it with her gift for words; basking in the adulation of his subjects for whom he was still the romantic young king of promise; basking, above all, in the love of women, young, beautiful, aristocratic and, on the whole, preferably, intelligent. Usually, they fell over themselves to enter the royal bed. But one who caught his eye did not, and casual interest turned accordingly to passionate desire.

Madame de Chateaubriant was happy in her country home with her husband and her little daughter. François invited her husband to bring her to court. She was too shy, replied her husband not knowing, perhaps, quite what to make of the situation: the husband of a royal mistress was not, in general, by any means to be pitied. It was at this stage, with his unrequited passion at fever heat, that François reminded himself that this beautiful, virtuous young woman was the sister of one of his gallant band, Odet de Foix, Count of Lautrec, a young man who had served gallantly, if not with particular distinction, in Italy. Gratitude, François reflected, might well begin to undermine the sister's defences. The royal edict accordingly went forth appointing the Count of Lautrec as Governor of the Duchy of Milan, so, in effect, constituting him viceroy for French affairs in Italy. As it happened, the office of Governor was already filled, the existing incumbent being Charles, Duke of Bourbon, Constable of France, who had been very largely, the architect of the French triumph in Italy. He was dismissed like a minor official without a word of explanation or thanks. Bourbon said nothing. The seals of office were handed over to Lautrec who thereby inherited the formidable military problem of providing for the defence of Lombardy against all comers, and the Duke of Bourbon went home, still keeping his own counsel. And that was the first of François' great mistakes.

In the same year that Charles, Duke of Bourbon, was so gratuitously humiliated by his King, Charles, Duke of Burgundy, became King of Spain. Not long afterwards, the Emperor Maximilian died and the crown of the Holy Roman Empire was available to the highest bidder: for this, theoretically the highest and holiest secular office in the world, was now simply an object of trade or barter. The right to choose the supposed successor to Caesar lay in the hands of seven powerful German magnates known, with unconscious irony, as the Electors. It was open knowledge that their votes were for sale, but so powerful was the lure of the debased crown, so firmly was it rooted in the mystique of Europe that there never lacked candidates for it. Three came forward now: Charles of Spain, François of France and Henry of England. Wisely, Henry backed out when he realised the colossal price being asked and Charles and François at last came into direct competition with each other for the first time. Both tried to put a patina of decency on the matter. 'We are both wooing the same mistress', François wrote to his brother king with what passed for a friendly smile. But no one was fooled. François wanted the crown most desperately; it was the only fitting diadem for a king such as he, who had already displayed his power and glory to the world. His mother, suppressing any private misgivings, backed him up and her financial advisers began the task of raising the quantities of gold necessary to satisfy the appetites of the Electors. But for every ten ducats Louise was able to squeeze out of an increasingly restless nation, Charles was able to produce eleven, for behind him he had the almost bottomless coffers of the Fuggers, the great banking house of Augsburg. In any case, the Fuggers, as Germans, might have been marginally in favour of a candidate who could at least prove German descent. But they were, first and foremost, bankers: that these coldly acquisitive men, skilled in the minutest dissection of character, decided to back the somewhat dull and pedantic Charles of Spain rather than the dashing, glamorous François of France was a good indication of the young men's characters. On 28 June, 1519, the nineteen-year-old Charles, Duke of Burgundy, and King of Spain was 'elected' Holy Roman Emperor of the German Nation at a total cost of something above half a million pieces of gold. François never forgot and never forgave.

Chapter III

The Triple Crown

Forty-one years before the Habsburg youth emerged as the legal lord of Europe, the Cathedral of Florence was crowded for High Mass on an April Sunday in 1478. Among the worshippers were the de facto Lord of Florence, Lorenzo de' Medici, and his handsome young brother Giuliano. At the moment of the consecration of the Host, assassins hurled themselves upon the two men, killing Giuliano, but only wounding Lorenzo.

The plot to topple the Medici failed because the conspirators had totally underestimated the family's popularity in the city. All involved were hunted down and slaughtered. But Lorenzo was not content with simple vengeance. He had loved his brother Giuliano with all the force of his generous, complex nature and his love now extended to embrace his dead brother's illegitimate child, a boy called Giulio. The boy was accordingly taken into Lorenzo's family and brought up with the rest. It was a happy, united family and young Giulio formed strong bonds with his relatives, in particular with the eldest boy, Giovanni.

In due course Giovanni became Pope Leo X. His cousin Giulio had followed him into the Church and now received his due reward, for Pope Leo, with that strong Medici love of family, ensured that his childhood playmate should accompany him as he ascended the heights of power. He created Giulio a cardinal and made him Vice-Chancellor – an immensely important office that was, in effect, that of deputy pope. It was by no means an unwise or dishonourable appointment, for Giulio was the ideal lieutenant, loyal, discreet, hardworking. Indeed, the two cousins perfectly complemented each other: where Leo was expansive, jovial, careless with money, Giulio was cautious, non-committal and frugal by comparison. Even their appearance was in contrast: Leo, the legitimate Medicean aristocrat, looked a plebian – short, fat, roly-poly; Giulio, the illegitimate, looked every inch an aristocrat, being tall and elegant, his swarthy good looks only slightly marred by a cast in the eye.

Leo's pontificate was the Golden Age of Rome and of the Papacy. 'God has given us the Papacy, let us enjoy it', he said. And he did. It was no crude debauch that he instituted, for he was, after all, a Florentine and a Medici. Rome became again the cultural capital of the West: artists, singers, sculptors,

43

musicians, scholars, any man who could gain the volatile but cultured Pope's interest was assured of a good living at the court of Rome, and they flocked in until the great city became a treasure house of talent. And not only of talent. Bullion poured into the city, gold and silver to be made into coins to pay the thronging artists and courtiers and artisans, gold and silver to be worked into ornaments and jewellery, cast in the form of statues. Precious fabrics from all the known world were heaped high in warehouses, waiting their turn to be transformed into costume both ecclesiastical and secular; gems glittered everywhere: rubies, diamonds, pearls set in great rings, sewn into clothing, studding goblets, reliquaries, crosses. Rome had not known such wealth since the collapse of the classical Empire. And it was wealth that was guarded by little more than a circuit of brown walls and a belief that the city within was inviolable.

For nine years Pope Leo X presided over this golden dance of pleasure, hampered scarcely at all by his priestly role. Balls, banquets, luxurious hunting parties joyously filled the days and most of the nights. There was always a new artist to be interviewed, a new painting to be commissioned, a new piece of jewellery to be chosen. He inherited from his predecessor the task of demolishing old St Peter's and building the new, a task which was to put a vast and unprecedented strain upon papal finances. Ears not totally deafened by the sound of music and laughter might have detected creakings in the ancient structure which he controlled, might have heard, above all, those hammer blows from beyond the Alps where the monk Martin Luther was nailing up his theses on the door of Wittenberg church. Leo handled the regrettable matter of Luther with skill and delicacy, assenting at last to the excommunication of this turbulent German monk with greatest reluctance before returning to more important things.

In the matter of Italian politics Leo was to gain a reputation for deviousness and double-dealing that was not entirely due to his Medicean, Florentine upbringing. To do him justice, he had but little choice. He was not only the spiritual leader of Christendom but also the lord of a large, rich, and very vulnerable, Italian principality, the States of the Church. The States were held like a nut between formidable jaws: for, to the north, the power of France had again established itself in the plain of Lombardy; while, in the south, the power of Spain was firmly established in Naples. Sooner or later the two powers must clash – those who were foolish enough to come between could not complain of being hurt. Leo's tactics, therefore, were to skip nimbly from side to side, never declaring unequivocally for one or the other. Or rather, those were his ideal tactics. They had to be modified because they affected the one certain object which could guarantee him unswerving loyalty and, if necessary, ferocious protection, and that was the well-being of the Medici family.

In order to ensure that well-being, he was perfectly prepared to stand papal policy on its head, in particular in the matter of those foreigners who were insolently using Italian soil on which to fight out their differences. As a good Italian Leo disliked Spaniards and Frenchmen impartially; as a good Medici he had to temper that dislike, since both his brother and his nephew had acquired

French brides. It was practical politics to make friends with France, while ensuring, of course, that one did not make an outright enemy of Spain. But, after the battle of Marignano, the delicate balance of Leo's esteem tipped with embarrassing, un-Medicean clarity towards France, so resounding and uncontrovertible had been young François' triumph. Charles, in Spain, was enraged: 'His Holiness has been playing a double game all along', he snarled to the nervous papal legate. 'All his zeal to drive the French from Italy is but a mask.' But still Leo contrived to hold a balance. He was even able to use the foreigners to create a dukedom for his unsavoury nephew Lorenzo: he persuaded the new French Governor of Milan to provide troops with which to drive out the Duke of Urbino in whose place Lorenzo was installed. The Duke of Urbino was Francesco della Rovere and he was to gain his vengeance at the expense of Leo's cousin and successor, and, above all, at the expense of the citizens of Rome.

Leo the fortunate was never so fortunate as in the time of his death in 1521. Outwardly, he was at the height of his power, a young man in his early forties, secure in his base, secure in his allies, his enemies suppressed or in exile. But those closer to him knew differently. They saw the empty coffers, emptied by an endless extravagance; they heard the mutterings behind the scenes of men waiting for revenge, of men who had been duped just once too often. Rome woke from a golden dream to the cold light of day. They were not to know it but the Golden Age had passed – for ever.

The Conclave to elect Leo's successor reflected the uncertainty. No one cardinal emerged as *papabile* – possessing those indefinable but real qualities which made him an obvious choice. So confused and conflicting were the currents that even Cardinal Wolsey entertained the thought that he might yet be the second English pope to ascend the Chair of St Peter. He was disappointed. So was one man after another who saw himself as the leader of a faction. There were, in fact, too many factions, all mutually exclusive.

It was Giulio de' Medici who suggested the traditional solution in such a situation: the election of a stop-gap pope. He proposed a man who was not even present in Rome, Adrian of Utrecht, the ex-tutor and life-long confidant of the Emperor Charles V. Reluctantly, the Conclave accepted the compromise. Adrian was elected, was summoned to Rome, and lasted just eighteen months, for Rome broke first his spirit then his heart. He had accepted the office with immense reluctance. The dissolute luxury of Rome startled and deeply distressed him. A story went round of how he had written ahead, asking if some small residence could perhaps be set aside for him. It is highly unlikely that even such a retiring man as Adrian would have been unaware that the vast and gorgeous Vatican Palace was placed automatically at the disposal of a new pope; but the legends of his frugality, transforming his natural austerity into barbarous ignorance, had gathered about him even before he arrived. By temperament, he had a natural antipathy for the spirit of the Renaissance. All the beauty that his predecessor, Leo, had created either was meaningless to him, or was regarded by him as a positive evil, a seduction of the Devil. The beautiful chambers of the Palace were closed; the exquisite, priceless vessels of gold and silver and gems were sold or locked away; the artists and cooks and singers and costumiers and poets, together with their innumerable hangers-on, were driven hence. The banquets ended: each morning, the gossips said, he took a single ducat out of his pocket and gave it to his housekeeper for the day's expenses.

And Rome, which had basked in the Medici glow for nearly a decade, which had grown fat through Medicean patronage, retaliated with that hatred which was its eternal and most potent weapon. Adrian, a foreigner and a Teuton, was totally at the mercy of the Italian bureaucracy which ran the papal court. The bureaucracy made the most of its power. There was no need for violent or overt action, no need to stage rebellion or assassination to get rid of an encumbrance. The same result could be gained by negative action: by dragging heels, by sullenness, by misinterpretation or by delay. Adrian came to his office at the age of sixty-three, comparatively young, for most popes achieved power in their late sixties and seventies. A life-time's austerity had given him a spare, healthy body. Reasonably, he could have expected to live at least another ten or fifteen years. Eighteen months as pope destroyed his health. Even as he lay dying he had no peace, for a group of cardinals, convinced that such a frugal man must have amassed a vast sum of money, brutally tormented him to make him reveal the whereabouts of his non-existent treasure. At his death the vicious wits of Rome had the last say: someone hung a wreath on his doctor's door with the inscription: 'To the deliverer of his country, of the senate and of the people of Rome.'

At the Conclave which met to elect Adrian's successor Giulio de' Medici did not repeat the mistake of suggesting a pope, who might turn out to be unsatisfactory. Medici emerged himself as Supreme Pontiff and Universal Pope, taking the name of Clement. At the age of forty-eight, Giulio de' Medici had just experienced the most traumatic transition: from a position of secondary authority to a position not merely of primary but of absolute authority. All monarchs assumed, as a matter of course, that they were where they were by the Divine will and that their writ ran in every corner of their sovereignty, controlling every detail of their subjects' lives from the cradle to the grave. But even they recognised that the writ ran out at the edge of the grave whereas it was precisely there that the writ of the Bishop of Rome came into its fullest power. At that moment in the Conclave when he had uttered the single word 'Volo' and had so become the successor of the Apostle, the Vicar of Christ on Earth, Giulio de' Medici, now Pope Clement, was charged not only with powers of life and death over his Roman subjects, but with powers of damnation or salvation over the souls of all human beings upon the planet. No matter that the majority of those human beings were either totally unaware of his existence, or fiercely derisive of his claims. No matter that his predecessors had so abused their powers that the awful sentence of excommunication was regarded now as one – and that, not the most potent – of the political weapons of the day. To his own mind, his spiritual powers and responsibilities were as real as granite and his every act was conditioned by his belief in them. That, perhaps, was Pope Clement's greatest disadvantage: he was a good man and a humble Christian, but he was also a man of his time, a dynast. The two halves of his nature conflicted endlessly with each other and, because he was a weak man, the immediate problems of the dynast only too often took precedence over the distant problems of the priest.

His election was welcomed with genuine delight throughout Italy, by Rome in particular. 'The city is filled with the greatest joy and all the world is returning', the Mantuan envoy, Castiglione, told his master. The Romans, admittedly, had a very down-to-earth reason for being delighted. The city was, and always had been, a parasite, from the days of the Caesars onward producing nothing. The Romans had always been dependent for their livelihood on serving – or exploiting – strangers, those attracted to the city first by the imperial court and then by the papal court that succeeded it. The rich pickings to which the Romans were accustomed had ended abruptly during the austere reign of the old Flemish barbarian, Adrian; now there was every hope that the golden days would come again, particularly under a Medici. It seemed that Giulio, now Pope Clement, did not intend to disappoint them. 'He granted more favours on the first day of his reign than Adrian did in his whole lifetime', Albergati, the ambassador from Bologna, reported to his government.

The cheers and compliments of those who benefited materially were naturally suspect, but added to the chorus were the voices of the wise and the virtuous, the sober and the industrious. Such a one was the noble matron, Vittoria Colonna: 'Praised be to the Lord for ever', she wrote on hearing of Clement's elevation. 'May he further this beginning to such ends that men may see that there was never wrought a greater blessing.' And if it be objected that Vittoria Colonna was merely a woman – even if a woman with an intellect to attract such a man as Michelangelo – then there is the testimony of the Doge of Venice, head of a government not usually given to excessive enthusiasms: the Republic would send its most illustrious citizens to honour the new pope 'as though he were a god on earth', the Doge wrote. In Florence the news of a Medicean pope was naturally received with very great pleasure and a brisk movement began among those more mobile sections of the populace who calculated that Rome's streets would be paved in gold for the compatriots of a Florentine pope. Not all these hopefuls were bankers and usurers: among them was the ex-Secretary, Niccolo Machiavelli, who was encouraged to hasten ahead with his *History of Florence* in order to place it in the hands of the new pope in return for much-needed cash.

Clement gave excellent grounds for optimism during the first few weeks of his reign. The frugal were pleased that he had turned aside from the spendthrift prodigality of his splendid cousin Leo: the vast, wasteful banquets were never resumed, neither were the balls and festivals in which Leo had delighted; instead, the new pope listened gravely to music at his simple meals, commenting and criticising intelligently, for he was an excellent musician himself. The religious noted how he kept all fast days and how all services at which he was present were conducted with devoutness. The uproarious hunting parties, which had used to take Pope Leo away from his duties for days on end, were in the past, together with the low comedies and troops of performers – dwarves, jugglers, minstrels, jesters, animal-trainers – which had been a feature of the Vatican Palace. But neither did Clement go to the other extreme, as did poor Adrian. For Clement, too, was a Medici and took pleasure in things of the intellect as well as the spirit. In his humdrum daily work as politician he was cautious. 'This Pope is the most secretive man in the world', the Spanish ambassador wrote to Madrid. 'I have never spoken with one whose sayings were so hard to decipher.' But that was no bad trait for a ruler whose lightest word could have such profound effects in the spiritual or temporal spheres in which he ruled. He worked hard and devotedly, spending hour after hour among the documents that poured in from all over the civilised world, listening to the nuncios and legates who were the ears and eyes of the Vatican in a score of countries. No ruler on earth was better informed of what was passing in the world than a conscientious pope, for his lines of communication did not end in gorgeous embassies or the homes of wealthy men, but continued down to the smallest towns and villages. And Clement was a conscientious pope.

He had need of the fund of goodwill and experience that was, briefly, so freely available to him. Each pope who ascended the Throne of St Peter had immediate and pressing problems thrust upon him, for each pope stepped immediately into the very heart of European affairs. But none had had problems quite so unprecedented as those thrust upon Clement VII, who seated himself upon the Throne at one of the great climacterics of world history. The world had widened immeasurably since his childhood and youth. He had been a young man of seventeen when the news had reached Florence that the ships of Messer Cristoforo Colombo had returned to Spain, bearing news of a world beyond the Atlantic. Those battered ships had been symbolic of a totally new age that brought with it a cargo of deadly danger as well as riches and delight. The kind of mind that could look across the Atlantic and visualise the curvature of the earth, and speculate what might lie beyond was the same kind of mind that could look at the established order of society and speculate what could perhaps take its place. Clement, as lieutenant to his cousin Leo, had been aware of the scale of the problems, but had not been particularly involved with them, for his talents had always been for the tactical rather than the strategic. But now, the problems were there, looming before him, as pope, like a hydra half veiled in the mists of the future.

There was first the tedious business of the ex-monk Martin Luther. Two years before, at the Diet of Worms, the young Emperor Charles had heartened all the orthodox with his firm elimination of that source of discord in the European harmony. But somehow Martin Luther refused to remain eliminated and bobbed up here, there, everywhere, with some new, crude piece of anti-papal propaganda. It was unlikely that his particular brand of heresy had any future to it (how many such heresies had there not been in the past?) but it was nevertheless untidy, a distraction for a mind that should be bent on other, more important affairs. In England, for instance, the braggart Henry seemed to be fancying himself as a theologian, edging into forbidden areas despite the respectful attempts of Cardinal Wolsey to keep his thoughts running in more fitting channels. So far, admittedly, the Englishman's pretensions had been useful. His absurd huffing and puffing against Martin Luther, in the pamphlet resoundingly entitled *Assertio Septum Sacramentum*, had even earned him the title of Defender of the Faith from Pope Leo – a cheap means of payment for his unqualified defence of the Papacy. But there were disconcerting signs that King Henry was, in fact, desirous of qualifying that defence, desirous of making other assertions regarding the roles of king and pope. Down Clement's marvellously sensitive grapevine had come hints that Henry was seeking some way out of an irksome marriage. Divorce was by no means impossible, Clement reflected: Holy Church was never inhumanly inflexible about any of the burdens she lay upon the faithful, and no important precedent would be established by allowing Henry to put away his wife. After all, it was scarcely twenty years since the late Holy Father, Alexander Borgia, had solved his daughter Lucrezia's problems by arranging a divorce for her, and there was no real reason why Henry Tudor should not have his problems solved in a similar way. But Henry would have to be patient.

At home, the domestic problems pressed thick and close. Not only was the papal treasury empty, but the revenues were mortgaged for the foreseeable future to the bankers of Florence and Sienna and Venice. Pope Leo had built his brilliant world on borrowed money and the bill was now presented to his cousin, Pope Clement. This burden of debt at the very outset of his reign was to cause Clement, unfairly, to be charged with parsimony and downright avarice. He was naturally sober and frugal and it seemed to him to be his obvious duty to apply his personal standards of financial morality to the affairs of the Church, in particular while that huge debt hung over it. He therefore began a policy of retraction in those areas where it was possible to economise. Those areas, unfortunately for him, included art patronage and social display; and those indignant – and articulate – artists, writers and assorted socialites who found that the Medicean fountain of patronage had dried up took their revenge in scurrilous gossip. Galling though it might seem, a pope's influence – his very ability to do his work as shepherd – depended in large measure upon his standing with the gossips and idlers and hangers-on of Rome, who manufactured his reputation for export as well as home consumption.

During the first few months of his reign Clement was at least spared the scourge of the great families which always afflicted all rulers of Rome. The Roman nobles were unique not merely in Italy but in all Europe. Elsewhere, the aristocracy had long since been tamed, either by the power of the king, as in France or England, or by the people, as in the republics of Florence or Venice. In the narrow confines of Rome some fifty great families maintained fifty miniature states. Their inter-tribal wars were not quite as ferocious and as frequent as they had been: to that extent, at least, they had been civilised. But still they were kept under only nominal control, regarding their earthly and spiritual lord, the Pope, simply as the first among equals, the man who had been able to rig enough votes in Conclave to emerge as Bishop and Lord of Rome. The barons could not affect the Bishop, but they could affect the Lord, for his power depended upon their support. Clement had already clashed with the most powerful of these clans, the Colonna, for in the Conclave his most determined rival had been Cardinal Pompeo Colonna. Cardinal Medici had triumphed over Cardinal Colonna because he was a better committee-man, but sooner or later he would have to reckon with a proud and arrogant man who believed he had been cheated of the tiara. For the time being, however, there was relative calm in Rome as the rival factions took stock of the confused situation in the north of Italy, where the troops of Spain and France were beginning to manouevre for position. It was a traditional custom of the great Roman families to use non-Romans – outsiders – as weapons against each other, and Clement, a veteran in the game of Roman politics, felt perfectly confident of his ability to maintain his balance. What he did not know was that, on the far side of the Alps, a great French magnate was sullenly contemplating the possibility of betraying his suzeraine. And even if Pope Clement had realised that Charles de Montpensier, Duke of Bourbon, was about to break his sworn oath, it would not have seemed of any particular significance either to Clement himself, or to the city of Rome.

Chapter IV

The Captains and the Kings

On the evening of 31 May, 1520 an armada of English ships docked in the English port of Calais on the coast of France and some 5,000 people disembarked. Although the crowd was vast, it was still exclusive, for it consisted of the entire upper layer of English society, including the twenty-nine-year-old King Henry; his queen Catherine, a pale, rather dumpy woman of thirty-five; the king's young sister Mary, widow of the late King Louis of France who still called herself dowager-queen of France though now happily married to the Duke of Suffolk; and, plebeian in appearance but arrogant in manner, the butcher's son from Ipswich, Thomas Wolsey, Cardinal, Legate and Chancellor of England, approaching the apogee of his power. On 5 June the King and Queen, together with their enormous retinue, travelled inland for some six miles, prudently remaining within the English Pale, and halted just outside the small town of Guînes where a camp of quite extraordinary luxury had been erected for them. There they waited.

Two days later a French cortège of approximately the same size arrived at the town of Ardres, a few miles from Guînes. This, too, was a royal escort travelling with the King François and his heavily pregnant Queen, Claude. Among the glittering figures were the Queen Mother, Louise, eagerly noting down every action of her beloved son; and his cousin and Constable, the Duke of Bourbon. As controller of all military forces, Bourbon was responsible for the King's safety, a task that was by no means a sinecure on this particular occasion, despite its outward appearance of gaiety. Also in the party, among Queen Claude's ladies, there was a little thirteen-year-old, black-haired, black-eyed maid of honour called Anne Boleyn or Bullen; her presence there was not thought worthy of remark until some six years later.

Between 5 June and 7 June envoys scurried between the two camps, wrestling with the minutiae of protocol concerning the meeting of two equal monarchs. It was at last agreed that they should meet outside a tent, supplied by the English and set up midway between the two camps in the Val d'Ore. The meeting would take place at 6 p.m. on Saturday, 7 June, and in that manner would be inaugurated the great tournament that was to go down in history as the Field of the Cloth of Gold.

The meeting was very largely at François' insistence. Over the previous months the personal relationship between himself and his great rival, the Emperor Charles, had taken on an increasingly bitter edge. War between France and Spain was inevitable when a man like François felt that he had been cheated of something and a man like Charles was determined to hold what he had. When that war took place, on which side would King Henry of England place himself? England, with a population of three million, and a beggarly income of 800,000 ducats, was a midget compared with France with her population of 14 million and an income of 6,000,000 ducats. But the application of even a tiny weight at a fulcrum could alter a balance of power. And Henry and Charles were on far too close terms for François' peace of mind: for were they not related by the strongest of all political ties – marriage? Admittedly, rumours were circulating that not all was well in the eleven-year-marriage between the King of England and the Spanish Emperor's aunt; but dynastic marriages were rarely happy and there was time yet for Catherine to present her husband with an heir. Young Charles had thought it worthwhile to pay a personal visit to England, slipping across just five days before the royal court left for France, and though nothing concrete had as yet come of the visit, François was only too keenly aware of the need to make a counter move.

Those were the political reasons for the meeting in the Val d'Ore, and they were sound enough. But the personal reasons were almost as strong. The two young men had never met, and each had the liveliest interest in the other's doings. Sharing much the same background, with much the same tastes, and of similar age, they were, in a very real as well as ceremonial sense, 'royal brothers'. Each knew the loneliness and headiness of absolute power; each knew the occasional temptation to let the burden of decision slide to other, professional shoulders. Each was fascinated by the other's royal splendour as demonstrated by jewels and brocades; by castles and artists; by prowess in battles and boudoirs. Henry, in particular, was eaten up by envy of François' military prowess, for he had nothing to put in the scales against Marignano; and François, for his part, was deeply impressed by the firm grip that Henry exerted on even the most turbulent of his barons. Each needed to display his splendour to the other, the only person who could really appreciate it. And so, while Wolsey in England and Duprat in France were beginning their devious lawyers' dealings; and while in France Louise minutely inspected every document that crossed the Channel, and in England Catherine conferred anxiously with her compatriots, Henry and François had turned their minds to matters concerning clothing and jewels and horses and tents and all the prodigal display that would make of this, the last of the medieval tourneys, the greatest of its kind.

The two royal camps erected outside their supporting towns were intended, quite simply, to stun with extravagance. The common materials used for the tents and pavilions were velvet, cloth of gold, satin; those who could not afford such splendours simply slept where they could in the decrepit, war-time towns. François' tent was an enormous pavilion, sixty feet high, of cloth of gold. Three broad horizontal bands of royal blue velvet were sewn with the golden lilies of

France; inside, the pavilion was lined with more royal blue velvet and divided into rooms. Supporting the royal pavilion were four more, only slightly smaller, serving as chapel, banquet hall, dressing room and council chamber, the whole complex forming an inner, royal enclosure. Nearby were the tents of the Queen's entourage, in cloth of gold and silver, and violet satin. Louise, too, had her own great pavilion in purple and crimson velvet, with supporting tents for domestic purposes. Some 400 other tents and pavilions surrounded this royal heart, covering acres of ground with gold and purple and crimson and violet, glowing and glittering in the summer sun, leaving an unforgettable impression upon those who were there. Years later, the Young Adventurer recorded the details as the richest display he had ever seen.

The English managed to upstage even this display, primarily through engineering ingenuity. François' pavilion, though luxurious, was still nothing more than a large tent: Henry had a portable palace, a confection of wood and canvas, painted to resemble brick and stone, made in England and shipped across to be erected outside Guînes. So proud were the English of this extraordinary structure, that a painting was made of it, a work by an unknown artist that was destined to survive and convey to posterity some impression of one corner of the Field of the Cloth of Gold. The prefabricated castle had windows of real glass and inside accommodation was on two storeys for the royal family. Their immediate followers were not spread out, like the French, but brought together under the one roof. The King, the Queen, Wolsey, Princess Mary: each had his or her spacious apartment in the palace. The great hall and adjoining chapel appeared absolutely solid, permanent, with golden statues, a floor of white and yellow taffetas, massive tables and a great throne. A graceful, flower-bedecked covered way connected the castle with the town, and in front of it two great fountains dispensed an endless flow of wine. In the opening days of the tournament, when François' edict that the mob was to be kept outside the valley was strictly enforced, the fountains added a luxurious but still decorous note. But later, when the policing arrangement broke down under the vast press of people, the area in front of the English palace became a squalid, drunkards' haven. Beyond the palace were the pavilions and tents of the English nobility, rivalling their French counterparts with their velvets and satins and cloth of gold and silk.

Such was the background, the stage-setting for an event that seems, in retrospect, to follow the pattern of a contrived drama which opened with the meeting of the kings. Despite the ostensible reason for the tournament, there was deep mutual suspicion between their followers. Wars still resembled chess: the king, no matter how personally worthless he might be, was still the heart and soul, the very reason for the existence of his nation and his army. Place the opponent's king under constraint and the most extensive concessions could be rung out of the opponent. Such were the thoughts which went through the minds of Charles of Bourbon, in François' following, and Abergavenny, in Henry's entourage. To an apprehensive eye, the royal cavalcades that gathered at each end of the Val d'Ore in the late afternoon of 5 June displayed an unsettling resemblance to an army, despite their banners and ribbons and ceremonial armour. It had been agreed that guns should fire simultaneously in Ardres and Guînes and that at that signal the two groups should move off, halting near the centre of the field where the two monarchs would advance alone. Barriers had been erected, closing off the entire valley to the thousands of commoners who had been drawn to this spectacle from all over France and the Low Countries.

Shortly before 6 p.m. the guns boomed and the two groups cantered into movement. To the distant spectators the glittering companies cantering down the sides of the valley and gaining speed as they approached each other resembled a cavalry charge. But though there were armed and suspicious men in the groups, there were also plump, elderly ecclesiastics who were only too anxious to dispel any warlike impression. Bourbon led on the French side, dressed in cloth of gold and silver, carrying his unsheathed Constable's sword. Flanking him was the Grand Esquire, the Italian San Severino, dressed in black and gold and carrying, also unsheathed, the great Sword of State with its damascened fleurs-de-lys. François followed, immediately accompanied by his favourite, the Admiral Bonnivet, and the heralds, Mountjoy, Normandy and Brittany. Behind them came a motley collection of nobles and high officers of state, among them the Chancellor Duprat.

Leading the English was the Marquis of Dorset with England's Sword of State. Henry rode immediately behind, almost abreast with Wolsey, enveloped in crimson velvet and riding a mule caparisoned in crimson and gold. Half way down the slope Abergavenny and Shrewsbury appear to have caught up with Henry, for even at this late stage Abergavenny voiced his uneasiness: 'Sire, you should stop. I have been in the French party and they be more in number – double as many as ye be.' Shrewsbury mocked the other's timidity: 'Sire, the Frenchmen be more in fear of you and your subjects than your subjects be of them. Your Grace should go forward.' 'So we intend my lord', Henry replied shortly, and the pace increased to a gallop. At the bottom of the hill both companies halted and the two kings galloped towards each other alone and in sudden silence. For the first time each could see the other in the flesh, as an individual, detached from his background, growing clearer, more distinct as he hurtled over the rich green field. Henry was dressed in gold and silver, a burly young man with close-cropped hair and a thick, soft, red beard, tough and proud of his toughness, although already inclined to flabbiness. François was glittering, on that bright evening, like a jeweller's shop, for while his basic costume was cloth of gold it was hung about and studded with scores of gems: diamonds, rubies, emeralds, pearls. The English were much impressed by him, 'a goodly prince, stately of countenance, merry of cheer, brown coloured, great eyes, high-nosed, fair breast and shoulders, small legs and long feet', the chronicler Edward Hall noted.

The young men thundered towards each other and drew up. Henry's horse reared; he controlled it with consummate skill. And then, still on horseback, the Kings of France and England leaned towards each other and embraced. Their followers cheered and mingled, Bourbon exchanging salutes with his opposite number, Dorset, both men doubtless relieved that the great naked

Swords were on ceremonial display only. The monarchs and their immediate followers dismounted and entered the golden tent where toasts and speeches were exchanged. There was a moment of embarrassment when the English herald, reading aloud from his prepared parchment, began: 'I, Henry, King of France . . .'. Henry interrupted him. 'I cannot be King of France while you are here', he said gracefully to François, and ordered the herald to begin again, dropping the style. The herald did so – but the style remained unaltered in the document.

Thereafter followed two weeks of incessant banquets and jousts and private visits. Henry and François displayed extravagant, somewhat adolescent, expressions of mutual trust and love. François gallops unattended to the English camp and rouses his royal brother from sleep. Henry thereupon declares himself François' loving prisoner. François airs Henry's shirt, announcing that he is the royal valet: Henry bestows a collar of gold worth 15,000 ducats upon him, and François promptly gives Henry a bracelet worth double that sum. They hunted together, drank together, played tricks on each other. Only once was the lovefeast marred when Henry boisterously grasped François as they were going into dinner, crying: 'I'll have a wrestle with you my brother.' François, though not so burly, was tough and wiry and skilful; despite the fact that he was taken by surprise he was able to throw Henry heavily to the ground. Red with rage, all the good humour wiped from his face, Henry arose and a nasty situation was averted only by their two wives' pleading with them to forget the matter and come to table.

The Field of the Cloth of Gold ended with the expected protestations of undying friendship between England and France. Henry took himself off to Calais, where he was to meet the Emperor, Charles, while François, his mother and the Duke of Bourbon made their way back to Paris. But they had scarcely arrived there when Louise, glumly totting up the astronomical costs of the tournament, learned that it had all been a complete waste of money except insofar as it had allowed her son to display his glory to the world. Henry and Charles had come to an agreement, and a treaty was even now being signed between Spain and England that would leave France isolated in the event of war. Bourbon heard the news without comment, then took his leave of his monarch, returning to his great estates in the south.

Ever since Bourbon had been summarily dismissed from Lombardy, the relationship between François and this laconic man, the greatest of all French vassals, had been, at best, strained and brittle. As befitting his office and his wealth, Bourbon had been a dominant figure at the Field of the Cloth of Gold, in particular attracting the speculative attention of Henry. During one of the tournaments Bourbon rode a splendid mount which could leap its own height, much to Henry's admiration. Bourbon immediately offered the horse to the King of England who graciously accepted it. Henry had a good eye for a horse, but also an extremely sensitive nose for survival; and regarding the splendid Bourbon, he came to certain conclusions. 'Were he my man', he remarked to François, 'I would have his head from his shoulders.' It was no idle boast: exactly a year later the Duke of Buckingham had his head neatly removed from his shoulders because Henry judged that it had grown too big. François made no response to the spectacle of the killer momentarily appearing behind the mask of Bluff King Hal. But he too was a survivor; he too was perfectly aware of the kind of threat a man like Bourbon presented. The fact that he had to take a roundabout, rather shabby means to neutralise that threat was due as much to his position as to his character. François was not the first, nor would he be the last King of France who had to undertake an undignified balancing act between the theory of absolute monarchical power and the plain fact that some of his vassals were richer, more powerful, than he.

Charles of Bourbon was trebly influential. His mother was a Gonzaga, daughter of the great Italian family who had ruled in Mantua for generations. He was born a Bourbon, and the Bourbons were a family who traced themselves back to the same St Louis as did the reigning royal house of Valois: should the Valois stock fail, then automatically the Bourbons would come to the throne. But Charles was not only Bourbon by birth: he had married a Bourbon, Suzanne, heiress of the major stem; and as though that were not enough, Suzanne's mother was the legendary Anne de France, daughter of Louis XI, and she approved whole-heartedly of her son-in-law. Inheritance and marriage had together given Charles Bourbon a virtual kingdom in the very heart of France. His titles were a territorial drum-roll: Duke of Bourbon, Auvergne and Châtellraut; Count of Clermont, Montpensier, Forez, La Marche and Gien; Dauphin of Auvergne; Viscount of Carlat and Murat; Lord of Beaujeu, of Combraille, of Morcoeur, d'Annonay, Roche-en-Regnier and Bourbon-Lancy. This kingdom within a kingdom was ruled from Moulins, high upon its beautiful hill on the river Allier, the home of the Bourbon princes ever since Robert, the son of St Louis, had chosen it as his home. The Dukes of Burgundy alone had kept greater state than the Dukes of Bourbon and now that the former had virtually vanished, Charles of Bourbon was the greatest beneath the King. He could raise an army within the limits of his own domains; he had the right to administer justice; he appointed a chancellor; he had his own pleaders. His household, while not equalling the Burgundian household in luxury and ceremony, was princely: a regular company of archers of the guard protected the Duke's quasi-royal person; his herald-at-arms, cup-bearers, stewards, secretaries, chamberlains, equerries, pages, reflected the state of his royal cousin, the King.

And at the heart of this splendour, at the centre of this massive power lived a curiously sensitive, complex personality. At the age of thirty this undisputed lord of vast territories, this ruler whose word was law for tens of thousands of human beings, this brave soldier and skilled general seemed essentially unsure of himself. Custom and inheritance had given him a role to play and he played it honourably and well; but within that shell of ceremony and power was an overscrupulous human being who can on occasion be seen peering out, as though in puzzlement at his own identity.

The Duke's hypersensitive, tortured personality is exactly captured in two sketches made by such widely differing artists as Jean Clouet and Titian. Clouet was the court painter for over twenty-five years, during which time he produced scores of paintings and drawings of the leading figures of the court, some carefully posed but most of them sketched with spontaneity. His favourite medium was red and black chalk and using that swift, flexible technique, he immortalised Charles Bourbon at the height of his power. Clouet has captured, in Bourbon's face, the contemptuously arrogant expression that sits like an illness upon the face of nearly all the French nobility. But he has captured something else too: a brooding, haunted look that is neither in the eyes nor in the mouth but seems to flit over the whole face behind its aristocratic mask. Titian sketched Bourbon after he had escaped from France: after he had lost his wife and betrayed his King and fled into that exile which, for people of his class, was scarcely preferable to death. In the face that Titian has sketched is an almost feral ferocity, the look of a wild beast cornered, with nothing to lose if it decides to rend its way out. Yet even here, deep down, is the expression of melancholy, almost of the little boy lost. The record that both Clouet and Titian left was neither that of a traitor nor even that of a soldier but one of a remote and haunted creature, an artist perhaps, thrown into a brutal arena.

It was common knowledge that Bourbon had lost his post of Governor in Lombardy because François had wanted to give it to his mistress's brother. It was a shameful enough reason for the demotion of a proud and powerful man, but worse was to follow. From that dismissal until the inevitable outbreak of war with Spain, François seemed to follow almost a planned campaign to alienate the subject from whom he had the most to hope and the most to fear. Bourbon had incurred immense expenses on the King's behalf while he was in Lombardy. His requests for reimbursement were met with vague promises, no more. Kings were ever more ready with promises than with payments and Bourbon might perhaps have contented himself with reflecting that, as one of the richest men in France, it was undignified for him to sue for payment from his king. But it was particularly galling to see how the vast sums extracted specifically for war expenses were frittered away on François' favourites. Bonnivet was one of these. François built him a splendid castle not far from Bourbon's own palace of Châtellraut and as though anxious that Bourbon should not miss a nuance of humiliation, he took the Constable on a visit to the castle and asked him what he thought of it. 'The cage is too spacious and too beautiful for the bird', Bourbon replied shortly. 'You're jealous!' retorted François. 'Jealous?' replied Bourbon. 'How can your majesty believe that I am jealous of a gentleman whose ancestors were only too happy to be squires of mine?'

Bourbon had won a debating point but lost the campaign which, for obscure motives, François was waging against him. So powerful was the impulse to humiliate Bourbon that François even imperilled the military defence of the country to gratify it. In 1521 war finally broke out between France and Spain, that generation-long war to which the Field of the Cloth of Gold had been the ironic curtain-raiser. Charles the Emperor attacked from his secure bases in the Netherlands. Every canon of military science argued that François should send his best general to the north. His best general was Bourbon and Bourbon was indeed sent to the north – but as second-in-command to the pathetically

incompetent Duke d'Alençon, François' brother-in-law. Why? François had
nothing but contempt for his sister's husband and no particular desire or
motive to do her a favour, in particular such a costly favour as this. As a direct
result of Alençon's incompetence, the French army lost a priceless chance to
capture Charles. François was shallow and selfish, and equated the nation's
good with his own well-being, but even so he would not deliberately have
alienated such a man as Bourbon purely for reasons of personal pique. Indeed,
his well-developed sense of self-protection should have impelled him to court
such a man as Bourbon during the perilous opening moves of a major war. He
seems to have been very much aware of the strains he was placing upon their
relationship. It was probably about this time that he asked Bourbon, half
laughingly, half speculatively, what kind of a bribe could tempt a magnate like
himself to treason. 'Sire, the offer of three kingdoms such as yours would not be
enough. But an affront would be sufficient.' The remark bears all the evidence
of a chronicler's polishing but it rings true enough, with its echoes of an almost
frantic amour-propre.

François' motive in baiting and humiliating his great vassal was to be made
embarrassingly clear in the near future, but Bourbon's motives for tolerating
the insults were complex and obscure. A mature, experienced man such as
himself would naturally have gone to great lengths to avoid a quarrel with his
king, particularly in such uncertain times. But equally, a mature, experienced
man would eventually have faced the fact that he must make a stand, that
François was probing him for tactical reasons and that the more he gave way,
the more difficult it would be to regain ground. Looking at the tragedy of
Bourbon's life as a whole, from the moment when he was first challenged to his
death outside the walls of Rome six years later, it becomes clear that his
toleration of François' insults was due to one constant, over-riding fatal flaw in
his character: procrastination. It was a flaw which cancelled his high
intelligence and courage and military skill; but it was by no means a
dishonourable flaw. It was the result of over-breeding, oversensitivity. Placed
in a situation that demanded physical action, he could react promptly and
firmly and efficiently, but when he found himself in a confused situation that
demanded mental action, he tended to put off making any decision in the hope
that the situation would clarify itself and so enable an honourable man to make
an honourable choice.

The probability is that the tussle between Bourbon and his king would have
been resolved had Bourbon played Achilles and retired to his giant estates until
such time as François came to his senses. Instead, the whole pattern of their
relationship was suddenly altered by two events, one tragic, the other bizarre.
Bourbon's wife, Suzanne, died and the mother of his king, Louise, urgently
and unmistakenly offered her hand to him.

Suzanne's death was a double tragedy to him. He had been married to the
gentle, crippled creature for eighteen years and was deeply fond of her. But he
had not only lost a loving companion: his very status as Duke of Bourbon was
suddenly eroded. The great Bourbon clan was a working model of the feudal
tangles that were strangling France. Charles was a Bourbon, but a Bourbon of

the junior Montpensier line, whereas Suzanne inherited direct as a member of the senior line. She had specifically left everything to her beloved husband; her mother thoroughly approved and all would have gone smoothly if a claimant had not suddenly appeared: the most formidable claimant of all, Louise of Savoy, the Queen Mother. She, too, was a Bourbon by birth and a Bourbon, moreover, of the elder line. Charles, in mourning for his dead wife, was faced with a shattering choice: to marry Louise of Savoy or to lose his inheritance.

Louise's love for, or infatuation with, the handsome, melancholy Duke of Bourbon provides the missing piece of the jigsaw. Almost certainly, this was the reason why François had both imperilled his state and tarnished his honour by humiliating his great vassal. Tacitly or implicitly, Bourbon was given to understand that he could regain the King's favour by divorcing his wife and marrying the King's mother. Suzanne's death had immensely simplified the matter, and a discreet messenger was sent hastening to Bourbon, intimating that the most powerful woman in France, a woman, moreover, of considerable charm and sexual attraction despite her forty-five years, was offering herself in marriage. Bourbon's reaction was uncharacteristically direct and uncompromising: the result of raw grief. 'Do you insult me by bringing me such an offer from such a woman? I, who have been married to the best woman in all France, am counselled now to marry the worst woman in the world?' It was an unwise reaction. The messenger faithfully reported the remark to Louise, and at that instant what appear to have been genuine affection and genuine attraction were replaced by a venomous hatred. She was beside herself with rage, screaming: 'The matter will not rest at that! By the creator of our souls these words will cost him dear.'

The tangled threads of the Bourbon–Louise affair make it impossible to assign any one motive as cause. Louise was a highly intelligent, worldly-wise woman and it is unlikely that she would have risked making a fool of herself in the eyes of all Europe by making her proposal without any basis at all for believing that Bourbon would respond favourably. The presumption is that Bourbon led her on for at least four years, from the time that he was dismissed as Governor of Milan to the time of the Field of the Cloth of Gold when François began putting oblique pressure on him. It is not a presumption that squares with Bourbon's supposedly chivalrous nature, but there is a certain poetic justice in that he, who had been dismissed in order to allow his king to pursue a love affair, should try and retain his power by pretending love for the king's mother. The French courtiers were very tight-lipped about the whole business, but there was sufficient leakage to give Louise good grounds for believing that she had lost face not merely in France but in Europe. Certainly, Henry in England knew about it: 'There has been much discontent between King François and the said Bourbon since he has refused to marry Madame, who loves him very much', he told the Spanish ambassador.

Louise determined on revenge and she got it to the last ounce, content with nothing short of Bourbon's total ruin. But even here the story is not a clear-cut one, of a ruin wrought by a woman's jealous fury. Working behind the bitter personal motivations, perhaps even unknown to the actors in this tragedy, was an impersonal motivation bigger than any: the well-being of France itself. Great magnates like Bourbon were a lasting threat to the stability of the State. One by one they had been extinguished or reduced: even the great Dukes of Burgundy were now simply a memory and a title. Bourbon had to be cut down to size for the country's good. It was his misfortune that he was the kind of man, and Louise the kind of woman, who could not accept half-measure. The lawsuit which began in the summer of 1521 was conducted in Louise's name, claiming the inheritance of the late Suzanne de Bourbon as a matter of family justice. But, in fact, the Crown of France was thereby drawing back to itself powers which had imperceptibly drifted away over the years.

Outwardly, the decencies were observed while the lawyers prepared themselves for their lucrative battle. Bourbon continued to attend the court and François continued to employ him on various lesser military tasks. Outside France, Bourbon became the object of speculation among those who wished France harm. Foremost among them, if reluctantly so, was the Emperor Charles V, seeking a way to weaken his determined enemy before the inescapable frontal clash. Charles, a brave man and a skilled soldier, nevertheless infinitely preferred the gains to be made by diplomacy to those made by the hazards of violence. If he could but detach the Constable of France from his King. . . . He had to move discreetly, delicately, for the touchy honour of a French nobleman formed a kind of minefield where a wrong move could create a violent explosion. The offer of money would be seen simply as a direct insult; even the offer of lands and the power that went with them would have little attraction for a man who still counted himself, legally, as one of the greatest lords of Europe. But an offer of marriage, the gift of a bride who would tie Bourbon to the great house of Habsburg, this would be acceptable for it was a reciprocal honour.

Charles therefore offered his sister Eleonor. Bourbon temporised, again seeming to act against both his knightly code and his personal concept of honour. There was no reason whatsoever why he should not accept Eleonore, widow of the king of Portugal, and a very attractive young girl in her own person; later, indeed, Bourbon was to plead for her. But at this early stage of the conflict between himself and François he was reluctant to make an open breach and, in particular, he had no objection whatsoever to Louise's assuming that he was still free to marry. But news of the Spanish offer came to François. Bourbon learnt of this abruptly, brutally. He was at court, paying his respects to little Queen Claude with whom, despite all the pressures and strains, he remained on good terms. François entered the room unceremoniously and when Bourbon rose to do him homage, he swung roughly upon him: 'I hear that you are to be married. Is this true?' Bourbon denied the charge but François refused to believe him, calling him a traitor, shouting that he knew all about the plots Bourbon was weaving with the Emperor. Bourbon protested, but the tirade went on.

That was the beginning of the final and lasting breach even though it had not yet taken a defined form. Bourbon retired to his estates but he still hesitated, still seemed not so much to be seeking a way out of an intolerable situation as to be seeking to understand how it had arisen. He had money, lands, influence: even now, François entrusted him with a military expedition, ordering him to attack and disperse a band of mercenaries who were terrorising the country near Paris. Bourbon discharged the task with his customary skill, but again returned to Moulins instead of waiting on the King in Paris. Shortly afterwards, he was visited by two smooth-talking gentlemen from Paris who assured him of François' undying love. He tried to pin them down regarding François' intentions: did the King really intend to deprive him of his estates through a rigged law-suit? The gentlemen raised their hands in horror: not at all, of course not. Ironically, Bourbon thanked them: would they be good enough to bear a letter back to the King, thanking him for his forbearance? Hastily, they declined the honour. As he had suspected, they were little more than spies, and clumsy ones at that, sent to discover his intentions and the disposition of his forces. Shortly afterwards, he heard that the all-powerful Chancellor du Prat had given as his opinion that the crown of France would not be safe until the Duke of Bourbon was reduced to the status of a simple country gentleman, drawing a modest income in rents.

And now the Emperor moved, still discreetly, but confidently and un-equivocally. He had already sounded out Henry VIII regarding the possibility of suborning Bourbon and Henry, delighted at the chance of detaching the greatest of François' vassals, had promised to share half the costs. Now arrangements were made for Bourbon to meet the Spanish chamberlain, Adrian de Croy, secretly in one of the mountain castles of the Bourbanais. Bourbon was still hesitant, still determined to treat the Spanish approaches purely as theoretical, but this secret meeting with a high representative of the king's enemy was the point of no return. No matter how accommodating were the concepts of a vassal's rights, this could not be construed as anything but treason and, in his heart of hearts, Bourbon must have known this.

On a sultry July evening in 1522 Bourbon and Adrian de Croy met in the castle of Montbrison. Stripped of the delicate nuances of bribery, de Croy's offer was an unequivocal invitation to violent treachery. Bourbon was promised the hand of Charles' sister Eleonore, together with an enormous dowry of 200,000 crowns. In return, he was to swear to support the Emperor in all things, including an outright attack upon François. Bourbon agreed: he agreed to the invasion of France by France's enemies, the Spaniards launching an attack from the south with over 25,000 men, while the English were to land on the coast with another 20,000 foot and horse. Bourbon agreed that this attack should take place as soon as François had left for Italy. He agreed that he, in his turn, would attack ten days after the main assault with a force of German mercenaries to be paid for by the Emperor and Henry VIII. He agreed to every condition save one: he declined to recognise Henry VIII as King of France. Compared with all that he had assented to, this seems almost a technical quibble, but Bourbon was already aware, and those who urged him on were already aware, that his treachery was all or nothing: if he were to survive, he had to destroy François, and by destroying François, he would have to take the crown himself. It was by no means an impossible goal. Both the Emperor and Cardinal Wolsey had done their homework and were convinced that quite half the nobility would side with Bourbon against the extravagant and frivolous François and his grasping mother. Whether the transference of the crown from Valois to Bourbon would necessarily be an unqualified good for France, nobody troubled to debate. With the wheel set turning, everybody involved had to run faster and faster to keep up with it, increasing their stakes until some decided to give up the race and others were at length dashed to pieces.

Bourbon threw himself into the task of arranging the widespread conspiracy with a frenetic energy. Allies had to be contacted, waverers talked over, the hostile identified and excluded. And in the midst of this activity, at the vital period when he needed to take all the threads into his hands, he fell seriously sick. 'Tertian fever', the physicians described it, and it may very well have been so, but there is little doubt but that this unusual bout of illness in a man who usually enjoyed excellent health had a psychosomatic cause. Intellectually he might have been able to convince himself that active rebellion was the only way out; emotionally, he backed away at the enormity of the thing he was doing. Powerful, virtually independent prince though he was, he was nevertheless still a vassal and the feudal tie between vassal and suzeraine was, according to the feudal code, stronger and more sacrosanct even than the tie between husband and wife, between mother and child. Bourbon took to his bed with a high fever and two of the men he had trusted hastened to François, giving the King the fullest details of the plot to overthrow him, embroidering it, indeed, with the statement that it was intended that he be put to death after his capture. And François, instead of immediately ordering the arrest and trial of his cousin as a felon vassal, visited him on his sickbed, the strangest twist in all this strange story.

'I slept at Moulins where I found M.de Bourbon very ill', François wrote to his mother. 'His face is very much changed. I spoke to him about accompanying me, which he seemed to wish very much, and he promised on his word that as soon as he could bear to travel in his litter, he would set forth at once. It would probably be in a week.' According to one of François' gentlemen, the two had a frank discussion in Bourbon's sickroom. François assured Bourbon that, whatever the results of the lawsuit, it had never been the royal intention to strip a royal duke of his estates. Only let Bourbon recover his good health and come to Lyons, and they could resolve the other matter of Bourbon's military appointments. François even seems to have assured Bourbon that he would again have a high place in the army during the forthcoming invasion of Italy. And Bourbon, on his part, assured the King of his undying loyalty, his love . . .

The cynical interpretation of this extraordinary conversation – which may very well be the right one – is that both men were simply manoeuvring for position, the King knowing that it would be impossible to arrest Bourbon in his own principality and Bourbon seeking to gain time. But it is equally likely that two essentially generous men had seen the brink towards which they were hurtling and tried to draw back. François, in particular, was an emotional young man, easily moved to anger or compassion, and the sight of his once splendid cousin lying gaunt with sickness, wracked with anguish, may have stirred him to pity. And Bourbon, demoralised by that sickness, would have responded to kindness by confession and protestation.

But the temporary rapprochement of the sickroom withered in the outside world. When François left for his court at Lyons he extracted a promise from Bourbon that the duke would follow in five days. But despite that promise, François took the precaution of leaving a loyal vassal, Pierre de Warthy, to keep an eye on Bourbon. Over the next few weeks Bourbon and Warthy circled round each other with manoeuvres which would have been comic but for the inherent tragedy. Bourbon pretends to be far more grievously sick than he is: Warthy tries to catch him out, anxiously shuttling between Bourbon and the distant court at Lyons to keep François informed. Bourbon slips away to another, distant and more easily defensible castle under a pretext; and displays wide-eyed surprise that Warthy should think him trying to escape. So the cat-and-mouse game went on with Bourbon ever increasing the distance between himself and François, trying to get into contact with his allies while Warthy flitted anxiously around, heading off the Duke, keeping François informed of his movements.

At last François' patience snapped and he ordered the arrest of Bourbon's most powerful, most loyal followers, the Bishop of Autun and the Sieur de St-Valliers. Simultaneously a powerful squadron was sent through the mountains of Auvergne to catch Bourbon in his last refuge and bring him forcibly to the King. Bourbon escaped. He was accompanied by an escort of nearly 300 gentlemen; in his saddlebags was a fortune in gold, but from that moment on he was a refugee. Instead of marching out at the head of an army from his own domains in order, as an equal, to meet up with the armies of his allies, he was simply a man on the run with a price on his head. He could not go south to the Spaniards nor north to the English: his sole route of escape lay eastward through Burgundy and Germany. Again and again he was within an ace of capture: he changed costume and horses with his valet – he experienced, in short, all the romantic vicissitudes of fleeing royalty. And he was to discover the bitterest truth about fleeing royalty: that a prince who runs for his life very rarely walks back. Arriving on neutral territory, he met a number of his old friends and allies who tried to persuade him to return and make his peace with François. He refused, turning his horse's head to the south, towards Italy, the land of his mother's people, the land where he had gained fame and honour as a soldier. He took nothing with him, apart from those 40,000 golden crowns in his saddlebags. Someone asked him, diffidently, what he intended to do about the Constable's Sword and the Collar of the Order of St Michael that marked his high and honoured position as his sovereign's bodyguard. 'Tell the King', he snarled 'that he took from me the Sword when he took from me the command of the vanguard and gave it to M.d'Alençon. As for the Collar of his order, you will find it at Chantelle under the pillow of my bed.'

Weary, gaunt, travel-worn, the Duke of Bourbon arrived at his kinsman's palace in Mantua in September after a journey of some six weeks. It was from Mantua that his mother, the gentle Chiara Gonzaga, had set out on her bridal

The Captains and the Kings

journey over the Alps to France forty years before in the summer of 1481. His mother's brother, the Marquis, had died three years before in 1519 and the ruling Marquis of Mantua was his cousin, young Federigo. An amiable, courageous, but inconsequent youth of twenty, Federigo held the proud title of Captain-General of the Church, but he was intelligent enough to know that he owed the honour more to his name than to his merits, and he received the veteran Bourbon, thirty-three years old, battle-scarred, bitter, with proper respect.

So did Federigo's mother, Isabella d'Este. At forty-eight, Isabella was entering that time of life which, for most women, was simply the onset of old age. But resolutely she declined to recognise the fact and so magnetic was her personality, so sprightly her conversation and insatiable her curiosity that people tended to accept her as a woman many years younger. She was delighted to see her French nephew, though shocked by the change in his appearance. The last time she had seen him had been during the days of the French triumphs in Lombardy, when Bourbon had ridden like a king into Milan. She had been intensely proud of him, telling all and sundry how much he resembled his mother, her dear, dead sister Chiara. Now the 'tall youth of handsome and majestic appearance', as she had described him, had changed into the gaunt, wild-eyed, wild-haired refugee who had arrived seeking the support of his kinsmen in their lakeland city.

The reaction of both the Marquis and his mother was warm, generous. But it was not entirely uncalculated. Charles of Bourbon was a fugitive at the moment. But he was on his way to join Charles the Emperor, the great Habsburg monarch with whom he would not only regain his heritage but increase it dizzyingly, for it was open talk now that he would seat himself upon the throne of France as soon as it was taken. It did not trouble his kinsmen that, in fact, he was a traitor to his king, because, for one thing, they were Italians who would have smiled at any concept of feudal ties and also because, for another, they genuinely believed that he had been grievously wronged and his king had thereby forfeited his loyalty. Not only the Italians took that view. The defection of the Duke of Bourbon was to be a talking point among his French peers for decades, a fascinating text-book case of the relationship between suzeraine and vassal. Was Bourbon justified in his rebellion? Was he goaded too far? Was he, in fact, more fool than knave? So much of the complex transactions between Bourbon, François and the Queen Mother remained secret that almost any gloss could be put upon their actions. Sexual attraction, feudal loyalty, personal humiliation, political necessity: all combined to place the Duke of Bourbon in an impossible position. A stronger, less sensitive, but more subtle man would have remained in France and fought it out with courtiers' weapons. Bourbon, too straightforward for his own good, acted too openly, too precipitately. But he had reacted according to the canons of his class. No less an authority than the Sieur de Brantôme, snob, gossip and passionately royalist chronicler, confirmed that. As a royalist, Brantôme might deplore Bourbon's action, but as an admirer of the nobility, he could not but defend it. 'What could Monsieur de Bourbon have done if he had not acted as

1 (*Top left*) Clement VII: "I tell you that in this world the ideal does not correspond with the real, and he who acts from amiable motives is a fool." *Painting by Sebastiano del Piombo*

2 and 3 The Emperor Charles V: "I will go into Italy and revenge myself on that fool of a pope." As a young man (*top right, painting by Strigel*); in maturity (*left, painting by Titian*).

4 (*Left*) Francois I, King of France: "All is lost, save honour." *Painting by Jean Clouet*

5 and 6 Charles de Montpensier, Duke of Bourbon. Before his disgrace (*below left, sketch by Clouet*); after his escape into Italy (*below right, painting by Titian*).

7 The Battle of Pavia. A highly decorative piece of tapestry by Van Orley, showing contemporary military tactics with admirable clarity, in particular the terrain which favoured the arquebusiers. A group of them emerges from the copse on the left.

8 Panorama of Rome in the sixteenth century. The viewpoint is directly above
Bourbon's encampment and clearly shows the two walled communities on this side of
the Tiber, the Vatican (left) and Trastevere (right), with the Ponte Sisto at centre.
A simplified Castello Sant' Angelo lies at the bend in the river (centre left).

9 (*Above*) The Ponte Sisto, the bridge by which the imperialists made their entry into the city proper.

10 (*Below*) The Siege of Sant' Angelo, by the imperialist artist Meemskerck. The architectural details are accurate enough, in particular those of Sant' Angelo, where

THE GENERALS

11 (*Right*) Georg Frundsburg, Prince of Mindelheim, commander of the *landsknechts*.

12 (*Below left*) Giovanni de' Medici, captain of the Bande Nere. *Painting by Bronzino*

13 (*Below right*) Francesco Maria della Rovere, Duke of Urbino, generalissimo of the papal army. *Painting by Raphael?*

THE POLITICIANS
14 (*left*) Francesco Guicciardini: "It is bad to make a bad decision, but worse to make none at all."

15 (*Bottom left*) Niccolo Machiavelli: "I believe we shall have war in Italy—and soon."

16 (*Bottom right*) Baldassare Castiglione: "The French are more afraid than they show." *Painting by Raphael*

he did?' Brantôme demanded rhetorically. 'Why, he would have been taken prisoner, tried, and had his head cut off and been dishonoured for ever, he and his race.'

So, convinced of his rightness, in the mellow autumn weeks of 1523 Bourbon knew a brief and honourable respite in Mantua – the last, indeed, he was ever to know. Heady plans were made for the future. The Emperor extended a warm invitation to him to hasten westward and join the crusade against François, and Bourbon's kinsmen the Gonzaga were eager to be associated. Had they but paused to consider the matter, they must surely have been disconcerted that scarcely one hundred gentlemen had accompanied Bourbon into exile: one hundred when it had been confidently expected that most of the nobility would indignantly rise in rebellion as soon as he had given the word. But the glamour of a Prince of the Blood still hung around the exile and Federigo the Marquis and his mother comforted and encouraged him as he made his preparations.

There was a slight diminution in confidence in November 1523 when Pope Adrian, the Emperor's old tutor, died and Giulio de' Medici took his place, for the Medici were traditionally the allies of France. Baldassare Castiglione, the veteran courtier who had learned his trade at the elegant court of Urbino and was now Mantua's most trusted diplomat, was sent to Rome to sound out the new pope. He sent back an altogether encouraging report: 'The Pope goes on his old ways, is most kind and benevolent. What his policy will be no one yet knows. The French pretend to be wonderfully well satisfied, but I do not believe these are their real feelings. As far as I can hear, His Holiness offers to do all he can to preserve the kingdom of France from foreign invasion, if only the French will give up meddling with Italy and abandon this expedition.' Everything seemed in the Duke of Bourbon's favour, and not long after the election of the new pope he took his leave of Mantua, making his way across Lombardy to Genoa where a great imperial army was assembling for the attack on France.

Chapter V

Servant of the Servants of God

Castiglione's assessment of Pope Clement's policy was accurate enough as far as it went. All the world knew that Clement, as Cardinal, had been a steady supporter of the Emperor. The Spanish ambassador, Sessa, had even sent off a jubilant despatch as soon as he had learned that Giulio de' Medici had become pope: 'The Pope is entirely your Majesty's creature. So great is your Majesty's power that you can change stones into obedient children.' But what both Sessa and Castiglione had overlooked, what every commentator overlooked, was that Cardinal Giulio de' Medici and Pope Clement VII were two entirely different men. The Cardinal had been a confident, honourable, highly competent negotiator. He had had the very real responsibility of accurately summing up a situation and presenting it to his cousin, Pope Leo, in so clear and precise a manner that Leo could then make the best possible decision under the circumstances. Giulio did this work well – but the decisions were Leo's, and behind his plumply affable appearance, Leo had a will of iron and a very clear idea of where he was going and what he wanted to do.

Clement had neither: it was his bitter misfortune that he became pope at the very moment when a clear-cut decision was necessary regarding those foreigners in the North. As Cardinal, he had been a supporter of the Emperor for the excellent reason that the French star was in the ascendant. But as Pope, his enthusiasm cooled considerably. All popes had the intractable problem of defining their relationship with the Holy Roman Emperor. A weak emperor meant a strong pope – but a pope without a natural ally. Conversely, a strong emperor was only too likely to regard the pope as his chaplain. It had been over a century since there had been an emperor strong enough to give sleepless nights to a pope, and it was yet another of Clement's misfortunes that his reign should coincide with that of one of the very few emperors capable of giving meaning to his high office and international claims.

Clement's initial attitude, on paper, to Charles and François was impeccable: he was the Holy Father of both, he announced, and therefore he intended to maintain a strict neutrality between them both. It was the most dangerous policy he could have adopted: neither believed that the Vatican really intended to stand outside power politics; each believed that Clement's announcement was a typically Florentine mercantile trick to raise the stakes; each was convinced that pressure applied at the right time and place would bring His Holiness to the proper frame of mind. Between January and August 1524 there was a constant procession of Imperial or French envoys to the Vatican, sometimes overlapping, all intent on bribing or threatening. Clement listened to both sides with a fine appearance of impartiality. He carried that impartiality to its logical extremes, for each of his two advisers in foreign affairs, the two men who shaped Vatican policy, were passionate partisans, the one of the Emperor, the other of the French. These two men, Gian Matteo Giberti and Nicholas von Schomberg, acted as magnets on the Pope's irresolution: his policy veered towards either the one or the other not only because one might have that time presented the better argument, but also simply because the one might have been present while his rival was absent.

Gian Matteo Giberti, Bishop of Verona and Datary of the Vatican, was the nearest to a friend Clement ever had in his life even though Giberti was twenty years his junior. They shared a similar social disadvantage for both had been born illegitimate, but where Clement had been the son of one of the rulers of Florence, Giberti had been the son of a Genoese sea-captain. His career had been a text-book example of the way an industrious young man could, with suitable patronage, make his way up the ladder of ecclesiastical success. He entered Clement's service while he was still a boy and was undertaking diplomatic missions for the Cardinal before he was twenty years old. He was reasonably well travelled: he went to the Emperor's court in Flanders and travelled back with the old Fleming who became Pope Adrian VI. He was only twenty-eight when his patron became Pope, but nevertheless Clement made him Datary, an office of vague definition but very wide powers.

Giberti was a bureaucrat, a diplomatist, and a scholar. But he was also a Christian of very high moral standards, a fact which would impress Clement. Giberti had already shown his courage and tenacity by tangling with no less a person than the notorious Pietro Aretino, swashbuckler, pornographer, blackmailer and poet. 'The scourge of Princes', Aretino called himself and it was true that he employed so deadly a pen that he was able to make a very comfortable living by blackmail: many a powerful man, lord absolute within his own city, was glad to pay Aretino to suppress a verse that showed embarrassing insight into his affairs, or even to pay him for a panegyric. While in Rome, Aretino became involved in the production of a number of obscene drawings by Giulio Romano, to which he supplied verse so lewd that the indignant Giberti swore to rid Rome of at least one source of corruption. The engraver of the drawings, who was also a friend of Aretino's, went to prison and Aretino himself escaped only by a precipitate flight from Rome.

Nicholas von Schomburg, the imperialist champion, was totally different from Giberti. He was a Saxon by birth who, on a visit to Florence, reputedly became converted by the reformer Savonarola. Certainly, he entered the Dominicans in Savonarola's convent of San Marco in Florence, but the master's influence does not seem to have penetrated very deeply or permanently. He was as skilled a diplomatist and careerist as Giberti – he was now

Archbishop of Capua – but he lacked Giberti's deep earnestness. He was the natural ally of Sessa, the Emperor's ambassador at the Vatican, but it was Sessa who left the unkind and succinct portrait of him as a man who combined the levity of a dandy with the pride of a friar, and one who was more fitted to write a fine letter than to govern a state. Nevertheless, Clement relied on him heavily as his adviser on foreign, in particular imperial, affairs and shortly after his accession to the Throne he sent the Saxon on a prolonged tour to the courts of Spain, France and England to see if there was any way of resolving the complex rivalries of the three young monarchs. Schomburg left with the deepest reluctance, well aware that in his absence Giberti would have total influence over the Pope. He returned in June 1524, when Charles and François were already inexorably set on their collision course: as Sessa remarked caustically, his journey was not worth his expenses.

Baldassare Castiglione had a long conversation with Schomburg on his return and from it prepared a precise report of the state of European affairs.

> The conditions which the Most Christian King [François] makes are very different from those on which the Emperor insists, especially as regards Monsieur de Bourbon, whom the Emperor is determined not to abandon. But the archbishop thinks that if the war goes on there will be much misery in France, and says he never saw a more wretched-looking set of men than these French soldiers, without shoes or stockings and as badly clad and equipped as possible. He tells me that neither the Chancellor of Spain nor any of the Emperor's servants has as much influence with His Majesty as the Queen Mother has with the King of France. He is also of the opinion that Cardinal Wolsey is not as absolute a master of the King of England as people say, but that the King attends to every detail himself and manages affairs in his own way. He says the same of the Emperor, and declares that the most confidential of his servants does not know his whole mind.

The Emperor's determination 'not to abandon Monsieur de Bourbon' had nothing sentimental about it for, so far, Bourbon had proved a very good investment indeed. The Emperor had offered him the post of Lieutenant-General in Lombardy – equivalent to the post that Bourbon had once held for his late master King François – and after some hesitation, Bourbon accepted. Despite the fact that the Emperor had delegated all powers in the north to him, his position was by no means clear-cut. It was, in fact, epitomic of the confused situation that reigned throughout Italy and would eventually result in tragedy.

In Lombardy with Bourbon was Charles Lannoy, the Spanish Viceroy for Naples, a skilled general and a confidant of the Emperor's. In Bourbon's command were Spaniards. Loosely attached to the imperialist forces was the Tuscan mercenary leader, Giovanni de' Medici, the young man commonly known by the mellifluous style of Giovanni della Bande Nere. He was the last of the condottieri, the first of the great modern Italian generals, the young man whom Machiavelli himself looked to as the saviour of Italy, the only Italian general who could purge the land of its arrogant foreign troops. Hastening to join the motley army was a band of some 10,000 German mercenaries, the landsknechts: their primary motive was pay and plunder, but they also owed allegiance to the Emperor for he was as much German as he was Fleming or Spaniard. In overall command of this army, dignified by the adjective 'imperialist' was the eighty-year-old Prospero Colonna. Bourbon somehow had to exert control over men who wielded far greater immediate power than he could muster. All he had was his name, the handful of men who had accompanied him in exile, and the Emperor's backing. But the Emperor was 800 miles away in the heart of Spain and a man like Giovanni della Bande Nere would have been merely amused to learn that a Spanish–Flemish–German in Madrid claimed any particular authority over him.

But during the first few weeks of the campaign in the north, the different cogs of the imperial army meshed smoothly together. Milan yet again changed hands, Bourbon again assuming the governorship of the city, though this time on behalf of the Emperor. There was, as yet, no fear that he might meet his anointed King head on in battle, for François still remained in France, embroiled in politics, much of it the result of Bourbon's defection. In command of the French army was the Admiral Bonnivet, brave but inexperienced, more adept at palace intrigues than in battlefield manoeuvres. Bourbon would have welcomed a confrontation with the man he suspected had done more than any other to turn the King against him. But such a confrontation never occurred, as Bonnivet hesitantly, indecisively, marched and counter-marched in Lombardy, uncertain whether to attack or retreat as the massive build-up of imperialist forces continued. He laid siege to Milan but was beaten off. Wounded by an arquebus shot, he thankfully handed over command to the legendary Bayard and hastened home. He had lost not only Milan but Lombardy for François, but still possessed his golden tongue and was even able to convince his King that Fate itself had destined Milan to be captured for the third time only by the King of France in person.

The tempo of the war in Lombardy changed. The aged veteran Prospero Colonna died and Bourbon, taking his place, swung over to a sustained and determined offensive. His old mentor and hero, Bayard, commanded what was now virtually a rear-guard fighting a retreating action, holding the enemy off as he tried to bring at least some of the once proud army back to France. But the arquebus that had given him command now took from him his life, a stone from one of the new weapons crushing his spine. It was the last blow for the French expedition, for Bayard's name alone was a potent force. The Emperor's envoy, Adrian de Croy, informed Madrid with genuine sorrow: 'Sire, although the said Sieur Bayard was in the service of your enemy, yet his death was a great misfortune for he was a gentle knight, well beloved by all and who lived better than ever did any of his condition, as indeed he showed at his end which was the most beautiful which I have ever heard of. The loss, indeed, is great to the French, and it is very overwhelming to them.' Martin du Bellay, a royalist chronicler, passed on a spiteful little tale to François, telling how Bourbon approached the dying knight, the last of his race, to offer his condolences. Bayard replied, according to du Bellay: 'Monsieur, do not pity me, for I die as an honest man. But I pity you, seeing you serve against your prince and your country and your oath.' It was exactly the kind of story François wanted to hear about his now hated cousin and, embellished, it went the round of the European courts. But the supposed condemnation of Bourbon by the noblest knight in Europe was a fabrication: du Bellay was nowhere near the battlefield and according to Bayard's own valet, the exchange between the two men was mutually courteous, with Bourbon, distressed, offering to send the best surgeon he could find and Bayard refusing as he composed himself for death.

In Rome, Clement heard of the collapse of French arms with dismay, for while it was bad enough to have to tolerate French influence in Lombardy, it was far worse to see the tightening circle of imperial power. Hastily, he sent off emissaries, still in his role of neutral Holy Father, urging the combatants to peace. Charles had entered into yet another alliance with England but he nevertheless listened courteously enough and, it seems, would have been happy to let matters rest as they were with the Habsburg double eagle once more flying over Milan. Even François might have been dragged, if unwillingly, to the conference table if Bourbon had not been involved in the proposed treaty. White with rage, François haughtily declined to take part in any treaty which involved the traitor Bourbon and the negotiations broke down.

Sweeping the French before them, the imperialists under Bourbon traversed Lombardy, halting at the barrier of the Alps. Logically, this was the time to reactivate the ambitious idea of the invasion of France, and Bourbon put the matter to Charles. He, too, saw the logic – provided his ally, Henry of England, could be drawn in. Henry agreed, not only to share the costs of Bourbon's southern invasion but also to launch an invasion himself from the north. He had only one proviso: Bourbon must first swear allegiance to him as King of France. And on that proviso, the grand alliance nearly came to an end. Such an oath would run counter to Bourbon's every instinct, make nonsense of his plans for returning to France in triumph. Henry was adamant, Charles non-committal. Spring slid into summer while Bourbon desperately sought a way out of the impasse. It was very clear now how limited his independence was, in fact: he was tethered to the Emperor by the strongest of leashes: finances. And at last he gave way, taking the oath of allegiance but stopping short at the ultimate physical gesture of placing his hands in that of his suzeraine. 'The Duke will not consent to pay homage', Sir Richard Pace, the English ambassador, wrote to Wolsey. Wisely, neither Wolsey nor Henry pressed the matter further, for Bourbon's highly strung tension might well have snapped at that.

With the oath taken, the imperial purse was immediately open to him. Charles sent him 200,000 ducats to feed and pay his army, and strengthen it with reinforcements. At the end of June he began the return journey home, marching through the Alps at the head of his international army composed of Germans, Spanish, Italians. He abandoned the Bourbon motto for the flamboyant 'Victoire ou mort', replacing the device of the flying stag with that of the flaming sword – all curiously theatrical and uncharacteristic of him. Crossing the Alpes Maritimes, the army descended down to the coastal plain, sweeping through city after city: Monaco, Vence, Antibes, Cannes, Grasse yielded to him and his spirits must have soared at this wholly unexpected triumphal procession. Unconsciously, he was following the old Roman route, the Aurelian way northward through Provence, his mens' boots beating upon the same road as had the sandalled feet of the legions.

They came at last to Marseilles and there the triumphant march ended, for Marseilles was not only in excellent military condition but its defenders were totally bound to the King of France, totally rejecting the Bourbon Duke who had entered their rich land at the head of a foreign enemy. Despite the use of artillery by the attackers, even now a city in good heart could keep an enemy long at bay; and the heart of Marseilles was sound. François had realised that this was where the crunch would take place and had sent his engineer Mirandel ahead to overhaul the city's defences, promising that the royal fleur-de-lys would be following in the very near future. The polyglot population was strengthened by Italian mercenaries under the command of Renzo da Ceri who, by a quirk of fate, would be defending Rome against the same army in a little over two years' time. The Massiliots received better value from him than the Romans were to receive. 'He set diligently at work repairing the walls, in making platforms and also in finishing the great boulevard, of which the walls were 28 feet thick and which was well furnished with artillery', a grateful citizen recorded.

The bombardment of Marseilles began in mid-August. It continued without pause into September, the citizens suffering from all the agonies of a city under siege but resolutely holding out. Touched with remorse, perhaps, Bourbon offered quarter to Renzo da Ceri. The offer was refused: the bombardment continued. But Bourbon's evil star was still rising and would not set again in his life-time. Daily he awaited news of the promised English and Spanish invasions. Nothing happened. Instead there came news that François himself was at last in movement, the crown of France advancing in majesty to the relief of its loyal city and the chastisement of its felon vassal. Bourbon redoubled his efforts: the rolling thunder of artillery echoed ceaselessly from the surrounding hills, yet still the Massiliots fought on, heartened by news of the advancing royal army. Even now Bourbon might have effected an entry through one of the great breaches which had appeared in the walls and, secure in Marseilles with a veteran army, he would have been impossible to dislodge. But at the moment of the crucial charge, his international army fell apart at its seams. It was the Spanish who gave way before the withering fire of the defenders. They were brave, skilful and loyal fighters and the probability is that their leader, the Marchese de Pescara, resenting Bourbon's role, deliberately undermined their determination. The German mercenaries who had actually gained the breach wavered in the face of the cannonade from the guns that the defenders had hastily dragged into position. The Spaniards were following and if they had pressed forward, the probability is that the Germans would have continued. But at this stage Pescara raised his voice, not to give an order, but to voice a fear: 'The besieged have made a fine table to treat those who visit them. If you want to sup in Paradise today, then go forward. But if, like me, you have no such desire, then follow me to Italy.'

That was the effective end of the great invasion of France. But it was more than that. One by one, the options had closed, both for Bourbon and for Italy itself. Ever since his escape to the south and throughout the campaign in Lombardy, Bourbon had had only one objective: his reinstatement as a royal duke. All else was but a means to that end. Now, with his definite repulse at Marseilles, he must have realised that there was no place for him in France, not now, not ever. No Frenchmen would ever raise the standard of rebellion on his behalf and certainly the prospect of a pardon from François belonged strictly to the realm of miracles. He did not, as yet, realise it, but from the moment that he turned his back on Marseilles he had lost control of his destiny and was now being swept along by the currents of chance and history.

The retreat from Marseilles was a disaster for the imperialist army. The stimulus of victory had so far proved an adequate factor to keep the disparate elements moving as one unit: defeat and privation broke the unit down into sullen, near-mutinous fragments. It was essential that the army retreat as a whole, for otherwise the enemy following hard on their heels could pick off stragglers. A group of German mercenaries, ignoring Pescara's urgent orders, settled down to a drunken orgy. He waited until they were sunk in alcoholic stupor in a barn, then set alight to it, forming a cordon around so that those who sobered up in time to escape were hurled back. The action admittedly helped to improve discipline but it weakened the already fragile bond between Spaniards and Germans. Bourbon became the scapegoat for their unhappy condition. Many of the soldiers were now in rags, hobbling on crude sandals made of the skins of freshly killed oxen. 'These are the brocaded shoes Bourbon promised us when he led us into France', was the bitter joke about these 'abarcas' or sandals.

But bitter though the condition of the imperial army was, worse was to come. In beginning the retreat from Marseilles they had at least had the hope of falling back eventually on Lombardy and, in particular, on Milan. But as they limped back by the coastal road, news came that King François, immensely heartened by the victory of his subjects at Marseilles, had determined that this was the moment to attempt the reconquest of Milan. His reconstructed army was already waiting for his orders at Lyons, more money had been extracted from a grumbling but still loyal populace, and there was nothing to prevent him attempting yet another brilliant feat of arms that would wash out the bitterness and defeat of the previous months. His mother Louise and her financial advisers protested, for even Louise had had enough of 'glory', but he ignored them. In October he set off, intent on repeating his mountaineering feat of nine years previously. And, incredibly, he succeeded, dragging his massive artillery through the high Alps, stealing a march on the imperialists. For while they were dragging themselves through the Maritime Alps, the fresh and confident troops of François descended upon Vercelli.

Bourbon had lost the race for Milan almost before he realised that it had started. He, Lannoy, the Viceroy, and Pescara had actually entered the city after it had formally surrendered to François, still some miles distant. But there was no time to prepare for a siege. The Milanese, though loyal enough to their puppet Duke Francesco Sforza, were in no fit state to fight a defensive war, for they had recently suffered severely from plague. The imperial generals retired to the nearby city of Lodi and, unopposed, on 24 October, 1524, François triumphantly entered his ducal city of Milan. A city just recovering from plague was not an ideal place to stay, however, and shortly afterwards he moved his camp to the beautiful hunting park of the Belvedere, just outside Pavia some fifteen miles from Milan. Pavia itself was still held by a military garrison, but they were already short of provisions and their surrender seemed only a matter of time. Meanwhile, there were the pleasures of the park to be enjoyed.

In a matter of days, François had turned defeat into victory – yet another dazzling example of the power of his personal presence, it seemed. Opposing him was simply a tattered, footsore mass of soldiers, scarcely deserving the name 'army'. Throughout Italy, governments and princes again hastened to pay homage to the rising star of France, even Pope Clement forgetting his careful balancing act and displaying every desire now to link his fortune with François'. There was nothing to stop the King of France chasing the mixed troops of his Spanish adversary out of Italy, showing up their 'imperial' claims for the hollow mockery it was. In October 1524, the ever-fortunate Valois king was the arbiter of Italian fate.

In February 1525 he was a prisoner of the Emperor.

Section Two

THE STAGE

Chapter VI

The Envoy

On 7 October 1524, at about the time that King François was triumphantly dragging his cannon through the Alps and Charles of Bourbon was dejectedly trailing back from Marseilles, Count Baldassare Castiglione was riding out of Rome's Porta del Popolo at the head of a rich cortège. The captain of the gate guard punctiliously saluted him, for the plump, gentle little Mantuan was not only universally popular: he had also become suddenly a person of very considerable consequence. Only a year before he had arrived in Rome as the ambassador of the Marquis of Mantua; he was leaving now as papal nuncio to the imperial court at Madrid, having accepted that office at the express, urgent and personal request of His Holiness.

About a mile or so from the Porta del Popolo the via Cassia heaves itself up in one of the gentle undulations of the Roman Campagna. Generation after generation of travellers journeying south down the great consular road got their first sight of Rome from this spot, and travellers leaving the city would, almost invariably, halt and look over their shoulders to gain a last glimpse. Castiglione followed custom. Behind him the city lay golden and tranquil in the most beautiful of all Roman seasons, the *ottobrata*. Most of the landmarks familiar to travellers centuries before and centuries after were visible to him. There was a gap where St Peter's should have raised its vast, brownish walls: the thousand-year-old basilica had been torn down ten years before and the new building had not yet broken the skyline, but the enormous, solid drum of Hadrian's tomb loomed unchanged and unchangeable over the Tiber; the Colosseum reared its bulk like a broken, jagged tooth into the blue sky; the roof of the Pantheon gleamed; the cypresses on the Palatine stood slimly elegant as they had in the days of Augustus and Nero and Domitian. There was far more greenery to the eye than there would have been in those imperial days, the greenery of vineyards and market gardens and small clumps of tangled country within the massive walls. But gleaming new palaces were springing up from the ruins, and workman's cottages and workshops were huddling alongside the palaces again, and the city was prosperous and busy. The Count could not help noticing that the Porta del Popolo was in a decidedly dilapidated condition. Although he was certainly no soldier, he had had command of his own detachment of lances, and

he knew enough about military ways to see that Rome's defences left a great
deal to be desired. But why waste money on rebuilding the fortifications? True,
a war was even now being waged in the north and his own appointment to the
court of the Emperor Charles was a direct result of all that martial to-ing and
fro-ing; but it was quite unthinkable that Rome should ever be caught up in any
actual conflict. The wars she excelled in, and invariably won, were wars of
words where the troops were lawyers and the weapons were parchment and
quill; fire, sword and famine were scourges reserved for lesser cities. And
having looked his fill, the Count nodded to the captain of his escort and they
moved off. He was not to know that he had looked for the last time on the city he
loved, 'my own Rome, the delight of Gods and Men'. The journey ahead of him
would take six long months during which he would pass through the embattled
armies of France and Spain, and, though only forty-six, he would never make
the return journey but would die in distant Spain, heartsick and worn-out in
the service of an unworthy master and an impossible cause.

Castiglione's feelings on leaving Rome were mixed. He was a career
diplomat and, proud though he was to have served the brilliant courts of
Urbino and Mantua, they were, after all, but toy states and to have been chosen
as Vatican ambassador to the Emperor himself, to have been chosen, above all,
from among the hundreds of place-hungry courtiers who swarmed in the papal
curia, was a great honour. He was, too, an imperialist. He was certainly not
fanatical in the matter: as a good Italian he could not but devoutly wish that
Spaniards and French and Germans and Swiss would take their pestilential
quarrels into their own countries but, since an Italian had to choose, he chose
the imperial side as the best in the long run for Italy. Nevertheless, though he
was delighted both as careerist and politician to be appointed to Madrid, it was
a decided wrench for him to leave home.

He had first come to the city, as Mantuan ambassador, some eight years
before. Those had been the great days, the golden days when Pope Clement's
cousin, the fortunate Leo, had been on the papal throne. The affable, roly-poly,
Medici pope with the short sight and the sharp mind had taken an immediate
liking to Castiglione, even allowing him to be lodged in the Vatican itself.
Castiglione took up his residence in the beautiful miniature palace known as the
Belvedere, set among fountains and lawns and orange trees. 'Would to God you
had as delightful a place to live in', he wrote to his mother, 'with this beautiful
view, these lovely gardens and all these noble antiques, fountains, basins,
running water'. And, though secluded and private, it was by no means cut off:
'All who enter Rome on this side pass through the streets below, as well as those
who go to walk in the meadows. And after supper I amuse myself watching the
crowds of boys and girls at their games.'

An ambassador was the eyes and ears of his distant master. Anything and
everything could have political significance: who had spent how much on a set
of gold buttons; who had quarrelled with whom; who had just arrived in Rome,
or was just leaving. He had to have a reporter's nose for news, and a
psychologist's skill in assessing character and calculating motives. Castiglione
had these skills and one additional, all encompassing talent – a brilliant literary

style that gave his descriptions of the most humdrum of daily events sparkle and interest. His main task, for which he was being paid reasonably well if invariably in arrears, was to keep his master the Marquis of Mantua minutely informed of political moves so that correct action could be taken in Mantua. But it was not only the Marquis who read the despatches: His Excellency's mother, Isabella d'Este, snatched them up as soon as they arrived, hungrily devouring their contents, feeding that restless, endlessly questing mind of hers with every detail that Castiglione could report of life in the great city.

So, therefore, the ambassador filled out his letters with colourful detail, providing an unrivalled picture of life at the papal court and the glittering, claustrophobic world that revolved around it. He writes of the supper given by Cardinal Farnese, where the principal course consisted entirely of peacocks, or of the prodigal banquet given by the banker Agostino Chigi when every one of the cosmopolitan company was given food and wines from his native country, served on gold plate. He writes of Pope Leo's vast hunting parties when His Holiness, clad in a snow-white costume and surrounded by a court kaleido-scopic with colour, glittering and clanking in gold chains and gold armour, brocades, velvets and silks, rides out over the Roman Campagna – a gay adventure with laughter and wine and song, but a dangerous one, too, for there might be a sudden charge of an enraged boar or bull or even wolf. He describes the marvellous alabaster organ which was presented to the Pope, and which Castiglione was able to obtain for Isabella after Leo's death. There are accounts of the plays and balls in which Leo so delighted, and also stories of more ribald occasions, such as the comic recitals given by the clown Strascino who specialised in animal imitations.

But Castiglione keeps the Marquis and his mother informed, too, of more serious matters that do not have immediate political significance. He tells of the reluctance of papal officials to accept the office of nuncio to Germany, 'where this Martin Luther's progress is very great. He himself is of small importance, but he has more than a hundred followers who are far more learned than he is, and who are all writing and preaching with the greatest fervour. Even women, we hear, do wonders, disputing with our friars and professing themselves ready to be martyrs.' There are descriptions of that perennial scourge of Rome, the plague. In the summer of 1522: 'Rome looks like a plundered abbey owing to the infinite number of persons who have fled from its walls. One very cruel thing is that many poor creatures who fall ill with other ailments or infirmities are abandoned and left to die of want. . . . The Pope is shut up in the Belvedere and refuses to give audience to any cardinals whose houses are not free of infection.' The Bishop of Grassi has had a vivid and macabre dream in which he says that 'he saw all the Cardinals who had died joining in a torchlight dance and that the Cardinal de Grassi came forward with the torch in his hand and presently handed it to Cardinal Santa Croce, who gave it to Soderini who, dancing in the Florentine fashion, passed it to Cardinal Fiesco, and he in his turn gave it to Cardinal Ancona. After Ancona it was Cornaro's turn and if these last two, who are still alive, follow their predecessors, I shall certainly believe this was not a dream but a vision.'

But the plague, though particularly severe in Rome, was also only too well known in Mantua as elsewhere. Far more interesting is the news that Castiglione has to tell of the marvellous city that is not only springing from the ancient soil, but also being discovered under it. Castiglione's great friend, the painter Raphael, has been specifically commissioned by Pope Leo to make a survey of the ruins of the classical city and make recommendations for its preservation. A neighbour of Castiglione, the Ferrarese scholar Celio Calcagnini, graphically describes the process of the survey which has taken every scholar's imagination: 'This is nothing short of a plan of the city of Rome, which he [Raphael] is producing in its ancient aspect and proportions. By digging out the foundations of ancient monuments, and restoring them according to the descriptions of classical authors, he has filled Pope Leo and all Rome with such admiration that they regard him as a god sent down from heaven to restore the Eternal City to its former majesty.' The work of excavation is all Raphael's, but Castiglione enthusiastically lends a hand with the drawing-up of the lengthy report which Raphael is preparing for the Pope, polishing the painter's unsophisticated prose so that the report became a potent plea for the preservation of those ruins which generations of Romans have either incuriously glanced at, or worse, plundered and cannibalised to make their own homes. Rome is rising from the dust of centuries, Castiglione rejoices in one of his elegant Latin poems:

> Now your eyes once more behold these wonders of a former age: the trophies of heroes are once more known by their names. Now the marble temples of the Vatican arise around you and the golden roofs of their porticoes glitter in the sun.

So the crowded, happy, hopeful years fled past. He left the city many times on various missions for his lord, but always he returned, his longest absence being during the unhappy reign of Adrian VI. He did not, like so many of his colleagues, join in the vilification of the honourable, austere, bitterly unhappy old Fleming, for he could understand, and sympathise with Adrian's deep-rooted sincerity and passionate desire for reform. But Castiglione, too, was a man of the new age: there was nothing for him in Rome under the new régime and the city was dull when his friends and acquaintances fled as though from the plague. He too shared in the delight when a Medici came again to the throne and Cardinal Giulio, whom he had known and admired, took the style of Clement VII. Willingly he accepted another mission to Rome, arriving back in the city in the November of 1523. It seemed, for a short time, as though the golden days were here again. Raphael had died two years before, cut short in the middle of a lifetime, for he was only thirty-seven, but though Castiglione deeply mourned his beloved friend there were many others to make up the circle: painters and goldsmiths and poets and sculptors hastening back to Rome to grasp their share of the new Medicean bounty.

However, times had changed. The cornucopia was empty and, in place of an affable pope jovially dispensing purses of gold for statues and paintings and rings and poems and banquets, there were only sour-faced auditors totting up bills that far exceeded income. The fairweather friends of Pope Clement rapidly melted away when it became evident that the papal coffers were empty. They were no great loss, and Castiglione knew enough of papal affairs to realise that it was the splendid Leo's fault that the papacy now was obliged to retrench. Even the failure to solve the nagging problem of Martin Luther could hardly be blamed on Clement. Castiglione heard with an amazement boarding on incredulity the story of how the papal legate to Germany had been greeted with jeers and insults in Augsburg and had been warned not to enter Nuremberg with the customary pomp and ceremony. Most people in the know were now convinced that large areas of Germany were lost to the Church for ever, but though the German heresy saddened Castiglione, he knew well enough that its roots lay deep in the past and that there was little that Clement could have done to eradicate the causes which lay in the very heart of the Roman Church.

All this the shrewd little envoy accepted; but it was Clement's handling of the feud between France and Spain that caused him ever greater anxiety throughout the spring and early summer of 1524. Pope Leo had managed to get away with his juggling act, partly because he had been Pope Leo but partly, too, because he had had both space and time. Now suddenly the two giants of Europe were preparing to grapple with each other just a few days' march from Rome and were demanding that Clement should declare, unequivocally, for one or the other. It would be dangerous to do so, but even that would be preferable to the teetering, tottering course Pope Clement was pursuing, Castiglione thought. Throughout the summer envoys from both sides arrived in Rome: Castiglione knew most of them through the international free-masonry of scholarship, and most took the opportunity to call upon him. Thus he learned from his old friend the Bishop of Bayeux that King François would consider no treaty whatsoever which included the hated traitor Bourbon, nor would the King ever relinquish his claim upon Milan. The Venetian Gian Francesco Valetio was of a similar, pessimistic opinion. 'I for one expect nothing from either the King or the Emperor. Two insuperable difficulties lie in the way of peace: one is Milan, the other Bourbon.' And Pope Clement, caught between the two, hesitated, advanced, changed his mind, hesitated again, retreated. Francesco Berni, a pampered, spoilt poetaster, one of those, perhaps, disappointed in his expectations, pinpointed Clement's irresolution in a vicious little sonnet:

> *A papacy made up of respects*
> *Of considerations and of talk*
> *Of yets, and then, of buts and ifs and maybe's*
> *Of words without end that have no effect at all.*

Not all of Castiglione's visitors during the restless, plague-ridden summer of 1524 were sober diplomats, come to share their worries with a colleague. On a June morning there burst into his comfortable lodgings the explosive figure of the young professional soldier known as Giovanni della Bande Nere. Massively built, with a cruel mouth and liquid, flashing, expressive black eyes, he made an incongruous figure in Castiglione's quiet, book-lined room. What was Pope

Clement up to? the visitor demanded. On whose side were they supposed to be fighting? How was he supposed to command his company when from one day to another his orders could be reversed? Giovanni della Bande Nere and the Pope were kinsmen, but they had only the Medici surname in common: there was no other affinity between the hesitant, intellectual Clement and this ferocious killer who commanded the only efficient Italian company to be found in all Italy. Swiss, Germans, Spaniards and French alike, whatever they might think of Italian soldiers in general, had nothing but the most wholesome respect for the Black Bands.

Giovanni's father had been a comparative nonentity, a Medici of the cadet branch. But his mother had been the famous Caterina Sforza, the woman for whom the term 'virago' had been coined, for she had all the courage and political competence of a man and the wiles of a very beautiful woman. She was a fascinating, tough, totally unscrupulous woman who took her lovers from wherever she pleased, ruled her little city-state of Forli with an iron hand, and flourished in the lethal masculine world of power politics. It had taken a man of the status of Cesare Borgia to bring her down, and it had taken even him a full-scale military operation to do so. Caterina had been supremely skilful at disconcerting her enemies by switching from feminine to masculine roles as it suited her, and Giovanni was the unborn star of one of these occasions. During a siege of Forli her enemies captured her children and threatened to kill them if she did not surrender. The virago easily triumphed over the mother. She appeared on the city walls, derisively raising her skirts to show that she was pregnant, and yelled 'Fools! Do you think that I can't make more?'

Orphaned at the age of eleven, Giovanni was brought up by a powerful Florentine family, the Salviati, allies and kinsmen of the Medici. But he scarcely needed protection. A violent, quarrelsome, headstrong young man, while still in his teens he was exiled as a public nuisance. But he was also more than just rowdy and a bully: he had within him a genuine military genius which his relative, Pope Leo, recognised. By the time he was eighteen he actually had his own command of a hundred lances, a company of three hundred tough, professional soldiers whose total acceptance of their young commander was the most emphatic testimony possible of his military competence. At the age of twenty, Giovanni recognised what was still hidden to the majority of even the most experienced and mature Italian commanders: that blood had been brought back into Italian wars. For over a century the battles between the city-states had been fought by foreign mercenaries, men for whom the prolongation of war and the avoidance of casualties were the major aims. The French invasion of 1494 had startled and horrified the Italians: French soldiers, bloodied in the long wars with England, well-supplied and well-trained in the use of the terrible new weapon, artillery, had cut a bloody swathe through the country. City after city had fallen to them and had it not been for the extended lines of communication, Italy would probably have become a French province. Cesare Borgia had been among the very few Italian generals to see that a new form of warfare had come to Italy, but he had been dead now for over a decade and his mantle had fallen upon Giovanni de' Medici . . .

To posterity, Giovanni della Bande Nere appears simply a brawling, whoring, violent killer whose first and last loyalty lay with the military machine that he had created. But contemporaries looked at him with a sudden hopefulness, and these contemporaries included men of the intellectual status of Aretino, who became his personal friend, and Machiavelli, who remained his admirer to the end. Varied and fanciful were the reasons given for the black ribbons which fluttered from the lances of his troopers and gave his company its name. The most likely explanation was that he ordered them to be used as mourning for his kinsman Pope Leo, and thereafter liked both their appearance and the sound of the name Bande Nere for his company. But there was no fanciful explanation for the nickname that he bore in his last years, Giovanni d'Italia. Even Machiavelli used it in allusion to Giovanni della Bande Nere as the one man who would be able to act as a military catalyst and, transforming the endlessly feuding armies of Italy into one national army, expel the foreigners who were battening on the vitals of Italy.

But this he was not allowed to do, Giovanni now exploded to the sympathetic but helpless Castiglione. As an Italian and as a general of the Pope's armies, he was eager to attack the invaders of Italy. But what, in fact, had happened recently? First, he had been leashed in during the short and dismal career of Pope Adrian, that Fleming who had also been the chaplain of the mongrel emperor, foreigners all of them. During that time he, Giovanni, had been obliged to dig into his own pockets to find the wages for his troopers and to keep them occupied during the tedious days of the so-called peace. Then, happily, Adrian had died and Clement taken his place and for a short and blissful period Giovanni had been given his head. The Bande Nere had torn into the French as they desecrated Lombardy. Heavily out-numbered though the Bande Nere had been, Giovanni's tactics had been supremely successful for he had disciplined his men to move in fast, hit, and move out again, appearing, it seemed, in a dozen places at once. The Grand Devil, the French had named him, and cursed him and his Black Bands as they began that lumbering retreat during which their particular champion, the Chevalier Bayard, had been killed. Pope Clement had warmly congratulated his young kinsman for that exploit and had even bestowed a small fief upon him. But now what? There was talk that the Pope was considering an alliance with those same French whom the Bande Nere had been fighting. Was it true? demanded Giovanni. Was he now to bear arms for King François, instead of against him? Castiglione could only shrug. In the present uncertain circumstances, and with the present uncertain pope almost anything could result. And on that unsatisfactory, inconclusive note the interview ended. Giovanni stormed out to expend his pent-up energy in drinking and whoring and brawling, so earning the severe displeasure of his august kinsman, and causing trouble, too, to poor Castiglione, as Mantuan envoy in Rome, because the Bande Nere clashed with Mantuan troops, to the Marquis of Mantua's rage, and Castiglione was hard put to it to satisfy all parties.

On 19 July 1524 Castiglione received a summons to attend on the Pope at the Vatican. He had been indisposed over the past few days, 'because of the great heat and the abundance of good melons which I have lately enjoyed', he naively informed his master and the Pope was kindness itself. 'He told me of the love he had long borne me and of the confidence which he placed in me, and after expatiating on this theme for some time, he said that he wished to give me a proof of the trust which he reposed in me.' Would Castiglione go as Vatican ambassador to the court of Charles at Madrid? The Emperor had already been sounded out as to whether he would accept Castiglione in such a role and had returned a warm affirmative. Castiglione pointed out that he could not accept such an office without the permission of his master Gonzaga, the Marquis of Mantua. 'The Pope replied that he had thought of this', Castiglione wrote to the Marquis, 'and that the fact of employing one of your servants on so important a mission would of itself do Your Excellency great honour.' The Count was not over-eager to accept the offer: 'To me, the idea is altogether new and I should never have dreamt of such a thing. I was aware that many favourites of His Holiness's chief ministers were scheming for the post and I, on my part, am anxious rather for repose than for fresh labours. Still, I would not refuse this office, seeing the Pope's firm resolve, and considering the advantage which this may be to Your Excellency's service.' Gonzaga, too, was perfectly well aware of the value of having such a faithful servant as Castiglione at the court of the Emperor and hastened to grant permission for his secondment to the papal service.

Castiglione spent the rest of the summer winding up his professional and personal affairs in Rome. Not the least of his difficulty was extracting money from Cardinal Armellino, the Chamberlain, a greedy, grasping man who was reputed to have paid 100,000 ducats for his office and was intent on making it yield the utmost possible. The Count needed money not only to finance his long journey and his indefinite but certainly prolonged stay in Spain, but also to support his little family here in Italy. He was a widower and his old mother was looking after his young children in Mantua; though she was proud enough of the honour paid to her son, yet she was also anxious as to how to provide for herself and his little ones during his absence. Almost every post brought a letter from her, adding a new worry to Castiglione's mounting problems. In mid-September he wrote to her, disabusing her of some of the optimistic stories she had evidently been hearing: 'If you are told the Pope has given me a salary of 150 ducats, do not believe it, because it is a false report which has spread all over Rome. It is true that the office of Papal Collector in Spain – which has been given to me – is useful and honourable, and carries with it important powers, but as yet there is no talk of a salary.' Castiglione was to find that his new paymaster was even more dilatory than the old, and the nagging business of obtaining funds from a distant and unsympathetic source was to bedevil the rest of his life.

But by 5 October all had been eventually, if not entirely satisfactorily, arranged. He took his leave of the Pope and received what he expected: instructions to visit both the Spanish Viceroy and the King of France on his journey through Northern Italy and to assure them both of His Holiness's paternal love. At the same time, he was to make the most of his privileged status and keep a sharp eye open for military preparations, reporting back to Rome on the strength of the contending forces, and the disposition of the Italian enemies and allies. He travelled slowly north, calling first at the shrine of Loreto where, in the Holy House that had been miraculously carried by angels from Jerusalem to Italy, he asked the blessing of the Madonna on his perilous and vital journey. At Mantua he stopped for a few days to visit his mother and children – the last time he would ever see them – and assured himself that they would be well provided for during his absence.

From Mantua he travelled onward into French-held territory. Giberti, Clement's pro-French confidant, was waiting for him at Parma in Lombardy, with a safe conduct signed by King François himself. There Castiglione learned that Clement's purpose like some weather-vane, had veered towards the French. Giberti was openly delighted, openly confident: His Holiness and His Majesty were in direct negotiation. Giberti's presence in Lombardy aroused Castiglione's deepest suspicions. What was this notorious Francophile doing so far from Rome and apparently on such very good terms with King François himself? Poor Castiglione was not to know that his master was engaged in deceiving him: that Clement was so desperate to pick the right side at the right moment that he was fully prepared to authorise a secret mission that would make nonsense of Castiglione's instructions.

News of the French re-conquest of Milan had reached Rome on 28 October, three weeks after Castiglione's departure, and had so terrified Clement that he had sent Giberti hastening northward with virtually a free hand. Giberti had first approached the Spanish with the suggestion of an armistice and, on the suggestions being rejected out of hand, he hastened to François. The young King also, confident of his ability to dispose of the 'imperial' forces then pent up in Pavia, had loftily rejected any idea of an armistice. It was almost certainly from this point onwards that Clement began his ultimately disastrous championing of François. Giberti, already well-disposed towards the French in any case, and comparing the confident, well-armed, well-fed army of François with the dejected imperialists, worked steadily towards persuading his master to conclude an alliance with the new Champion of the West.

Castiglione knew nothing of this. But he understood Giberti sufficiently well to realise that the weather-vane of Vatican politics had swung yet again towards France. There was no certainty even now that Clement would commit himself to anybody, but Giberti's confidence deepened Castiglione's conviction that some underhand work was in process, and made him more dejected as he crossed the wintry Lombard plain.

In Cremona he met young Francesco Sforza, brother of the exiled Massimiliano, and now himself an exiled Duke of Milan – although 'Duke' was a grandiloquent term to use for a young man whose capital was occupied by one set of foreigners, and whose continued existence was guaranteed by another set. Castiglione was favourably impressed by this youngest son of Beatrice d'Este, the long-dead sister of Isabella d'Este. He had known the young man's father, Ludovico il Moro so-called, the wily Duke of Milan who had proved too wily for his own good and ended his days in a prison cell in France, and he found that the young man seemed to have inherited the d'Este intellectualism rather than the Sforza cunning. But, though impressed, Castiglione could give no comforting answer to young Francesco's question: why was His Holiness standing aside with folded hands while the armed might of Spain and France manouvred for their inevitable clash? Surely His Holiness must see that whether Milan remained in French hands, or was captured by the imperialists, the balance of power must be totally altered in Italy? Castiglione could only repeat the weary, pious platitude that Clement, as the Holy Father of all good Christians, could not take one side against the other.

Listening to the conversation was a swarthy, sturdy man, Girolamo Morone, the Duke's secretary and manipulator, a hardened, veteran intriguer who nodded knowingly to Castiglione's hesitant explanation and afterwards took him on one side. His Holiness really ought to throw in his lot with the imperialists, Morone pointed out. The French could not possibly defend Milan, send an expedition to Naples as they were planning to do, besiege Pavia and defend their King, all in a foreign and hostile country. Privately Castiglione agreed, but, true to his instructions, he announced his intention of continuing on to Milan to visit François in person. En route he waited upon Lannoy, the Imperial Viceroy, who was at pains to tell him that the poor condition of the imperial army was only temporary: that even now the Duke of Bourbon was hastening towards Germany to recruit landsknechts, and that Germans and Spaniards combined – even without those Italian allies who would infallibly join the larger side – would much outnumber the French.

Castiglione spent Christmas Day with the French Viceroy in Milan, then, the following day, rode the fifteen miles to the camp outside Pavia where François was busily establishing his siege. They had last met nine years earlier after François' victory at Marignano. The intervening years had done little to subdue François: he was still the gay, ebullient, courteous cavalier that Castiglione remembered. The Mantuan was pro-imperial: he disliked French politics, in particular the politics which brought the French on to Italian soil. But he deeply admired and liked the French King who seemed to embody all those qualities which he most highly valued and which he was to enshrine in his book *The Courtier*. The last time they had met, in fact, François had politely enquired as to when he proposed to publish the book. Nearly a decade had passed and the book was still gestating, but François was still pre-eminently the kind of gentleman Castiglione had had in mind when he framed his work which fixed for all time the Renaissance concept of courtesy.

Their conversation on this occasion was political and amiable, rather than productive, judging by the report which Castiglione sent back to Giberti. But from other sources the envoy was able to build up a picture that was rather closer to the facts than Giberti's own account of French potentialities. 'The King's affairs are most prosperous', Castiglione agreed,

And indeed Pavia is closely besieged by the French, although now and then those in the city make a sally, as they did in my presence today, when a troop of foot soldiers marched out through a breach in the wall and attacked the

French troop vigorously. The King himself is very gay and confident and determined to carry out this enterprise to the bitter end. . . . But I tell you that though he and his nobles speak so bravely, I hear that they are very short of money, as may be seen by the cruel way they are extracting gold from the Milanese. Several merchants have been thrown into prison and shamefully treated. Milan is very much discontented, and the French are more afraid of the imperialists than they admit.

With that perspicuous assessment of affairs, the envoy took his leave of Milan, travelling on to Turin where the Duke of Savoy welcomed him warmly, and so on through the high Alpine passes. With his departure from Turin it was as though a curtain had descended between him and Rome. Again and again, in letters addressed for the most part from rough Alpine inns, he complained to his friends that he had had no news, either from them or from his principals. The lack of news from his friends was mildly hurtful, particularly for such a gregarious, vulnerable man as Castiglione. But the lack of news from the Vatican was totally demoralising. He seemed to be working in total darkness, not knowing whether the ground before him was solid, or a morass into which he might disappear.

He reached Lyons on 9 January and found, to his surprise, that the city was *en fête*, though the festive season was long past. He was not long left in doubt as to the reason for this unseasonable rejoicing. On presenting his credentials to Louise, the Queen Mother who was acting as Regent, he learned that 'Madame and all this city are filled with joy because of the news that the Pope and the Venetian Signory have entered into a league with the Most Christian King François, and promised to be friends with his friends and fight against his foes.' The long silence was at last explained. While Castiglione had been toiling through the Alps, bound ultimately for the court of the Emperor Charles V, the enemies of the Emperor had triumphed and the wavering Pope had thrown in his lot with François.

Castiglione was in despair: but had he known of the strength of Charles' reaction, he would probably have turned his horse's head about and gone back home. For once, the Emperor's cold, formal exterior cracked. Beside himself with rage he cried 'I will go into Italy myself and be revenged upon that villain of a pope. Martin Luther, perhaps was not so far wrong.'

Chapter VII

The Battle of Pavia

Matteo Giberti, Datary, friend and confidant of Pope Clement, had all the humanist scholar's love of a fine phrase. Towards the end of the long-drawn-out negotiations with François, which had ended to Giberti's entire satisfaction, his conscience urged him to give the King a warning, but a warning suitably wrapped up in rhetoric: 'As no sailor ever risks the storm of the open sea with only one anchor, so the Pope – confident though he be in the strength of François I – will not stake all upon the single throw of his success before Pavia.' Stripped of rhetoric, the message was clear enough: if François insisted on a military trial of strength with the Emperor and was worsted, then he would be abandoned – immediately.

François paid no heed to the warning for why should he? The King of France was riding on a wave of triumph that engulfed his enemies with scarcely any exertion on his part. Milan, that great prize, had fallen to him without a battle, the demoralised enemy force falling back on Lodi after hastily garrisoning a number of cities, Pavia amongst them. At this very moment, a picked detachment of French troops was marching briskly southwards to attack Naples, the imperial stronghold in Italy. To reach Naples, his troops had to cross the territories of sovereign states, including the Pope's own States of the Church: all such had willingly granted permission, showing how clearly the French star was rising. The garrison of Pavia was proving stubborn, but it was only a matter of time before starvation forced its surrender. And meanwhile he had for headquarters one of the most delightful pleasuregrounds in all Italy.

Pavia, some fifteen miles from Milan, was about to find itself in the middle of a battlefield, because it had the misfortune of being a singularly beautiful place, as well as being strongly fortified. It had always been a loyally pro-imperial city; that was why it was holding out so stubbornly. But its physical setting was so attractive that the rulers of Milan had developed it as their favourite place of residence. A century before, one of these rulers had built himself a superb palace or castle there. Francesco Petrarch, poet, connoisseur of good living, and first of the modern breed of tourists, stayed there shortly after it was completed and described it enthusiastically to his friend Boccacio:

I have now spent three summers in this city of Ticinum, now called Pavia, which the grammarians tell us means admirable or wonderful, and do not remember ever to have experienced anywhere else such refreshing showers, such freedom from heat and such delightful breezes. The city stands in the middle of the Ligurian plain upon a little hill . . . and enjoys a wide free prospect on every side. By turning one's head ever so little in one direction may be seen the snowy crests of the Alps and, in the other, the wooded Appenines. The river Ticino itself, descending in graceful curves and hastening to join the Po, flows close by the city walls. It is the clearest of streams and flows very rapidly, although just here it moves more deliberately and has been deprived of its natural purity by the brooks which join it. Lastly in order of time, though not in importance, you would see the huge castle standing on the highest point of the city. I am convinced, unless I am misled by partiality for the founder, that you with your good taste in such matters would declare this to be the most noble production of modern art.

The castle stood on the northern side of the city, towards Milan, and was now firmly in the hands of the imperialists. But stretching away from it was the immense, walled park known as the Mirabella. It was carefully landscaped with clear streams running through lawn-like meadows dotted with groves of planes and cypress and myrtles, and even in the depths of winter it was a delightful place, teeming with game that simultaneously provided sport and a plentiful supply of food. The French army occupied the Park, François taking up his headquarters in the Belvedere (the duke's hunting lodge); and from this ideal spot he directed the siege of Pavia, refreshing himself from time to time with the pleasures of the chase, whether of game in the Park, or of women in Milan. It was here that Castiglione had visited him just after Christmas and had been so impressed with the external appearances of the French force. Amply supplied with provisions, his troops well rested and in good heart, and militarily secure behind the stout walls of the Park, François was totally confident of the outcome. The enemy had one choice: to be starved into surrender or to be overcome by superior numbers in a pitched battle.

Even Giovanni della Bande Nere was now fighting on the French side. He had ridden into the Park at the head of his Black Bands and offered his sword to the French King as part of the deal made between Clement and François. Giovanni's nascent nationalism, a concept for which there was still no term, and which he would have had difficulty in defining or defending, had not been wholly smothered. He had, for instance, refused François' offer of the decoration of the Order of St Michel, for to have accepted such an honour would have entailed the swearing of fealty and he had no intention of tying himself down in such a manner. But he was also a condottiere, a mercenary leader of mercenary soldiers who must needs pick up their pay where they could, and King François had offered very handsome terms indeed, delighted to commission the legendary Italian hero. His mere presence turned the French army from an invading force into an ally, giving a gloss to François' claim to be legitimate Duke of the Italian State of Milan as well as King of the realm of France.

Giovanni arrived with a boon companion: a big, thick-set man with flowing beard, expansive gestures, deep thirst and a quicksilver tongue. Pietro Aretino, a man who thoroughly disliked being physically hurt and would run miles to avoid a fight, seems an unlikely companion for a professional soldier who rarely opened a book, scorned all scribblers and regarded physical courage as the highest form of virtue. But though the friendship seems to have been rooted merely in a mutual liking for wine and women, it was strong and enduring and Aretino – the same foul-tongued Aretino who could ruin a reputation with a letter – was to write one of history's most moving and tenderest of epitaphs for his young friend when Giovanni was brought to an early grave. François was just as delighted to receive the writer as he was to commission the soldier, for he prided himself on his own skill with the pen and so knew the worth of Aretino's. He threw a massive gold chain around the writer's neck and sat him at the high table along with Giovanni and they drank and laughed and danced and afterwards went hunting and all went merrily in the great Park of Mirabella.

Far different was it within the massive walls of Pavia. The city had been under siege now for nearly four months, ever since the early November of 1524, and the grim spectre of famine began to raise its head. Normal supplies of meat had long since disappeared and the flesh of horses, mules and asses was substituted, ominous harbinger of later privation. That winter was particularly cold and, denied access to the normal sources of fuel, the citizens had no choice but to burn first their furniture and then actually to rip up the beams and floors of their houses and churches. Yet, curiously, the Pavese remained steadfast. Outwardly, this was simply another Italian city occupied by a foreign force, for the governor, Antonio de Leyva, was a Spaniard and the garrison consisted of Spanish soldiers and German mercenaries. Nevertheless, the people of Pavia seemed to regard themselves primarily as imperial subjects whose loyalties took precedence over their rights as Italian citizens. The nobles and merchants lent money for payment of the mercenaries and, when that proved insufficient, the precious plate from the churches and the University was melted down and turned into bullion.

In Pavia, during that bitter winter of 1524, was re-born the old Ghibelline spirit. For a century and more the old rallying cries of Guelf and Ghibelline had been little more than pretexts for civic brawling, but the citizens of Pavia now gave their party dignity, at least, by their self-sacrifice; and by their individual actions demonstrated loyalty to an emperor they had never seen and who, even now, was scarcely more than a concept. Charles the man, the Burgundian–Flemish–Spaniard, could have meant nothing to these Italians, but they were prepared to suffer and die for Charles the Emperor. One of those who entered legend that winter was the beautiful Ippolita Fioramonda, a friend and correspondent of Castiglione's. She used to wear a skyblue satin vest embroidered with gold moths – a warning symbol, it was said, to her vainly sighing lovers to keep their distance or be scorched. The satin vest was exchanged for drab workaday clothes as this delicate, aristocratic intellectual threw herself energetically into the defence, exhorting and encouraging the soldiers and militia, making the circuit of the walls to hurl ritual defiance at the enemy below. She, however, was one defender who was quite safe from the missiles of the enemy, for the fame of her beauty and courage had spread through the French camp and every knight of spirit had, in hope at least, joined the legions of her admirers.

François conducted the siege energetically and imaginatively. An impressive attempt was made to divert the Ticino, an attempt which was defeated only by nature itself when a violent rain-storm caused extensive flooding. Miners and artillery played their part and the frequent clashes between besiegers and sortie parties were bloody and violent. But François had made a fundamental error by indulging himself in a siege, even for such a prize as Pavia, when the main body of the enemy army was still at large. It was demoralised but still in being, still capable of being welded into a fighting whole, given reinforcements and the right spirit. Admittedly, the Viceroy Lannoy himself seemed to have lost heart, bluntly warning his emperor: 'Take care what you are doing for you might yet lose a crown in order to gain a ducal hat – a dear bargain.' Lannoy had wanted to retreat to the safety of the Spanish kingdom of Naples, forgetting the Milanese enterprise, but Bourbon and Pescara had persuaded him to remain in Lombardy. Bourbon had everything to lose, and nothing to gain, by abandoning the campaign in Lombardy and it was therefore he who undertook the delicate and dangerous business of raising reinforcements in Germany.

At the beginning of December 1525, at about the time that Castiglione arrived in Lombardy and François was settling himself for the winter in Pavia, Bourbon crossed the Alps and entered Nuremberg. There he waited upon Georg Frundsburg, Prince of Mindelheim, a huge old oak of a man who was in his eighties yet still rode at the head of his troops, towering above them. It would be interesting to know exactly what passed between this dramatically dissimilar couple: between the Lutheran German for whom loyalty to the tribal leader surpassed all other loyalties, all other virtues, and the Catholic Frenchman whom all the world now regarded as a renegade. But Frundsburg's very loyalty would have obliged him to welcome Bourbon, for Bourbon had come on behalf of the emperor, and though the rest of the world might regard Charles V as being a Burgundian or a Fleming or a Spaniard – and a Catholic at that – for Frundsburg he was simply Kaiser Karl, grandson of Maximilian, head of the house of Habsburg. It was unfortunate, perhaps, that Kaiser Karl had not yet seen the light and still held to the pernicious doctrines of popery but that was, strictly, irrelevant. Frundsburg's tribal leader had called for help and Frundsburg must obey that call or be for ever dishonoured in his own eyes, and in the eyes of the men he led.

It was Frundsburg's men that Bourbon wanted. The old man himself had no particular political value but he was venerated by the landsknechts whom he had trained and led throughout his long and explosively active life. The landsknechts were a new force on the military scene. They were mercenaries, but linked together by a far stronger tie than the usual common desire for pay and booty and, under certain circumstances, they would be prepared to fight and die for love of their leader alone. They had been founded by the emperor

Maximilian, that brilliant, contradictory, impecunious Austrian who had once toyed with the idea of being pope himself, fancied himself as a writer and, on those frequent occasions when his fortunes were at a low ebb, did not disdain to carry a lance for pay. What was good enough for the Emperor Maximilian III was good enough for many a landless lordling with an empty purse, a good sword and a taste for adventure. Returning home, laden with gold and booty after some successful campaign, they were the best possible advertisement for the military life, and eager young men in their hundreds would hasten to the town square when some commander raised his standard as sign that a company was being formed.

These companies of landsknechts were virtually military republics. Discipline was absolute: significantly, every company had its official executioner; but the humblest soldier had a voice in the control of a company, for officers were appointed by popular vote, and articles of service defined, with Germanic precision, the rights and duties of each man from the commander to the newest recruit. In appearance, the landsknechts must have been among the most picturesque soldiers in history. They disdained any appearance of a uniform: jerkins, doublets, coats of mail were worn according to the taste of the wearer; and, in addition, it was they who introduced the custom of 'slashing' garments, one of the very few examples of a fashion moving upwards in society, for it was to be adopted even by the aristocracy by the end of that century. The Swiss had begun the fashion, very possibly making a virtue out of necessity. The landsknechts carried it to extremes, developing the incredibly baggy breeches which employed twenty yards or more of gaily coloured material falling in loose strips from hip to knee. It seems remarkable that they were able to control, much less fight in, these loose, swirling ribands, and some, in addition, sported hats with monstrous plumes.

The Swiss supremacy in battle had disconcerted the landsknechts and it was probably from this point, and under the iron control of Frundsburg, that they had begun to employ the deadly new weapon which they called the hakenbusch and which the rest of the world was to know as the arquebus. The earliest form of handgun had been simply a tube mounted on a pole, the charge being ignited by a match – a three yard length of cotton cord soaked in saltpetre and kept constantly alight. Later, a mechanism was developed which brought the smouldering match into contact with the priming powder by means of a lever action, and from this single weapon developed first the arquebus and then the musket. The arquebusier faced a peculiar hazard for he was obliged to carry upon his person a length of smouldering match in proximity to quantities of powder, and many a man blew himself up before he was even able to charge his piece.

Charging was a complicated task. Black powder was held in one flask, finer priming powder in another. A measure of powder, together with a bullet taken from a leather bag, was rammed home, priming powder placed in the pan and ignited – the whole operation taking a length of time during which the arquebusier was totally defenceless, relying either upon his comrades' being armed with traditional weapons, or upon fellow arquebusiers' firing in an exactly timed sequence. The general who, in the heat of battle, could protect his arquebusiers during their vulnerable periods, was the general most likely to emerge as victor, but only the Germans, and Spanish as yet, had fully appreciated the potentialities of the new weapon and devised a technique for its use. Even the flexible Italians, normally so quick to adopt an innovation, seem to have overlooked its possibilities. Giovanni della Bande Nere made no particular provision for arquebusiers, and some of the more old-fashioned Italian generals still hanged them when they were captured, indignant that a coward armed with a gun could bring down a brave man armed with a sword.

Bourbon, therefore, had excellent reason to feel pleased with the result of his mission when, in mid-January 1525, he and Frundsburg rode down into Lombardy at the head of eleven companies of landsknechts – barely 6,000 troops in all, but together forming an immensely effective, compact fighting unit. They joined the imperial army at Lodi to find a heated argument taking place among the Allied leaders. The Viceroy, Lannoy, still wanted to wash his hands of affairs in Lombardy, being anxious to hasten south and ensure the safety of Naples, his base in Italy, even at the price of abandoning Pavia and all within it. The Neapolitan-born Marquis of Pescara was undecided: he had personal reasons for wanting to return to Naples, but he also had enough military good sense to know that it would be courting disaster to turn south while a large French army, numerically their superior, was roaming free in Lombardy. The young Duke of Milan, and his adviser Morone, were not unnaturally insistent that the enemy should be cleared out of Lombardy. The situation was made even more confused by the activities of Clement's legates. One of them was even now giving aid and comfort to François in Pavia while another, the supposedly pro-imperial Schomberg, galloped into Lodi, charged with the task of persuading the imperialists not to attack the French. Frundsburg settled that particular problem by drawing his immense sword and personally chasing the terrified ecclesiastic from the camp. He and Bourbon, less personally involved than the others, were better able to assess the military situation and between them they succeeded in convincing Lannoy that the battle for Italy must be fought here in Lombardy.

The army marched out of Lodi on 24 January, a bitterly cold day, gloomy with the threat of an approaching snow-storm. Against all tradition and military usage, the imperialists were marching to war during the close season of winter. Provisions were low, money scarce, morale at its very lowest by the time they arrived at Pavia where the pessimistic Lannoy immediately decided to dig in, reluctant to challenge the militarily superior French. In the opposite camp, François was bursting with confidence. 'According to the view I have always held, I think that the last thing the enemy will do is to fight, for our strength is too much for them', he wrote to his worried but still admiring mother. 'Pavia will be lost to them unless they find some means of reinforcing it. So far they have tried everything, determined to hold it to the last gasp – which can't be far away. For more than a month now those inside have not drunk wine or eaten meat or cheese.' Despite the fact that time was indubitably on the French side, still Lannoy stubbornly clung to his waiting game. The two armies were so close to each other that the sentries could hear each other being relieved. Short, bitter skirmishes took place, during one of which Giovanni della Bande Nere was badly wounded – significantly enough by a stone bullet from an arquebus – and had to be shipped out down the Po. His company remained under François' control, commanded by the English exile the Duke of Suffolk, but not long afterwards 6,000 of François' Swiss mercenaries refused to renew their contract and marched out. François still had the advantage in numbers, in provisioning, and in morale, but the more sober of his officers, reflecting that a hungry and desperate enemy was the most dangerous kind of enemy, counselled a withdrawal to Milan.

, The egregious Admiral Bonnivet mocked their caution: 'You propose to our brave king to avoid a battle so greatly desired of all? We French have never refused battle – above all when we have for our general a valiant king.' Turning to François, he delivered precisely the kind of exhortation that would appeal to his romanticism: 'Kings bear their fortune with them. . . . When he leads the way, his men at arms will follow and trample down this paltry enemy. Therefore Sire, give battle.' Alarmed, the papal legate Aleander tried to reduce the dangerous exaltation. Perhaps it was unfitting for a king of France to retreat from an apparently inferior enemy, but just wait, he implored: Let the imperialists exhaust themselves, shivering and starving in their muddy, icy trenches, while François took his ease behind the stout walls of the park and the even more dependable sword arms of his men.

It was the imperialists who decided the matter, for a desperate and hungry enemy was, indeed, the most dangerous kind. Lannoy had no choice but to attack: from within Pavia, de Leyva sent despairing word that he could no longer hold the city, while within the camp the men were growing mutinous. The landsknechts of Frundsburg might willingly die for him in battle, but they declined to starve to death like rats in a hole. On 23 February, the imperial leaders held a council of war.

It was a gloomy meeting, with much left unsaid among the six men. They were an ill-assorted group of men for a high enterprise, divided by race, religion and private motivation. There was Bourbon, the French renegade, whose only hope lay in the total destruction of his King and cousin; there were the two Italians, the pliant young Duke of Milan and his devious counsellor, Morone, who was only too well aware that by throwing the French out of Milan they were probably only facilitating a Spanish conquest of the city; there were the two imperialists, Lannoy and Pescara, both of whom tended to regard Lombardy as the first line of defence for their base, Naples; and there was Georg Frundsburg, ill at ease among these Latin papists, and probably the only one inspired by a simple sense of loyalty to his Emperor. But the six men were able to come to a common decision under pressure of a common threat: an attack must be launched under pressure of a common threat: an attack must be launched immediately. As it happened, the following day was the twenty-fifth birthday of their titular leader, the Emperor – as good a day as any for risking the remains of the imperial army. It was agreed that a picked band of pioneers should make a breach in the Park wall large enough to allow the passage of the main body of the army. A message was also sent to the anxiously waiting de Leyva: on receipt of a signal – two blank cannon shots – he was to lead the garrison in an attack on the French rear. The garrison were to wear white shirts over their armour so that they could be distinguished in the gloom of a February night.

But the white markers were not needed: the massive wall of the Park proved far tougher than had been expected and daylight had broken long before a large enough breach was made. The long and noisy work had given François ample warning. He was delighted: a full, head-on clash in the open was the proper way to fight wars, and not this tedious business of waiting for an enemy to starve himself into submission. Long before the breach was complete, François and his nobles were drawn up in splendid battle order, glittering towers of steel upon their immense chargers, their banners and ensigns brave in the cold spring morning. The French cannon began their shattering roar, the stone and metal shot ploughing through the imperialists as they poured through the gap. But that was just an overture to the impatiently awaited drama that could be played out only by human beings. The King clutched his great lance, his face, with that almost comically long nose, alight and quivering with eagerness. His noble friends and relatives were no less eager to hurl themselves into the only activity worthy of an aristocrat. Behind them and on their flanks, the remaining Swiss mercenaries grouped themselves with dour precision: this was just another job in hand and they would give a good account of themselves, but there was no profit in their own death – a sentiment shared by their Italian comrades-in-arms, the Black Bands of Giovanni de' Medici, on the opposite flank. The cannon ceased their roar: the French vanguard began its remorseless advance. Lannoy, a brave man but a logical one, made the sign of the cross when he caught sight of the enemy force and, turning aside to his men, said coldly: 'There is no hope but in God: follow me and do what I do.' At the first clash the imperial vanguard was thrown into disarray. François killed the Marquis of Civita Sant' Angelo with his own hands, and as Lannoy and his armoured knights fell back, the King cried out exultantly: 'Now indeed I can call myself Duke of Milan.'

However, the battlefield that François had chosen so many months before did not favour the stately groupings and splendid cavalry charges which he had been brought up to regard as the true spirit of knightly warfare, in which he excelled. The little rivulets that kept the Park green in the hottest summers, and the carefully landscaped copses broke up the armoured charges, turned the great steel wave into groups of individuals suddenly fighting desperately for their lives. For that same terrain was most favourable for the new, un-glamorous, but immensely effective warfare based on firearms. The great cannons of France that had wrought such terrible destruction in the past were now suddenly obscured by their own allies, the Black Bands galloping forward to meet a sudden onrush of landsknechts under Bourbon's command. Germans and Italians clashed fiercely and the Black Bands, though fighting for pay for a foreign paymaster, honourably acquitted themselves. But at this crucial point the absence of their leader proved fatal and they disappeared at last under the

German charge. Meanwhile, the main body of François' knights had en-countered the deadly fire of the arquebusiers. The gun-men were fighting on ground perfectly suited to their trade, for the trees and hollows gave cover during loading and they were able to send volley after volley screaming into the massed knights. Even plate armour was not equal to the force of explosively propelled missiles: pierced through and through, the towering steel castles crashed to the muddy ground, taking an era with them.

The battle was approaching its climax, with the issue still in doubt, when the balance was tipped against the French by two disasters in swift succession. On the flank François' incompetent brother-in-law, the Duke of Alençon, lost his nerve and in that heightened, almost telepathic, mutual awareness which marks a battle at its climax his panic infected those around him and spread like a disease. Whether Alençon ordered a retreat, or merely followed, no one afterwards either knew or cared: all that was known was that he and his fellows abandoned the King. Some of them, Alençon in particular, did not stop running even after they had fled the field, but continued until they were safe within the frontiers of France. Safe, but totally dishonoured, their flight never to be forgotten nor forgiven. In vain, Alençon tried to justify himself to his beautiful and indignant wife, François' sister Marguerite. She contemptuously rejected him, and though he is a dull, lack-lustre figure, it is impossible to avoid feeling a tinge of pity for the little man as, drably, his life came to an end. He died two months later, and if ever remorse brought a man to his grave, that man was François, Duke of Alençon.

The second disaster for the French at Pavia proved final. The demoralised knights, reeling back from the deadly volleys, crashed into the ranks of Swiss pikemen. These held for a moment then, in their turn, they broke up and began to stream from the field. The disintegration of his army took the King completely by surprise. He had broken his lance but was still doing terrible execution with his sword; he was blood-stained, wearying fast after two hours' violent activity, but remained cheerfully confident that this battle would make him arbiter of Italy's fate. Then, out of the corner of his eye, he became aware that the orderly mass of pikemen on his flank was turning into a jostling, panic-stricken crowd. 'My God, what's that?' he cried, and forced his horse towards the fugitives. They ignored his commands. They were good soldiers but, like the armoured knights, they quailed at last before the withering fire of arquebuses. François' personal friends and household cavalry remained steadfast around him but they formed a diminishing island in a raging sea as the entire French front collapsed before the charge of the suddenly heartened imperialists.

Most of the 10,000 French dead fell in that last quarter of an hour or so of the battle: Bonnivet himself, whose disastrous advice had been largely responsible for the tragedy; La Pallise, the first Marshal; La Tremouille; the Italian Galeazzo San Severino, François' Grand Esquire who fell almost at his master's feet. François himself nearly joined the mounting pile of dead. His horse was killed under him, he was wounded in face and hand, and, distinctive in glittering armour decorated with the fleur-de-lys and surcoat of cloth of silver, he was the natural target for ransome-hungry mercenaries. Haughtily, he refused to surrender to inferiors, enraging them with his contempt. The Sieur de Pomperant, one of Bourbon's officers, recognised the King from over the heads of his assailants and cried out to him to surrender to the Duke of Bourbon. 'I know no Duke of Bourbon but myself', François snarled back. He slipped to his knees and would have fallen like a stag among hounds had not the Viceroy Lannoy arrived. Beating off the mercenaries, he dismounted, raised François to his feet and urged him to surrender to the Emperor. It was a bitter end to the high and splendid hopes but an honourable one. 'All is lost save honour', François was to write that night to his mother, and now he gave up the great gold-hilted sword and was escorted to a monastery where his wounds were dressed.

That night Lannoy gave a banquet in his honour and he had the magnanimity to accept the overtures of Bourbon who served his royal cousin and feudal lord at table. The imperial officers, Spanish, German and Italian alike, crowded in to see the man who, though defeated, still carried the magic aura of kingship, and François received them graciously. This was but a temporary setback; soon his brother monarch would arrange his release and, though there must naturally be a ransome, it would be according to the usages of chivalry, for both he and Charles were, after all, Christian knights. As far as François was concerned, the Battle of Pavia was simply a move on the chessboard of international chivalry, a move which had gone badly for him but which could be redeemed by skilful play in the game at which he excelled.

However, François was wrong, for what he did not know was that not merely the rules, but the game itself, had been changed overnight. The Battle of Pavia marked the end of warfare as a knightly exercise. And, by a supreme irony, François – paladin among knights – was himself to besmirch ineradicably the ideal by which he lived.

Chapter VIII

The Gathering Storm

'The Pope is as one dead': so, starkly, a foreign observer recorded Clement's reaction to the news from Lombardy. His first state of astonished disbelief then changed to one of sheer panic in which he sought advice from all those around him, changing his mind minute by minute, hour by hour, and then finally sunk into a numb despair in which he sat passively awaiting the turn of events. Clement had grounds for despair and terror, for before his eyes there was materialising that spectre which, for over seven hundred years, had haunted all popes: the spectre of an armed, insolent and dominant emperor claiming suzerainty over the throne of St Peter. Most emperors had been prepared to make that claim but very, very few had ever been in a position to enforce it. Overnight, the Emperor Charles V, still in his twenties, had joined that select and dangerous band. The Battle of Pavia had by no means made Charles Lord of Italy. There were half a dozen Italian states, including the formidable republic of Venice, prepared to dispute such a claim. But the Battle had established him as emperor in the north. Already, as King of Spain and therefore ruler of the Spanish kingdom of Naples, his writ ran from the Gulf of Taranto almost to the gates of Rome. Now the imperial powers could begin to forge the northern half of the pincers that would hold Italy – and with Italy, the Papacy itself – in a steel grip.

Or so it appeared to the wretched Clement. To the quaking Pope, and to most of his allies and enemies, it seemed as though the Emperor Charles was proceeding deliberately, majestically, along a clearly defined path, suffering occasional setbacks, certainly, but with a single, all-encompassing goal in view. But the view from Rome was over-dramatic, over-simplified: the reality was far more confused and thereby, though Rome did not yet appreciate it, far more dangerous. Charles was reacting exactly as his opponents were reacting, on a largely ad hoc basis. The most extraordinary demonstration of this was that, while all Italy was buzzing with the news of the Battle of Pavia, the titular victor was himself totally ignorant of the fact that the balance of power in Italy had tipped irrevocably in his favour. The Battle took place on 24 February, ending at about noon; it was not until late in the afternoon of 14 March that a messenger galloped into Madrid with the news. Quite evidently, Charles had made no particular arrangements to maintain communications with his invading army, and soon it became only too apparent that he had made no particular arrangements to pay the troops: for the first act of the victors of Pavia was to demand a ransome of 100,000 florins from Rome, a demand which Charles was later to ratify by treaty. Even when he knew all that had happened and realised that the destiny of Italy lay solely in his hands, he was content to operate by remote control. François had, at least, paid Italy the honour of coming to invade it in person; Charles left it to his subordinates to try and add this brightest of jewels to his imperial crown. Years later, when he came to write his cold and stilted autobiography, he was at pains to let it be assumed that the so-called 'imperial' army in Italy had been raised, led and maintained, in fact, by the Duke of Bourbon, who happened to be dead by then and so could not deny responsibility for the disastrous chain of events that followed the Battle of Pavia.

It is just possible that had Charles come immediately to Italy and taken personal control, order might have been established in the peninsula. Behind the young Emperor's cold, restrained façade there lay a deep religious faith and its product, a strong sense of personal responsibility: when he had at last received news of the defeat and capture of François, he immediately withdrew to pray and afterwards sternly forbade all rejoicing, except for a solemn service of thanksgiving. His astute and subtle brain, coupled with that sense of responsibility, could have enabled him to thread his way through the tangle of Italian politics. As it was, however, in all Italy there was no one man with the sensitivity to discern, and the power to control, the pattern of events. The internecine rivalry of Italians, where brother would betray brother for the sake of temporary advantage and which would eventually place the whole land under foreign dominance, now flared up, the princelings and republics allying themselves with Pope or Emperor as dictated by expediency.

Venice cautiously threw in her lot with Clement, but the Duke of Ferrara, who was disputing possession of certain territories with the Church, became automatically an imperial supporter, if a lukewarm one. Florence had no choice but to support Holy Mother Church for the high priest of Holy Mother Church was a Medici. Clement might be the greatest vacillator and postponer ever to hold papal power, but in all that related to his family inheritance he was a man of steel. Florence, theoretically a republic, was ruled as arbitrarily and as firmly as any despotism: it had even been the Florentines who had found the vast sum of 100,000 florins to buy off the mercenaries after Pavia. Milan swung uneasily between the two poles. There was again a duke in Milan, for young Francesco Sforza had returned with the triumphant imperialists. But they, and he, and Clement knew that he held the proud title by grace and favour of Spanish arquebusiers and spearmen. The Gonzaga family of Mantua was split neatly down the middle, for while the Marquis was a Gonfaloniere of Holy Church, his brother Ferrante was serving with their cousin the Duke of Bourbon in the imperial army. Their mother, Isabella, was even now making arrangements to go to Rome to obtain a cardinal's hat for her third son – a move which, if successful would very nicely complicate dynastic loyalties. And in

Rome itself the ancient rivalry of the two leading families, Orsini and Colonna, decked itself out with new symbols, with the Orsini swearing loyalty to the Keys of St Peter and the Colonna adopting the eagle of the Habsburgs. As it happened, the Colonna were traditionally Ghibelline, pro-imperial, but they would have sworn loyalty to Martin Luther himself if that would have helped them to harass Pope Clement, for their clan leader was the same Cardinal Pompeo Colonna who had loudly and bitterly claimed that the Medici bastard had stolen the crown of St Peter from him, and made no secret of the fact that he would not shrink from violence to redress the wrong.

Immediately after the Battle of Pavia the imperial army fell into its components. The Germans, having saved their Kaiser's honour and obtained their share of the ransome squeezed out of the Pope, marched off home. The Italians did the same, but the Spaniards remained firmly established in Milan. Rapidly it became evident that they regarded themselves as conquerors in a conquered country, however they might be described by imperial propagandists.

The Spaniards had first come into Italy as a fighting force some sixty years before when the dynasty of Aragon had wrested Naples out of the hands of the Angevins. Northern Italy had been given a sharp taste of Spanish customs during the short and violent reign of Cesare Borgia. And throughout these sixty years Spaniards and Italians had loathed each other with a deep, racial loathing. Xenophobia was not an Italian characteristic. They far preferred exploiting the foreigner to fighting or persecuting him, and their attitude to the strangers who thronged into Italy ranged from curiosity to an amiable contempt for those unfortunate enough to be born outside Italy. Traditionally, Italians reserved their greatest hatred for each other – except in this matter of the Spaniards.

Until now, only the Neapolitans had been exposed to Spanish rapacity and Spanish cruelty, and the Neapolitans had had nearly 2,000 years' experience of coping with arrogant conquerors, giving as good as they got, if in a more subtle form. Now it was the turn of Lombards and Tuscans and Romagnols to learn how to deal with this ferocious enemy in their midst, and they were caught off balance.

Spaniards and Italians hated each other with the fervour of close relatives, but also despised each other as representatives of opposite poles of European culture. Each was clearly the product of their differing environments, the one the most austere in Europe, the other the most voluptuous. Italians had known over two millenia of civilisation during which the most dangerous enemies they had encountered had been people of their own blood. A sophisticated, subtle race whose loyalty rarely went beyond the immediate family circle, they measured every act in terms of its expediency and regarded warfare as an inescapable but unsatisfactory extension of politics. The Spaniards, in particular the infantry, were barbarians compared with their Latin relatives: simple, uncomplicated men whose loyalty was tribal and who regarded warfare as the highest expression of civic and personal virtue.

Their idea of warfare was conditioned by their centuries-long running battle with the Moors in Spain itself, and like soldiers the world over, they were influenced by their enemy – particularly such a courageous, cunning, resourceful enemy – and they adopted and adapted the Moorish tactics and weapons for their own use. Spanish cavalry was the first to abandon the plate armour which turned horse and man into a moving tower of steel, but at the cost of mobility. Mounted upon their agile horses, the Spanish cavalry could be used with astonishing flexibility and operate in conditions which virtually immobilised the conventional men-at-arms. The rapid development of the arquebus soon cancelled the advantage once bestowed by plate-armour (Pavia had clearly demonstrated that fact), and for a brief while Spanish horse had the field to itself.

The Spanish infantry, too, had been modified, in particular in the use of firearms. Spanish commanders shared with the Germans an awareness of the value of the arquebus, and now one Spaniard in every six in the army carried the weapon and was skilled in its devastating use.

Common to both horse and foot was their Spartan life-style: accustomed to campaigning in the gruelling conditions of their own country, they could march and fight long after the soldiers of more sophisticated nations had sunk, exhausted. And a corollary of their courage and endurance and indifference to personal well-being was a refined and dedicated cruelty which took the Italians completely by surprise. The Italian code of honour certainly enjoined the taking of vengeance for an insult, and the planning of that vengeance might occupy months or even years; but its physical execution was swift, sword or dagger settling the matter in seconds. The Spaniards took pleasure in extended physical torture, particularly if it could be used for the extracting of ransome, thereby combining pleasure and profit.

Finally, the psychic differences between the races was compounded and exacerbated by the physical, specifically by the profound if irrational disgust felt by the washed for the unwashed. In Italy, the bath had been for centuries a centre of social life; in Spain, it was still a symbol of decadence or luxury. The Spanish soldiers' fondness for pungent foods (garlic, chillis, onion and cucumber mixed with olive oil and breadcrumbs was a staple diet), combined with their dislike of washing, made them one of the most odorous armies in history. It was said that the identity of a Spanish force could be established by nose alone if the wind were in the right quarter.

It was the Milanese who first felt the Spanish Fury. In theory, Milan was again part of an independent state with the young Duke Francesco Sforza owing only technical allegiance to the Emperor. In practice, Milan was an occupied city subject to the savage desire of Spanish troops who felt, with reason, that they had so far gained singularly little from their invasion of Europe's richest country. The ransome of 100,000 florins extracted from Clement after the Battle of Pavia had not gone very far when divided between some 25,000 men, most of whom had received only starvation pay for months. It seemed that no more money was coming from Rome, at least in the foreseeable future, and the Spaniards thereupon set about obtaining what was necessary from their nearest victims, the Milanese. The citizens appealed to

Rome, but the only help they received from their Holy Father was to be involved in an inept conspiracy which further debased the credibility of the Vatican and delivered the Milanese over, finally and totally, into the power of their enemy.

Lannoy, the imperial Viceroy, was absent in Spain whither he had gone, dragging his royal prisoner François, to gain the Emperor's congratulations. Bourbon had gone, too, correctly deducing that his interests were best served at the imperial court. The major imperial officer in Italy was the Marquis of Pescara who, though a Spaniard, was Italian-born, and who, moreover, thought he had been ill-rewarded by the Emperor.

It was young Sforza's secretary, the devious Girolamo Morone, who first had the idea of suborning Pescara and hastened to put his proposition to Rome. If His Holiness would offer to invest Pescara with the crown of Naples, surely it would be a simple matter to persuade Pescara to abandon his master. And if Pescara abandoned the Emperor. . . . Clement listened eagerly, assented eagerly and Morone trotted off no less eagerly to Pescara: who listened impassively, asking for details, guarantees, names, and when all concerned had thoroughly betrayed themselves to him, informed the Emperor. Morone was arrested and thrown into a dungeon under threat of imminent death. His protégé, the young duke, was deposed as a felon vassal. The Spanish formally took over Milan, and in Rome a jubilant Cardinal Colonna made it known that 'with 100,000 ducats I could drive the pope from his capital'.

All through that summer and autumn of 1525 Italy waited helplessly while its future was decided by foreigners. There had been, at first, great hopes that François' redoubtable mother Louise would take up the championship of Italy against the Emperor, but it soon became apparent that Louise's only interest was for her son's well-being. She would have betrayed the world to ensure that.

In Spain, Charles and François endlessly bargained the terms of François' release. Charles, so modern in his approach to most aspects of government, curiously still clung to the medieval concept of monarchy, in which the king was not simply the personification or the symbol of a people, but their whole purpose of existence, so that, like the king in chess, if he were removed or constrained, then the game was totally in the victor's hand. Charles really seemed to believe that, because an accident of war had placed a gallant but not particularly intelligent young man in his power, then several million French men and women and children and several million acres of French territory were his to command.

His terms appeared preposterously unrealistic, in particular his demand that François should again open a gaping wound in France's side by detaching the Dukedom of Burgundy and ceding it back to Charles, titular Duke of Burgundy. François, for all his frivolity, baulked at so destructive a concept. He was willing to concede, on paper at least, almost everything else that Charles demanded. He even agreed that the Duke of Bourbon should be pardoned and reinstated in his possessions. But he would not yield the Duchy of Burgundy. On and on went the weary argument in Madrid, month after month while François grew thin and pale, and even Charles feared for his health and agreed that François' sister Marguerite should be granted safe-conduct to visit him. François was delighted to see his sister and his health improved under her solicitous care, but still he stubbornly refused to countenance any diminution of his royal authority. Nevertheless, Marguerite's presence began to weaken his resolve. He had quarters befitting his rank: he and Charles were, indeed, on amiable visiting terms; he was allowed contact with his ambassadors and, through them, with the outside world. But he was still a prisoner and, judging by Charles' own iron inflexibility, likely to remain so for the rest of his life.

In December, after nearly a year's captivity, François abruptly capitulated, much to Charles' surprise. He agreed to everything: he agreed to marry Charles' sister Eleonor; he agreed to the restoration of the Duke of Bourbon: he agreed to withdraw French troops from Flanders and to abandon French claims in Italy. He even agreed to the cession of Burgundy. It seems extraordinary that Charles should have suspected nothing. But he was, after all, dealing with a fellow monarch, a fellow knight, and it was to him virtually unthinkable that such a man should break his pledged word. François planned to do exactly that. When his French advisers displayed horror at the sweeping terms of his capitulation, he smiled, assured them that he had not the slightest intention of keeping such a promise and promptly obliged them to swear to keep his intentions secret, blithely ignoring the fact that he had himself substantially contributed to the devaluation of sworn oaths. Despite the protestations of his own advisers, Charles accepted François' promises, though stipulating that as hostages he would require François' own little sons. The King agreed even to that.

François regained his freedom on 18 March. Twice more he gave his solemn word to recognise the treaty. The first occasion was when he parted from Charles, who had ridden part of the way to the frontier with him. At the very last moment Charles drew the King on one side and asked him earnestly whether he would keep his promise. 'I swear to you that I will keep all that I have promised as soon as I reach my kingdom', François replied as earnestly, and Charles was satisfied. A few hours later, the Viceroy Lannoy asked him much the same question. François took Lannoy's hand in his and then, speaking in French, he said solemnly and forcefully: 'I, François, King of France, Gentleman, give my faith to the Emperor Charles, Catholic King, in your person, Charles de Lannoy.'

The precise moment of François' freedom came when he crossed the frontier river Bidassoa. Half way over his barque passed the craft taking his two children into captivity – the little Dauphin aged eight, and his young brother – but the spectacle seems to have left him undisturbed. As his own boat touched the French shore he leaped out with a great shout: 'I am again a king!'

It was not long before Charles discovered that he had been duped: none of the conditions were fulfilled; and the Emperor's reaction was a burst of rage in which he challenged François to single combat and, when that was contemptuously ignored, sullied his honour by venting his rage upon the defenceless children in his power. They were removed to a grim, airless, lightless cell where they passed the three years of their captivity. One of their grandmother's servants, a M. Bodin, visited them shortly before their release, and described their situation in harrowing terms. Their sole plaything was a little dog. They were unable to speak French and their room 'was very dark without carpet or decoration save a straw mattress. The said lords were seated on stone stools beneath a window barred inside and out with great iron bars, the windows so high that scarcely could my said lords have air or the pleasure of daylight.' Bodin declared that he burst into tears at the sight.

Nobody emerged with credit from the sorry episode, but Bourbon was the most injured. For months he had buoyed himself up with the hope and belief that François would, finally, be forced to restore him. He had even agreed, if reluctantly, that François should have the bride that had been promised to him, but as weeks merged into months after François' release and his own reinstatement seemed as far off as ever, he seemed actually to have a nervous breakdown. Castiglione, who had been a close observer of the whole train of events in Spain, was seriously concerned by the deterioration in Bourbon. 'Monsieur de Bourbon is in despair and talks at random', he noted. The Emperor had kept faith with his still valuable ally, offering to install him as Duke of Milan in place of the unfortunate young Sforza, but though it was honour enough, it was little to Bourbon's tastes, as a great magnate, to rule a turbulent foreign city as a puppet duke. And yet, there was nothing for him in Spain and he could not return home to France and so the Spring of 1526 found him again in Italy, officially Captain-General of the imperial forces, charged to keep the Emperor's peace in those Italian territories which now, perforce, recognised the Emperor.

However, Italy had changed during the months in which he had been absent. For the first time in many weary years a feeble but distinct wind of nationalism was blowing across the peninsula.

'Whatever happens, I believe we shall have war in Italy and soon. Hence we must have France with us and, if we cannot, we must decide what to do. In that case we must follow, it seems to me, one of two courses: either submit and buy ourselves off, or arm and help ourselves as we can. Buying ourselves off will not serve, I believe – if it did, I would say let us go no further. But it will not for either I am stone blind, or they will take our money first and our lives next, so that it would be a kind of justice to find ourselves destitute and destroyed, when we would be no worse by defending ourselves . . .'

So Niccolo Machiavelli wrote to his friend Francesco Guicciardini, Lieutenant-Governor for the Pope in those regions which, perforce, recognised the Pope as earthly lord. Machiavelli seems an improbable figure then to hold such martial sentiments: fifty-seven years old, though looking ten years older, with his face bearing the imprint of failure and imprisonment and debauchery. Behind the high and splendid forehead there worked ceaselessly the most brilliantly logical mind, perhaps, of the Renaissance. That ice-cold succession of 'either/or' choices which he presented to Guicciardini was typical of the mind that had created *The Prince*. Yet poor Machiavelli was quite incapable of applying the remorseless logic of his political theory to his own personal career and of so joining the right party at the right time. Lurching from personal crisis to personal crisis, he was only just able to keep his head above water while far less talented men soared effortlessly ahead to amass comfortable fortunes. Disappointment, frustration, hostility; Machiavelli had learned to live with them in a wry self-mockery. The face that he turned to the demanding world might be downright obsequious, at times, indeed, furtive and even hangdog, but it could be lit in unguarded moments with flashes of contempt and, in repose, was self-reliant enough.

Among those who knew and valued him – and they were many – he could be a delightful companion: witty, lightly wearing his immense erudition, and with a gay courage that never deserted him whether in a prison cell or, as now, contemplating the collapse of his world. Guicciardini read his letter with close attention, for he knew his friend to be no armchair soldier. Machiavelli was proud of his book *The Art of War* but he was even prouder of the fact that during one of Florence's endless upheavals he had resurrected the noble concept of the militia. For too long Italians had relied on hired soldiers, he argued: native or foreign, the mercenary was treacherous, unpredictable and useless, for he was fighting only for money whereas the citizen-soldier was fighting for his fatherland and could, on the whole, be expected to die for it if necessary. During the present crisis Machiavelli had tried to sell the idea to Pope Clement but His Holiness, in his usual way, had blown hot and cold, entangling the idea in a web of afterthoughts and qualifications.

Now Machiavelli was trying to persuade his influential friend Guicciardini to persuade His Holiness to adopt another idea. 'These times require bold and unusual resolutions. You know – as everyone who thinks knows – how fickle and foolish the populace is. Nevertheless, it sometimes puts into words what should be done. In Florence a few days ago I heard people saying that Signor Giovanni de Medici [Bande Nere] was raising a company to make war where he liked.' They should use him as a guerilla until open war was declared, Machiavelli went on. 'There is no leader among the Italians whom soldiers follow more willingly or whom the Spanish more fear and respect.' Giovanni della Bande Nere could ride and strike at will, demoralising the Spaniards without compromising the Pope, perhaps even encouraging King François to come back to Italy . . .

It was a good idea and Guicciardini faithfully passed it on to Rome, but Clement turned it down as Guicciardini knew he would. In his way, Francesco Guicciardini was an even more unlikely person to be found chivvying a nation into war than was Machiavelli. Handsome, cold, restrained where Machiavelli was all warm impulse, he had had a far easier life than his old friend and fellow-Florentine. Although a layman, he had prospered under three such different popes as the ebullient Leo, the austere Adrian and now the hesitant Clement – a fact which argues that, despite his self-righteous air, he was able to trim his sails considerably to the prevailing wind. As governor of the Romagna, he was a very important man indeed:

If you had seen messer Francesco, in Romagna with a houseful of tapestries, with power over the entire province which apart from the Pope – who left everything to him – knew no authority above him: with a guard around him of more than a hundred pikemen, with halberdiers and other mounted guards. If you had seen him go through the streets always surrounded by hundreds of men, never riding out with less than a hundred or one hundred and fifty horse, smothered in 'lordships', in titles, in 'most illustrious', you would never recognise him as your fellow citizen, your fellow man, but considering the greatness of his affairs, his unbounded authority, his vast power and importance, you would have thought him nothing less than a duke. . . . His speech, his manners, his haughtiness, his desire to be understood and obeyed at a gesture were no different from what is found in a man who had been and always lived a prince.

But neither did Guicciardini lack self-knowledge: that corrosive portrait was written by himself.

And, even more important, he was able to look above and beyond the narrow parochial loyalties which were strangling Italy and think in national terms. During all these turbulent, exciting, dangerous years he was quietly amassing material for his immense *History of Italy*, the first portrait of the Italian race which saw them not simply as forming a multiple of petty states which happened to be sharing the same landmass, but as a people sharing a common heritage, common blood, common hopes, fears, loves – and dangers. It was fortunate for Italy that such a man was in a position of authority during the critical months of 1526. It was unfortunate for Italy that that authority was subject to another's, that Guicciardini had to use as instrument the flawed Pope Clement VII.

Guicciardini was summoned to Rome in the early days of 1526 to act as adviser to Clement. There was nothing unusual in that: Clement sought advice from everybody and, having received it, turned to the next on his list. What was unusual was that this particular adviser had a steely will behind his courtier's charm; viewed the whole deplorable affair as an Italian rather than as a partisan of the Pope's, the King's, or the Emperor's; and, with the historian's compulsive itch to record, noted down almost daily his dealings with Clement. Those notes, some of them merely hasty scribbles to act as aide-memoire, others detailed essays in which he sought to put the matter clear in his own mind before attempting to influence Clement, lay gathering dust for over four centuries until Guicciardini's biographer Ridolfi discovered them and arranged their contents into a coherent whole. They displayed nothing startlingly new: indeed, their impact lay precisely in the fact that they corroborated minutely what had been suspected or assumed for centuries. The incredible portrait of Pope Clement VII which had been handed down through generations had not been founded upon hostile propaganda but upon sober fact. At this critical stage in Italian history the keys of St Peter, with all their incalculable effect upon Europeans, were held in a palsied and trembling hand. Clement really did change his mind from hour to hour, from minute to minute sometimes. The levers of power really were available to whoever happened to be passing. Guicciardini had known Clement as a cardinal and, like so many others, had liked and respected him. He was dismayed by the change that the crushing weight of the Triple Crown had made upon a competent, honourable and compassionate man. The absolute power conferred by the papal tiara only too often resulted in moral corruption; in Clement's case the responsibility which went with that power produced intellectual corruption. Where, as cardinal, he could see a precise limit to his responsibility, for it was always the Pope who made the final decision, now each decision he made had endless repercussions. In the position he now occupied, imagination and sensitivity were dangerous luxuries; a pope could not afford to look down the receding vistas of cause and effect. Every day, every hour he had to choose one decision out of an apparent infinity of potentiality, and having chosen it, stick to it. And that Clement could not do, his high intellectual qualities being betrayed by lack of a corresponding power of will.

Guicciardini understood this only too well and minced no words. Surveying the chaotic field of international and national affairs, he agreed that the situation was unclear, and that venal men were moved by ignoble motives so that a decision to support one against the other might itself lead to ignoble results. Nevertheless, 'it is bad to make a bad decision but worse not to make any'. There was no coherent policy, so that energy and enthusiasm were dissipated: 'Everything is done haphazard, and often today's action is contrary to and ruins yesterday's.' In a remarkably frank series of memoranda, Guicciardini dissected the Pope's character: 'These scruples of his often keep him helpless in affairs and with people where fear is of no avail.' The Pope should endeavour to recapture the reputation he had as cardinal, and if it really were impossible for him to remould his character and go against nature, 'he should try at least to force it in most things and in those that matter most: if he began to form but different habits and enjoy the good results, I am quite sure it would be harder for him to return to his old ways than it would be now to get used to the new one', Guicciardini concluded, unconsciously echoing Hamlet:

Refrain tonight
And that shall lend a kind of easiness to the next abstinence
The next more easy:
For use almost can change the stamp of nature.

Did Guicciardini really speak in this bold manner to his lord and master and spiritual father? His use of the third person makes it seem likely that his report of the one-sided conversation was born of the *esprit d'escalier*, corresponding more to what he would like to say than what he actually said. Yet he was a tough, self-confident man, much accustomed to dealing with high-ranking but shifty politicians, and it may very well be that he did treat Clement to some such homily face to face.

Certainly, from February 1526 onwards, Clement's attitude hardened. He had, perhaps, little alternative, for like the Duke of Bourbon, he saw his options fading away one by one. He and the Emperor, a thousand miles distant from each other and both regarding war as a distasteful admission of intellectual poverty, were drifting towards an inescapable confrontation, each forced to overbid his hand. Thus the conspiracy of Morone had obliged Charles to take over Milan in an act of naked conquest. Badly frightened, Clement had turned to François as soon as the King had regained his liberty. Like everybody else, the Pope thought Charles a fool for agreeing to the conditions of François' freedom and, though, doubtless, he did not personally urge François to break an oath that had been sworn solemnly on the altar, he entered into an alliance with François which casually assumed that the oath was meaningless. On 22 May 1526 His Holiness Pope Clement VII, the Most Serene Republic of Venice, His Excellency Francesco Sforza titular duke of Milan, and His Most Christian Majesty François I formed a mutual protection league against the Emperor, dignified by the title of Holy League.

Enraged and, perhaps, frightened too, in his turn, Charles became openly aggressive. Ugo Moncada took over the negotiations in Italy. He was the most hated of all Spanish generals, a man who had been one of Cesare Borgia's trusted lieutenants and who regarded Italy simply as a fat and degenerate land to be plundered at will. Moncada's first act was to contact Clement's most bitter personal enemy, Cardinal Colonna, and come to certain secret arrangements with him. Clement, encouraged by the more martial of his advisers, prepared for open war.

In vain, poor Castiglione in Madrid sent urgent messengers to his master, Clement, pleading with him to draw back from the abyss whose depths only he could see clearly. He had witnessed Charles' growing rage and growing bewilderment at Clement's unpredicted and unpredictable reactions. He himself was the recipient of contradictory instructions: now he was instructed to offer disdain and defiance to the Emperor and then, having scarcely done so, he received another messenger, hard on the heels of the first, bearing orders for him to sooth and propritiate. Charles treated the poor, harassed little nuncio with the utmost courtesy. Castiglione was convinced that the Emperor really was a loyal son of Holy Church, and really did prefer peace to war. Nevertheless, he warned Rome, Charles would fight to the death if necessary:

> The Viceroy is sailing to Italy with the strictest injunctions to offer favourable terms of peace to His Holiness before he engages in war. If they are accepted, they will be in the name of God. If they are rejected the most strenuous measures will be taken to advance the Emperor's cause and long and endless war will come. Even if he is defeated, he will never yield as long as there is breath in his body, and universal ruin will be the result. His subjects will not fail to support him and if they once lose their sense of shame, and begin to taste the liberty of disobedience to the Apostolic See, I know not how they will ever return to their old allegiance.

The looming war had all the characteristics of classic tragedy, for it was the conflict not of right and wrong but of right and right. Charles was, indeed, going to war with the utmost reluctance. He had, indeed, just grounds to be aggrieved, for of the four members of the misnamed Holy League one

(Clement) had betrayed him whenever it was expedient to do so; another (François) had broken his oath to him; a third (Sforza) had attempted to corrupt his servant; while the fourth (Venice) had no real quarrel with him but was following the well-tried Venetian policy of fishing in troubled waters.

Yet the Italians, too, were justified. For a generation now, they had watched while foreigners trampled to and fro over their land, killing, burning, destroying, in pursuit of their own, frequently incomprehensible goals. Those Italians with the wider historic perspective of Machiavelli or Giucciardini could look down over centuries of such frustration, which had been present, indeed, ever since the fall of the great Roman Empire itself. The foreign Spanish dynasty which now ruled nearly all Italy south of Rome had merely chased out the foreign French dynasty that had ruled there before, and this in its turn had merely dislodged another set of foreigners, and so on, back and back in a receding perspective of servitude. 'This war is not for a point of honour, or for a vendetta or for the occupation of a city. This war concerns the well-being or the eternal servitude of all Italy.' So wrote Clement's confidant, Giberti, and though Giberti was notoriously pro-French and anti-imperialist, yet he spoke truly enough. The Ghibellines (the imperialists) might preach a noble ideal where an all-powerful emperor compassionately ruled over all Christian subjects, granting each the protection of an unbending law: all that reality saw was the spectacle of greedy Spaniards and time-serving Italians dipping their hands into a bran-tub.

Guicciardini joyfully rode north out of Rome to take over military control, exchanging his scholar's quill for a general's baton. But only for a brief while, for Venice sent her general, the Duke of Urbino, and, because Venetian aid was desperately needed, Guicciardini gracefully gave way, non-committally noting that 'though the Duke of Urbino was only General of the Venetians, to avoid disputes – and because there was nothing to be done about it – the Ecclesiastics had decided to receive his orders as Captain-General'. This was the first and worst mistake that 'the Ecclesiastics' made.

But for the moment all was triumph. The imperialists were again in a very bad way even though they had Milan as base, being short of money, short of troops, short of food, while 'the Ecclesiastics' had all Italy to draw upon. Giovanni della Bande Nere joined the march northward, overjoyed to find that the long days of doubt and speculation and inertia were behind. Other condottieri made their way to Lombardy, lesser men than Giovanni de' Medici but still good fighters with Italian blood in their veins: Guido Rangoni, who had fought for and with the late Pope Leo and Renzo da Ceri, last heard of fighting for King François in Marseilles, but now, it was rumoured, heading south bringing the banners and power of France. So it was said.

Machiavelli heard the trumpets and fretted among his books and papers and at last he, too, took the road north, joining the camp of that young Giovanni de' Medici whom he had so long championed. Giovanni welcomed the shabby scholar, the ageing author of the *Art of War*, the only book in which Giovanni had the smallest interest. Partly in jest, but also in gratitude and admiration, he granted Machiavelli his dearest wish, the command of a company on the parade

ground. The armchair soldier's experiment ended in pure farce. For two hours
he tried to drill some 2,000 men under a blazing sun. By the end of that period
tempers were stretched to the utmost, the disciplined ranks of the Bande Nere
had been reduced to a shambles and Machiavelli, watched by a sardonic
Giovanni, admitted at last that military practice differed considerably from
military theory. Ironically asking permission, Giovanni took over and, using
the drummers, with a few brisk orders untangled the chaos and had the soldiers
marching off within minutes. Machiavelli, ever able to laugh at his own follies,
took the incident well. At dinner that night he toasted his young companion:
'Signore, I firmly believe that if you had not relieved me we would be out there
yet.' Then, when the laughter had died away, he launched into one of his
funniest and most salacious of stories, vicariously becoming a soldier.

Italy was geared for war with the splendid banners rippling into Lombardy,
the drums thundering around the beleagured city of Milan and the trumpets
shrilling high at Pavia. But it was Rome, not Milan, who first felt the shock of
battle, and that shock was delivered not by a Spanish mercenary soldier but an
Italian priest. In September the shocked armies of Holy Church heard that
Cardinal Pompeo Colonna had led a raiding party into Rome, desecrating the
very basilica of St Peter and, it was rumoured, taking the Pope prisoner.

Cardinal Pompeo Colonna belonged to that pernicious race of Roman
nobility which, more than any other single factor, condemned the great city to
centuries of anarchy and deprived Italy itself of its natural head and leader. The
Colonna were old: they claimed descent from the Etruscans of nearby
Tusculum and this may well have been true. Their antiquity had given them
pride of family but no particular pride of race, a common attitude among the
Roman nobility. Their lives were centred in the family; Rome merely
happened to be the place where the family was established. Loyalty lay to the
family, not to the city, and the Colonna, like any other baronial family, would
betray the city as a matter of course in order to promote the family.

The fact that Pompeo was a cardinal had no religious significance whatsoever. The College of Cardinals was the most powerful organisation in the city,
and therefore it was inevitable that every family would want to have its
representative there. A pope might choose a cardinal because of his merits.
More commonly, the candidate either bought his hat, or obtained it as part of
the complex wheeling and dealing which went on endlessly between the
different branches of the Curia and between the Curia and the outside world.
Above the cardinals was the pope, created by the cardinals and usually drawn
from their ranks, and it was natural and inevitable that each Roman family
should seek to grasp this prize and resent it when 'foreigners' from Florence or
Milan or Venice usurped what they regarded as their hereditary right. Pompeo
Colonna, having failed in two successive conclaves, had been fully confident
that he would emerge from the last conclave as pope. The fact that another
Medici had done so ensured his unremitting hatred. No matter that the new
pope hastened to give him the office of Vice-Chancellor, the most important
office below that of pope itself and carrying with it Rome's most beautiful

palace, the Cancellaria. Pompeo felt that he had been cheated: he wanted the papacy and was fully prepared to kill for it.

The Colonna raid on Rome in September 1526, curtain raiser to the Sack itself, was the result of the secret negotiations between Pompeo and Ugo Moncada, the imperial general. It was Moncada who provided most of the 800 horse and 3,000 infantry which stiffened the cardinal's retinue, but they were scarcely needed. The commando and his men arrived at the great gate of St John Lateran at dawn to find it hospitably open. They galloped through and thundered down the long straight street which led to the Forum. There the main body encamped on the turf that now hid the ancient heart of the city, and a detachment led by the cardinal himself galloped on to the sleeping Vatican. Far from being opposed, they were cheered by the early risers abroad in the city. Clement heard the advancing uproar and after finding that he had no support, began to prepare with some dignity for his death.

The ease with which a flying column composed mostly of foreign soldiers could take over the great city was testimony to Clement's perilous situation in his own stronghold. And yet the Roman citizens who betrayed him now did so from no sense of high principles. Propagandists might cry that the troops of the Emperor brought freedom to a priest-enslaved city; the Romans were indifferent to such stirring calls, for the priests had brought them a fat living for centuries. Neither were they impelled by any great hatred of Clement himself. Their refusal to defend him, and their welcome for their raiders, was based on an ignoble but highly potent factor: their dislike of taxation coupled with their disappointment that a Medici rule was proving to be so frugal, colourless and lacking in glamour.

The supreme spiritual power conferred upon Clement could not by any means whatsoever be alienated, shared or diluted: from the moment of his accepting office to the moment of his death he was the unique Vicar of Christ on earth, successor to the Apostle, holding the keys of heaven and hell and confirmed in all this by canon law. But the nature of his earthly power was decidedly different: he held just exactly as much as he could grasp. Like any other monarch's, that power ultimately depended upon a web of intangibles, in particular on the interaction of his personality with those around and beneath him. Clement was, in fact, a far better man than his cousin and predecessor Leo: in his personal life he was dependable, for there his decisions affected him alone; he was honest, following a clear-cut moral code, whereas Leo had conducted his entire personal life as well as his state affairs strictly on a policy of expediency. Nevertheless, Leo had had that unknown quality summed up under the term 'magnetism': he could make people like him even while they distrusted him. Those close to him were only too well aware of his defects: but the public adored him. They admired his personal magnificence: vicariously they enjoyed his banquets and entertainments, and sufficient of them were able to pick up patronage and pickings to spread the general impression of his generosity. There is no knowing how far Leo's popularity might have helped him had he been in a similar situation to Clement's now: the Romans very rarely indeed thought themselves obliged to defend any particular principle to the death. But their very unpredictability made them dangerous: sometimes they would rise in defence of some obscure principle, some improbable hero; and a Roman mob on the rampage was a terrifying sight. Their love for Leo had been a cupboard love, but any would-be aggressor had to take into account the fact that it was love of a sort. Now, Colonna, like everybody else, knew that the Romans had no time for Clement and was able to act accordingly.

It was the Venetian ambassador, Marco Foscari, who best summed up the reason for Clement's unpopularity. Foscari was an objective observer, simply mapping out the overall situation for the benefit of his government, and his analysis of Clement's character was an essential, objective part of the survey. He admitted Clement's very real qualities, particularly when compared with Leo's: 'He is just and God-fearing. If he signs a petition he never revokes it, as did Leo who signed so many. He withdraws no benefices, nor gives them in simony.' But these were all negative qualities, and the Romans wanted large, positive, gold-plated gestures. 'He gives nothing away and neither does he bestow the property of others. But he is considered very avaricious. Pope Leo was very liberal: this Pope is the opposite and therefore the people grumble in Rome. He gives largely in alms, but nevertheless is not liked.'

Such was the Venetian's opinion. Paolo Giovio, the smooth courtier-historian, would have agreed wholeheartedly with Foscari had the ambassador's despatch come his way. Some years later, when writing his own account of these turbulent days, Giovio speculated on the reasons why the Colonna were able to menace the Bishop of Rome in his own palace and why, just eight months after this warning of Rome's vulnerability, the city yet fell easy prey to a ragged marauding force. The people were totally alienated from their leader, Giovio thought, partly because of his 'fatal avarice', but mostly because of his unfailing ability to appoint the wrong person to the wrong job at the wrong time. Giovio was informed enough and honest enough to admit that Clement's notorious parsimony was not really his fault 'but because of the deplorable condition in which he found the treasury. And the shabby fiscal measures resorted to were not to be imputed to the Pope, but to his Chamberlain, the minister of finance.' Nevertheless, the appointing of the Chamberlain was entirely Clement's responsibility and in choosing Cardinal Francesco Armellino he had made a very grave mistake.

Clement may have felt that he was discharging a family debt when he made the grasping Armellino Chamberlain, for the cardinal had been one of those almost ruined by Pope Leo's sudden death. He had been owed 150,000 ducats when Leo died and the 100,000 ducats Armellino was supposed to have paid for the post of Chamberlain was probably little more than a paper transaction. The path of Pope Clement VII is strewn with ironies and paradoxes, but it was more than an irony that he, a hater of simony, should have appointed a polished simoniac to this vital post: it was a tragedy. Armellino was loathed by high and low alike. On one occasion, in full consistory, when another round of Armellino's taxes were being debated, Pompeo Colonna snarled that if Armellino were to be flayed and his skin displayed for payment, money would flow in. Giovio's own dislike of the man was undoubtedly coloured by the fact that his own pay was cut when, 'to eternal shame', a tax which had always been intended to pay the professors of liberal arts was diverted to other purposes. But Armellino went far beyond a mere juggling with accounts. His treasury set about cornering the entire supply of wheat, trebling the price; and through its control over the *Maestri delle strade*, Armellino added yet another source of income at the cost of very real hardship to those who could least support it. The *Maestri* were responsible for the safety and accessibility of the streets of Rome and one of their duties was to demolish any dangerous structure, or any building which jutted too far out into the street. It was a sensible and long-accepted provision, but now entire rows of houses were pulled down under the pretext of improvement, and in the subsequent bargaining over the sites more cash flowed in. Surveying the demolition, Giovio remarked that it mostly affected the poor, those who were unable to go to law to protect themselves: 'The cruelest barbarian could not have wreaked greater ruin.'

Much of the Roman hatred for Armellino, and therefore for his master, was the normal dislike of any taxed population for the taxmaster. Marcello Alberini cited, as evidence of Armellino's inhuman greed, the tax he placed upon wine. Wine was no longer the necessity it had been before the repair of the ancient aqueducts had again brought wholesome drinking water into the town, and such a tax strikes an outsider as being an irritant rather than an injustice. But Alberini had his finger even closer on the popular pulse than did Foscari or Giovio. He was, after all, an ordinary Roman citizen himself, and he was in complete agreement with the two non-Romans that the Curia's miserly, money-grubbing tactics had totally alienated the bulk of the population.

The troops of the Colonna therefore had a totally free hand as they swept through the city. 'Liberty!' the citizens cried, voicing the parrot cry of all disenchanted citizens. 'Liberty! Colonna!' and even 'Espagna!' The Colonna captains responded sensibly, sending trumpeters through the city, announcing that they had no quarrel with ordinary honest citizens, and the ordinary citizens cheered them on. Near St Peter's there was a brief clash with the papal troops but it was soon resolved, for even the handful of Colonna troops outnumbered the defenders. Armellino had been only too successful in persuading Clement that no Christian would commit sacrilege by attacking Christianity's holy city and that there was therefore no need to keep a large garrison eating its head off.

On news of the Colonna raid, Clement had hastily sent out to demand – to plead – for the protection of the militia. Rome was divided into Regions, and by ancient custom, the Captains of the Regions were supposed to rally all fighting men under the Region banner on a call from their bishop. Nothing happened: there were no speeches either of justification or of protest – a significant lack in a city where the smallest public action was accompanied by impassioned debate and high-flown rhetoric. Clement's messengers were met simply with a shrug: the destruction of their bishop was apparently something not even of passing interest to the Romans. Now it was that Clement decided, with tardy but courageous dignity, to die if necessary. He would meet these sacrilegious Colonna robed, crowned and throned as the Apostolic Successor in the

Apostolic Palace, he told his alarmed courtiers. Neither is there any reason to doubt his courage or, indeed, his intention, and perhaps if he had been allowed to stage a dramatic confrontation, he might have been able to reinstate himself with the Romans. He was, after all, their bishop and anti-clerical though they were, as were all Italians, the anti-clericalism was only the reverse coin of a profound religious faith. The Romans, too, reacted strongly to drama and the spectacle of Clement, in full canonicals, defying the forces of the World, would have appealed to them. They might, perhaps, have stood on one side and enjoyed the spectacle to its climax, admiring the brave display of their bishop's blood against his gold vestments. Equally, they might have moved to his defence, then, or to avenge him, afterwards.

The matter was never put to the test, for Giberti volubly persuaded Clement to give up the idea and at the last moment he agreed to seek shelter in Sant' Angelo. The papal party scuttled across the walkway to the shelter of the great castle scant minutes ahead of the advance party of the Collonna. They were doomed to humiliation even in the heart of Sant' Angelo, entirely due to Armellino's passion for saving money. There was no known limit to the length of time that Sant' Angelo could hold out, provided, of course, that it was adequately provisioned. It was not adequately provisioned, neither in food nor in ammunition. The great cannon boomed out their defiance, sending a few scattered shots with a brave show into the ranks of the invaders, and raising spirits in the castle, but soon they fell silent. And a hurried stock-taking of food supplies disclosed that there was sufficient only for the regular garrison. The hundreds of frightened servants and priests who now milled restlessly round the dark chambers of the castle could be fed only for a day or so.

But even that scarcely seemed to matter, for there could be no possibility of a prolonged resistance. From the castle Clement and his court watched helplessly, scarcely believing what they saw, as the Vatican Palace was put to the sack by the troops of Cardinal Pompeo Colonna. Amongst the horde staggering away laden with plunder could be discerned men wearing the livery of the papal household. By mid-afternoon, the Palace had been cleared of its portable values: even the altars were plundered of their precious, and consecrated, vessels. Raphael's great tapestries were carefully taken down from the walls of the Sistine Chapel by someone who was fully alive to their financial as well as aesthetic value. Chalices, mitres, croziers, candelabras, and the very papal tiara, were heaped up and carried off by men for whom they were, supposedly, objects of superstitious reverence. On that September morning in Rome was neatly demonstrated the theological proposition of accidence and substance, the Catholic troops of Moncada and Colonna experiencing no difficulty in distinguishing between the accidence of the precious object, which could be sold for a handsome profit, and its spiritual substance, which happily remained unaffected by the indignity of the transaction.

Cardinal Colonna and his ally – or his master – Ugo Moncada withdrew to the Colonna palace and it was there that two of Colonna's fellow cardinals waited upon them. Although Sant' Angelo was scarcely ten minutes' walk away, the two unhappy men had had an alarming journey, being obliged first to scurry across the unnervingly long, open bridge over the Tiber, and then to make their way through a city that suddenly seemed to be at war. The heady effect of total success, combined with a limitless supply of wine, had turned the reasonably well-behaved commandos of the morning into swaggering, threatening bandits. Fights were breaking out as householders suddenly realised that they had to defend their property or their womenfolk, and the two cardinals had become the target for abuse and worse as they hastened through the streets. At the palace Colonna listened to their plea that a representative should be sent to Sant' Angelo to discuss an armistice with Clement. Haughtily he refused to do any such thing.

Colonna's motives for refusing an interview with Clement were of a piece with his motives throughout the extraordinary episode. But they are, for all that, no less mysterious. There is little doubt that he hoped – possibly planned – that during the confusion of the assault, when bullets, arrows and spears were flying through the air, one or other of them would find its goal in the body of Pope Clement. There is also no doubt that he hoped that, after a fortunate accident had removed the present occupant of the throne of St Peter, he would be invited to take the vacant place. But did he plan the entire sequence, or simply take advantage of a collapsing situation? It seems remarkable that a politician of Colonna's experience would not have realised that the Sacred College would have been fiercely opposed to his election. The most abject, the most blinkered of his supporters and creatures must have been appalled by the unleashing of such irresponsible violence for such a limited aim. Clement had few friends among the cardinals: but neither did he have many enemies. No man could possibly say that the Colonna raid was justified by the need to remove such a man as Clement. The Sacred College was, for the most part, composed of world-weary men, who had won their political spurs in many a dubious battle and who could be surprised or shocked by very little. But even these would have reacted to the spectacle of Cardinal Colonna attempting to lift a blood-stained tiara on to his own head. The probability is that Colonna had long since left logic behind: that his jealous hatred of Clement blinded him to everything except immediate aims, immediate gratifications. In this matter he was very much the Italian, reflecting in his own personal life the pattern of hatreds and rivalries which characterised all Italian politics.

On this occasion Colonna at least was given no chance to take the next step, for Ugo Moncada decisively took over. Moncada had planned this raid with Colonna not to further some wretched little Italian conspiracy but to aid the Emperor. And here, too, Moncada was as much a representative of his own race as Colonna was of the Italian: the Italian could think only in terms of immediate, family loyalties; the Spaniard could transcend his own desires and feelings. Courteously but firmly, Moncada put Colonna in his place and accepted Clement's overture. He did more: instead of sending a representative to the Pope, he would go in person.

Thus, as dusk was falling, a detachment of Spaniards formed outside the Colonna Palace to escort their general in a disciplined, soldierly manner through the disturbed ant-heap that was Rome. Crossing the Tiber bridge, they were admitted into the modern outworks of the castle and made their way to where the vast drum soared up into the darkening evening. It was, perhaps, symbolic of Rome that this, Rome's final defence, was merely the shell of an emperor's tomb. Inside, a broad passageway spiralled upwards through the solid stone heart of the drum, its slope so gradual that it was possible for the party to proceed on horseback. The passage was lit at intervals with flaring torches that cast a lurid light for a few feet, leaving the darkness between deeper by contrast. There was no sound but the echo and clatter of the horses' hoofs, for the garrison was above and below. The ramp led through the sepulchral chamber, empty now save for Hadrian's despairing epitaph, and spiralled onwards and upwards. As a soldier, Moncada was vividly aware that he could be going deeper and deeper into a trap, for this castle was quite impregnable to direct assault. He had taken the obvious course of demanding a hostage, but his only real protection was the intangible shield of an Emperor distant half a continent away.

The spiral passageway ended on the upper surface of the drum and they came out under the night sky nearly 200 feet above ground level. Moncada noted the guard chamber and adjacent armoury with a professional eye and took particular interest in the massive cannon: from here, it would be possible to drop a ball into almost any part of Rome or aim a devastating broadside at any force assailing the Vatican Palace. If those guns had been handled with skill and dedication a few hours before then he himself might not now be standing here but could have been a bloody smear on the street in front of St Peter's.

But Sant' Angelo, though primarily a castle, was also a comfortable retreat. Successive popes had built on this drum, creating a little community high above the dusty streets of Rome; and Clement was waiting to receive his guest throned in one of the handsome public rooms. Scores of brilliantly burning candles drove back the night, illuminated the frescoes on the high walls and gave a soft glow to the polished marble underfoot. Moncada, in full armour, and his armoured men struck a harsh, discordant note as they clanked forward through the ranks of courtiers and priests to where Clement was seated. He was dressed in the white of his office, a spot of vivid purity of colour among the blacks and violets and crimsons of the curial costumes. Arriving at the throne, Moncada briefly genuflected as well as he could in armour, carefully observing etiquette, for, though Clement was in a desperate state, yet, with the obstinacy of the weak, he could still impose serious obstacles. Vehemently the Pope upbraided the Spaniard. Was this the way that His Imperial Majesty showed filial regard to his Holy Father? Did the Emperor really authorise his troops to be used like bandits to raid Christendom's sacred city? The world knew the worth of Cardinal Pompeo Colonna, a man so mad with ambition that he would destroy his own city to achieve it. But the world – and Pope Clement – had expected more, far more, from the Emperor Charles.

Moncada listened with every appearance of contrition. Later that day he would write to the Emperor, urging him to pretend to be angry at the indignity to which Clement had been subjected. Now he developed that theme: it was all a mistake, the fault of the Colonna. What had been intended simply as a ceremonial display had got out of hand. The guilty should be punished. He would disassociate himself from the sacriligious Colonna. Meanwhile, as earnest of his good intentions, he begged permission to restore the papal tiara and crozier which had been taken from the Vatican by impious hands. Two of his attendants now came forward, bearing the glittering symbols of spiritual power. It was a shrewd move and the probability is that Moncada had himself arranged for the illegal removal of the objects from the Vatican. He who bestowed a crown could also take it back, and if Clement accepted its return from the hands of the Emperor's representative, it could be taken to imply recognition of the Emperor's superior status. Clement either did not see the trap, or was anxious to obtain the return of the precious symbols, for he accepted Moncada's gesture without further discussion.

Pressing his advantage, Moncada urged His Holiness to disassociate himself from the warmongers who had dragged him into this ruinous contest with His Imperial Majesty. Let His Holiness merely sign a treaty in which he would withdraw from the League, and remove the papal troops from Lombardy. The imperial forces under the Duke of Bourbon would very rapidly settle the business of the rebellious and violent men in the north, and peace would return to all Italy. Dubiously, hesitantly, Clement agreed. There was perhaps little else he could do, with armed soldiers swarming through the Vatican Palace and unarmed, hungry papal officials falling over each other's feet in the castle; but, with a stoke of the pen, he yet again dizzyingly turned his policy upon its head. Again he became the loyal ally and loving Father of the Emperor and those who had striven to bring him to the test as leader of an Italian alliance were disowned.

Not all of his opponents were pleased with the result of that night's negotiations. When Moncada returned to the Colonna Palace, triumphantly brandishing the signed parchment, Cardinal Pompeo was beside himself with rage, crying out that Moncada was a traitor both to his Emperor and to his ally. For Moncada had effectively called a halt to whatever plans Colonna might have been hatching, using Spanish armed aid. But the Spaniard merely smiled as he bowed ironically, withdrawing from the grudging shelter of the Colonna palace. He had much to do during the few remaining hours of darkness, for the treaty would be signed on the morrow and there would be neither need nor pretext to keep his troops in Rome. Calling to his equerry, Moncada rode out into the dark and restless city to begin the task of rounding up some 3,000 soldiers, most of whom would be the worst for drink.

The raiders marched out in good order on 22 September, carrying with them some 30,000 ducats-worth of booty – an excellent profit for barely a day's work – and Fillipo Strozzi, husband of Clement's niece Clarice, as hostage for the Pope's good behaviour. Strozzi had been highly reluctant to accept the dangerous honour: as a relative of the Pope's, he knew better than most the true value of his word. And Clement had been deeply offended at Strozzi's unwillingness. After they had gone, a shame-faced calm fell upon the city. Clement was agitated, simultaneously humiliated and enraged. He swore that he would withdraw permanently from Rome and establish the papacy in a new-built city untainted by treason and ingratitude. 'They will see what the absence of the Pope means to Rome', he burst out. He changed his mind, for a pope without Rome was no pope; but he still wanted revenge. In affairs international, Clement might endlessly hesitate and waver, but where Italian affairs were concerned, he was very much the papal monarch. He had been deceived and attacked and humiliated by the clan of a rebellious cardinal and the ink upon the treaty that Moncada had forced upon him was scarcely dry, before he was breaking it. Troops were assembled under the command of the condottiere Vitello Vitelli and hurled against the Colonna strongholds in the Campagna. It was the kind of bitter, vicious fighting only too familiar to Italians where vineyards and wheatfields and the homes of ordinary people were the 'military' targets. Oblivious to the mounting menace in the north, where Spanish and German mercenaries were assembling for as yet unclear purposes, oblivious to the menace in the south, where a Spanish fleet had landed another army, Italians fought Italians in Rome's ancient landscape.

The Romans, as was their wont, returned to their everyday activities, not knowing that they had themselves created an irreparable breach in Rome's defence. They had proclaimed, in the clearest, most unequivocal manner possible, that they were no longer capable of defending themselves.

Chapter IX

The March on Rome

Revenge, the Italian proverb ran, is a dish best tasted cold and Francesco Maria della Rovere, Duke of Urbino, Generalissimo of the Holy League in the war against the Emperor, was in the process of tasting the dish prepared in the classic manner. Ten years before, in 1517, he had been robbed of his dukedom by Pope Leo who, after dispossessing the rightful duke, had placed the ducal coronet upon the head of his abominable young nephew, Lorenzo de' Medici. Time had provided della Rovere with a revenge of sorts: both Lorenzo and Leo had descended to the grave, and della Rovere was not only back in Urbino but, as the Captain General of the Venetian troops, was pre-eminent among the oddly assorted 'ecclesiastics'. In his serious and balanced prose Guicciardini recorded that it was the general belief that Urbino, 'retaining still the memory of the injuries which he had received from Leo, and from the present pope when he was cardinal . . . was out of either hatred or fear unwilling that the war should soon be brought to an unhappy conclusion'. Guicciardini was admittedly writing with the benefit of hindsight. At the time he had only his suspicions, but it is curious that, though so many and unequivocal were the grounds for those suspicions, he gave no warning to the wretched Clement.

It was all of a piece with Clement's bad luck and bad judgement that not only should his life be threatened by a rebellious cardinal, his foreign policy made a nonsense by the tugging of rival advisers, and Rome itself made almost uninhabitable for him by a miserly and dishonest Treasurer, but that also he should confide his protection to a devious man whom his family had grievously injured. And having done all this, in swift succession he dismayed his friends by making that treaty with the Emperor, so destroying his credibility, and then promptly enraged the Emperor by breaking the treaty and taking again the path of war.

The tactics of Urbino, the generalissimo on whom everything depended, were simple: to avoid conflict at all costs, even though he had under his command some 24,000 troops (including those of the formidable Bande Nere) and the enemy was both weakened and demoralised. Yet, again and again, the army of the League was in shameful retreat. 'Veni, vidi, fugit', some wit remarked when the Leaguers, having advanced to within attacking range of

Milan, promptly retreated under cover of nightfall. Giovanni della Bande Nere refused to take part in the humiliating withdrawal: instead he deliberately kept his men standing at arms until broad daylight, then retreated slowly and defiantly to join up with a fuming Urbino.

But, though the army of the League was bedevilled by an equivocal leadership, the imperialists were in a far worse condition. When Bourbon had landed in Italy, he had brought with him some 800 soldiers and 100,000 ducats. In Milan, 9,000 Spanish and German soldiers were waiting impatiently for him, but by the time essentials of food and ammunition had been purchased, there was sufficient left over to give each man only two or three ducats. Savage with disappointment, the garrison abandoned what little restraint they had practised and there began for the Milanese a reign of terror, as a soldiery, not noted for its humanity in dealing with the defeated, were now driven out of sheer necessity to force their reluctant hosts to provide the means for their sustenance. A deputation of the citizens waited upon Bourbon, bitterly complaining of the savage treatment that was now meted out to them as a matter of course. Bourbon listened to them sympathetically, then offered to lead the troops out of Milan if the citizens would scrape together 30,000 ducats – sufficient for a month's pay for the troops. 'He knew they had been deceived at other times with the like promises but they might very safely depend upon his word and honour, adding an imprecation that his head might be taken off with the first ball from the enemy's cannon if he should not make good his promise to them', was how Guicciardini later described the transaction. The Milanese somehow got the money together, but Bourbon was quite unable to keep his word, 'either making no account of his promise or unable, as it is supposed, to resist the lawless will and insolence of the soldiery'. The 30,000 ducats were very soon exhausted: again the cycle of privation and torture began with a desperate soldiery battening on a desperate citizenry. And it was at this stage that old Georg Frundsburg again stirred himself in his northern mountains and prepared to descend into impious Italy to fight his Kaiser's battles, even though it was in the depth of winter, and an unusually cold, wet winter when men far younger than he were glad to huddle before the fire. But this was to be the last battle, he swore, and packed in his saddlebag a length of silken rope with which he intended to hang the Bishop of Rome before his own palace in Rome.

Or so the gossiping chroniclers said. That piece of rope suffered more than one metamorphosis with some writers swearing that it was gold, others silver, others claiming that it was not rope at all but a golden chain while yet others turned it into a bundle of ropes, all silver except for one golden one, with which Frundsburg intended to hang the entire Sacred College after disposing of their head. But whatever its form, the rope was a potent symbol, the badge of a rampant Protestantism that scarcely as yet knew its own identity but was sure of its bloody goal. To the strong brew that was simmering in Italy Georg Frundsburg, Prince of Mindelheim, was about to add his own ingredient: sectarian war.

Frundsburg had need to consider himself a crusader for there was, as usual, scarcely any money available for soldiers' pay. Bourbon had managed to acquire 35,000 ducats by playing on the fears of the wretched Morone, the Sforza chancellor who had languished in prison since the failure of his conspiracy. Deducing, correctly, that such a man would always have access to money, Bourbon put him under increasing pressure, even dragging him to a scaffold in pretended preparation for his execution. In exchange for his freedom, Morone paid over a ransome that went some way towards paying Frundsburg's landsknechts. But it was only a little way, each man receiving a ducat – less than a week's pay. Here again, however, the tribal loyalty of the German, in particular the loyalty which these young men felt for their own chief, was sufficient to get the army together and moving. There was, too, the lure of Italy herself, that lure which never failed to work upon northerners, be their contempt for Italian corruption never so great.

The last German expedition had certainly not proved outstandingly successful in financial terms, the landsknechts returning with very little more gold from Italy than they might have earned honestly in their own country. But the warm, scented lure remained undiminished because it was virtually a racial memory, something compounded of hope and imagination and ancient stories of the siren land: of warm seas and brilliant skies and splendid buildings; of the memory – even if it were only a pseudo-memory – of the rich scent of dust and oranges and olives piercing the glacial cold of a northern winter. There was, too, the lure of Rome. Their chief on this occasion would not be content with Milan or Lodi or Pavia, great and splendid though these cities were: Rome, mythical Rome, would be their goal. The city whose existence was co-terminous with European civilisation: the city which had taken in their shaggy forebears sometimes as hostages, sometimes as conquerors, sometimes as slaves, and left its ineradicable mark upon them; the city which had all the fascination of Sodom and Gomorrah, which was ruled by Antichrist and garrisoned by demons; the city, above all, which had made all the world tribute and was bursting with gold and silver and jewels and precious stuffs and unimaginable delights: this was to be their goal this time.

So the young men flocked to Frundsburg's banner: men like Sebastian Schertlin, a swash-buckling youngster who found space for paper and ink in his pack and somehow contrived to keep a diary of sorts which in his maturity he would work up into a swaggering memoir. With Schertlin there was his comrade-in-arms and fellow-scribbler, Reissner, a gentler, more modest soul than Schertlin but, like him, imbued with the desire to record so that between the two of them they provide for posterity a worm's eye view of a vast historical process. In Schertlin's staccato, and Reissner's more fluent, more penetrating record the observer moves briefly from the libraries and palaces of the great to the camps of the common soldier, seeing, briefly, the road winding ahead in white dust or freezing mud; feeling, if only momentarily, the bitter resentment of a hungry man who knows that his next meal depends upon politicians' manoeuvrings or, at the other extreme, the mad, savage elation of unexpected victory, an elation made all the more potent by the knowledge that the morrow or the day after could bring defeat and, with it, injury and death.

Frundsburg had a justifiable grievance against his Emperor. It had been his landsknechts who had turned defeat into overwhelming victory at Pavia, his massive loyalty which had throughout tipped the scales in the Emperor's favour. But where Bourbon had been offered the dukedom of Milan and Lannoy had been summoned to Spain to share the imperial confidences, and even an assassin like Moncada had been entrusted with delicate and vital negotiations, he, Georg Frundsburg, had had to be content with thanks and vague promises that the arrears of pay would be paid off. Money! Charles V, theoretically temporal lord of the entire planet, was as preoccupied with money, or the lack of it, as any little shopkeeper. There was never enough to keep pace with his vast responsibilities, or his now soaring ambitions, and it was perhaps inevitable that the most loyal of his people should be treated the worst.

However, despite his mean treatment, Frundsburg did not once hesitate to answer the call. There was not sufficient money to finance the projected expedition? Then he, the Prince of Mindelheim, would mortgage his own estates, placing his family in danger of want and imperilling the very seat of his family. There was a hostile army, spread over a vast wintry plain between himself and Bourbon? 'The more enemies, the greater the honour', he grunted: his eager, disciplined young men would carve their way through the ramshackle army of the League, an army commanded by bureaucrats and timid generals. 'With God's grace we will succeed in saving the Emperor and his people.' But which God? The Catholics'? Or the Protestants'? What would happen when his Lutherans, some of whom were serving without pay simply for the honour of slaughtering Catholics, joined forces with their allies, the Spaniards who, whatever they might think of Pope Clement, were faithful sons of Holy Church? There was no answer to that conundrum, save a shrug.

The Prince of Mindelheim, at the head of some 14,000 landsknechts, marched out of Trento on 12 November 1526. They were not only leaving three months later in the season than François had left when he made his epic march through the Alps; they were also tackling a far more frightening route, literally scrambling over the high peaks and across the gorges above Lake Garda. Autumn rains had turned to blizzards; the rocky paths and ledges along which they crawled were armoured with ice; sudden fierce gusts of freezing wind sent more than one unwary man toppling to his death hundreds of feet below. The crossing took nine terrible days. Above the tree-line they were without fuel for campfires, and so they ate cold food and at night slept in uneasy snatches, shivering with cold, wet, exhausted. It was their giant leader who kept the young men moving onward, upward and southward, encouraging, threatening, promising, keeping before their eyes the one glowing goal 'nach Rom'. Frundsburg was a big man, but he was also old and burdened with the corpulence of the old, and at places along the route his landsknechts were propping the old man up, pushing and heaving as at some precious but unwieldy parcel. The landsknechts would never have made the crossing without Frundsburg's courage and dedication but he would probably not have survived without the devoted strength of his young men. They put themselves at risk to ensure his safety, standing linked arm to arm, or clutching each other's lances, to form a living balustrade on the edge of the more perilous footpaths. And at last, on 21 November, they stumbled down into the plain of Lombardy.

But the nightmare for the landsknechts was not yet over: it had, indeed, only started. Those young men who had never been out of Germany before and for whom Italy was synonymous with warmth and wine and sun had their first bitter disillusionment. The plain of Lombardy can be as bleak and hostile in winter as any German plain, and the winter of 1526 was as bad in northern Italy as it was beyond the Alps. Frundsburg's men found themselves fighting in a place and under conditions that favoured the defenders. Between them and Bourbon, now impatiently awaiting them in Milan, were some hundreds of miles of open country, traversed by swollen, swiftly flowing rivers, each of which presented a major obstacle. The ground under foot was the Lombard clay, viscous, glue-like stuff that wearied a man immeasurably to just lift one foot in front of the other. The blizzards of the high Alps had given way to bitter rainstorms when, for hours on end, the sky would empty itself without cease. Their food was what they could carry, or extract from frightened peasants, and again there was no money, and in consequence a shortage of the cheap, harsh wine which would, at least, give a man a few hours' relief from misery. And always there was the watching enemy, a not very energetic enemy, it was true, but always a suspended menace.

In the marshes around Mantua the landsknechts were almost wiped out, partly through treachery, partly because they came into contact with the only effective fighting unit in the League's army, the Bande Nere. They repelled eight determined attacks in one short winter's day, one attack coming on the heels of its predecessor. The attackers were driven off by arquebus and musket, for here the landsknechts were still superior even over the Bande Nere; but it was a near thing. Three centuries later the great German historian, Gregorovius, recording the passage of his fellow countrymen through Lombardy, compared it to the march of the Ten Thousand under Xenophon and though Gregorovius was prone to see all things German in a flattering light, his simile was true enough. There was here the same dogged determination which scarcely masked a deep despair: few of the men thought they would survive what now appeared to be a trap.

The landsknechts had had the initial advantage of surprise: these gaunt, shabby men scrambling over the Alpine ice wall, 'that barrier placed by nature itself to keep the barbarians at bay' had disconcerted the Leaguers on their first appearance, and they had been able to fight their way through into the heart of Lombardy before their impetus was checked. But thereafter it should have been a relatively easy matter for the well-equipped, well-prepared army of the League to destroy these desperate men before they made juncture with Bourbon. But the Duke of Urbino, pursuing his own ambivalent aims, kept at arm's length from them, and it was now that Giovanni de' Medici, alone of all the expensively maintained captains, salved something of Italian honour, proving to be the final bulwark between Italy and the 'barbarians' outside.

Limited though he was in his loyalties and his intellect, Giovanni della Bande Nere was precisely the man Italy needed at this time and in this place, and he rose heroically to the challenge. This was the leader which Niccoló Machiavelli had in mind when, at the end of that coldly factual blue-print for tyranny, *The Prince*, he suddenly spoke from his heart: 'Italy seeks and must find her redeemer. Oh, with what love he would be received in all those provinces which have suffered from the floods of these foreign invasions, with what thirst for revenge, what unshakeable fidelity, what piety, what tears! What gates would be shut against him? What jealousy would oppose him? What Italian would deny him respect? This barbarian rule stinks in our nostrils. Up, up, take up this task with spirit and hope, so that under the banner of so great an enterprise Italy may be ennobled, and what Petrarch wrote may come true:

> *Virtue will counter fear*
> *Take arms! The contest shall be brief*
> *For the ancient valour is not yet dead*
> *In Italian hearts*

The plea had been addressed to Lorenzo de' Medici, at that time Lord of Florence, and he listened only coldly and dismissed it, having other and more important things to do, such as eroding the freedom of his fellow Florentines and killing the more aggressively independent. But Giovanni de' Medici, roughneck of the junior branch of the Medici, in the fullness of time responded. It was the element of greatness in the young man which drew Machiavelli to him, away from the relative comforts of Florence to the rigours of campaign in Lombardy. Doubtless, Giovanni was merely following his own instincts and desires, without any conscious intention of fulfilling Machiavelli's prophecies, but the combination of the soldier's courage, and the scholar's vision of a great nationalist leader, gave a brief touch of nobility to a campaign that was otherwise characterised by a squalid incompetence and treachery.

Given the irony that seemed to be the guiding principle throughout these last convulsions of a free Italy, it was perhaps inevitable that Giovanni della Bande Nere, last bulwark of Italian freedom, should be killed; and that the medium of his death should be one of the modern weapons which he despised; and that it should have been given to the enemy by an Italian nobleman.

Alfonso d'Este, Duke of Ferrara, like Francesco Maria della Rovere, the Duke of Urbino, had grounds to fear and hate the distant Bishop of Rome. Two successive popes had hurled armies against Ferrara, attempting to wrest territory from the dukedom, and d'Este had excellent reasons for believing that Clement would keep up the pressure as soon as he himself was free of pressure. Unlike the Duke of Urbino, however, who preferred to follow the traditional path of Italian vengeance, the Duke of Ferrara came out into the open, allying himself with the Emperor and holding out a hand to Frundsburg's starving heroes as they stumbled across the Lombard plain. Among the supplies he had sent them were twelve falconets; guns mounted on swivels, much lighter than a cannon but heavier than an arquebus, which hurled a solid stone ball at close range. They were a viciously effective anti-personnel weapon.

On the afternoon of 19 December the Bande Nere were harrying Frunds-burg's rearguard. Unaware that the landsknechts had been supplied with artillery, Giovanni took no precautions against such an attack and his company was, in fact, returning after a highly successful skirmish when he was hit by a shot in the same leg that had been wounded near Pavia nearly a year before. So terrible was the wound that he could not immediately be moved and the same Jewish surgeon who had attended to him before was now brought hastening to him. Stripping off what remained of the leg armour, the surgeon found that the stone had pulverised metal, bone and flesh inextricably: amputation might – just – save Giovanni's life.

The short winter's day was coming to its close as they placed him in a litter and, beneath a black sky, picked their way through the frozen marshes towards Mantua, eight miles away, Pietro Aretino had heard the news and raced to Mantua in time to meet his dying friend. It was there that he wrote the long and moving letter to their mutual friend, Francesco degli Albizzi, describing the last hours of Giovanni d'Italia – and, incidentally, leaving one of the most vivid and horrific descriptions of contemporary surgery.

At the surgeon's request, Aretino told his friend that amputation was essential.

Let it be done at once, he said to me. Upon this the surgeons entered and, praising his strength of purpose, said they would do what they must that evening. They made him take some medicine and went to prepare the instruments they needed. It was now time to eat, but he was assailed by vomiting and said to me: 'The omens of Caesar! I must think of other things than those of this life.' But then the time arrived and those worthy men appeared with the implements needed for their purpose and said that eight or ten people had to be found to hold him while he endured the violence of the saw. 'Not even twenty', he said 'could hold me.'

The patient dominated the sickroom as he dominated the battlefield, personally taking the light and holding it so that the surgeons could best go about their bloody task. Aretino's nerve failed at this stage: 'I fled from the scene and stopping my ears, I heard only two cries, and then he called for me.' Upon going back into the tent he found that not only was Giovanni conscious but, with barrack-room humour, wanted to arrange a macabre tableau with the amputated foot.

But the pain that had ebbed attacked him again two hours before daylight with every imaginable torment. And when I heard the agitation which shook the room, my heart stood still and, dressing in an instant, I ran to him. As soon as he saw me he started to say that the thought of cowardice, troubled him more than his pain.

Aretino stayed talking to him, trying to distract his mind from the well-nigh intolerable pain. It speaks much for Giovanni de' Medici's incredible self-control that he was able to maintain a semblance of civilised conversation; but it speaks much, too, for Aretino's love and loyalty that he, the cynic and hedonist, remained in that evil-smelling sickroom, while the wan dawnlight strengthened into the cheerless light of a winter's morning, reminiscing, gossiping, putting on a bold and confident front though it was now known that gangrene had set in and that the end was only a question of time. He remained with Giovanni all that day, while friends and servants and allies came in and out of the room, some to weep, some to proffer cold-eyed condolences, and most of them to speculate what would happen should the leader of the Bande Nere die. At nightfall the pains returned and at Giovanni's urgent request, Aretino read to him like a father reading a restless child to sleep. Giovanni did fall asleep, then woke: 'I dreamed of making my own will, and I am cured. If I continue to improve like this I shall teach the Germans how to fight and show how I get my revenge.' But it was only a temporary rallying and shortly before the end he demanded to be lifted out of the sickbed and put in a camp cot. 'I'm a soldier, and will not die among these sheets and bandages.' They obeyed his request and it was there that he died. 'Such was the passing of the great Giovanni de' Medici. . . . And both Florence and Rome (though would to God I lied) will soon know what it is to be without him.'

Giovanni's death was like a breach in a dyke: energetic action could have blocked that breach; but under the Duke of Urbino's lead no such action could take place. Frundsburg's men poured through, crossing the vast natural barrier of the Po with ease, marching steadily southward in torrential rain. Yet their position had not really improved: they still lacked money and provisions and above all a secure base. Bitterly Frundsburg wrote to his ally Bourbon in Milan:

> In the face of great dangers he had crossed high mountains and deep waters, had spent two months in the country, enduring poverty, hunger and frost: that owing to the great patience of his soldiers and with the help of God he had divided and driven back the enemy. He lay there now in the enemy's country, attacked every day, and desired further instructions.

Behind the stilted words of a field commander 'desiring instructions' from his commander-in-chief was the bitterness of a fighting soldier against the staff. Compared with the perilous situation of the landsknechts, encamped in the heart of enemy country, Bourbon was simply taking his ease safely lodged in one of the great fortified cities of Europe.

Yet the situation in Milan was only better by comparison: in reality, Bourbon and his mixed Spanish and Italian troops were in almost as desperate a state as the Germans in the field. Bourbon wanted to march out and link up with Frundsburg, but his men refused to move until they had received some payment on account. A few more thousands were squeezed out of the wretched Milanese, a garrison was chosen and on 30 January 1527, the 'imperial' army marched out to join up with the Germans near Piacenza a week later. And with that juncture it was as though a critical mass had come into being: 22,000 soldiers were now assembled in Lombardy, waiting for they knew not what, certain only that daily their privations grew greater.

Meanwhile, in Rome the pendulum of Clement's hopes and fears was swinging with a wildness that would have been comic were it not for the underlying tragedy. When he had heard the alarming news of that Lutheran avalanche in the north, Clement had turned to the man who had started all this – François. His Nuncio in France wrote in the most vigorous terms to the King: 'If your majesty does not now use all the might of France . . . Italy will soon be subject to the dominion of the Emperor and your sons will remain in prison all their life. . . . The coming of the landsknechts across the Po, the death of the Seigneur Giovanni de' Medici are mortals blows for the Pope. . . .' François expressed sympathy, made large promises, and forgot them. As the Nuncio remarked in a letter to Giberti: 'Pleasant things blot out serious matters from his mind so that most frequently the words remain with us, while the deeds go to his amusement.'

Frustrated there, Clement turned again to the idea of bribery – if he could raise the money. The Venetian ambassador was summoned to the Vatican: would Venice provide gold with which to divert Frundsburg? The Venetian was barely polite in his reply. It was highly unlikely, he pointed out heavily, that the same Prince of Mindelheim who had mortgaged his very estates to serve his Kaiser could be tempted with Italian gold. Almost immediately afterwards there came news of an imperial success – dramatic but local – in the south of Italy. In a panic Clement abandoned his allies, his hopes and what little remained of a consistent policy, to sign a treaty with the Emperor on 31 January. In France, the King proclaimed himself astonished: 'We are greatly amazed for we expected quite other conduct from His Holiness. It is strange that he is willing to put himself in the power of the Emperor who will make of him a simple priest.'

But the ink was scarcely dry upon the document before Clement repudiated it. On the very day that he had signed the document there had been a success of papal arms – resounding but local – in the south of Italy, and Clement hastened to tell the world, and France in particular, of his undying enmity for the Emperor, his undying love for liberty, France and his bewildered Italian allies. François accepted the new protestations with admirable restraint, but could not resist adding: 'For the love of God he must keep up his courage, and meddle no more with truces or negotiations. To tell the truth, his incessant practice of making terms, his projects of flight, have kept us undecided and made us always afraid that we should lose our time and money.'

But though Clement did not realise it, his options, like those of the Duke of Bourbon, had for some time been closing one by one. Outwardly there was no change: the papal couriers sped across Europe; splendidly dressed nuncios waited in gorgeous palaces to confer with kings and princes; the ambassadors of these great ones waited upon him respectfully, with careful protocol, in the Vatican. But behind this glittering screen of conventional high-level diplomacy was the gritty reality of that huge and hungry army in the north, an army moving southward still with no great sense of purpose, but gathering momentum. In each elaborate treaty there occurred ever more references to this army – again, references with no great sense of urgency but presenting an irritating problem that would not go away.

In the treaty of 31 January Clement had promised 200,000 ducats to be paid to the landsknechts – not to the Emperor, nor to his Viceroy, but simply to the soldiers. Even this vast sum would give less than eight ducats apiece to the men, but it was something. It would put food and wine in their bellies and slightly improve the quality of the camp-followers; and, more important, it would retain the men's faith in their commanders, for he who paid, commanded. Then, with the breaking of the treaty, the promise to pay even this sum was also broken. This may have been merely a broken promise to the Apostolic Treasury but it was a severe and personal disappointment to already resentful soldiers in a foreign land. Their morale had been astonishingly good: even Guicciardini, their enemy, recognised this:

> We cannot sufficiently admire the resolution and fortitude of the Constable [Bourbon] and his army who, without money, without ammunition, without pioneers, without any assurances of provisions, undertook to pass through the midst of so many foes and of troops much superior in number to theirs. Perhaps the firmness of the Germans was still more surprising than that of the others. They had set forth from their country with a single ducat each, and after long sufferings in Italy, where they had only two or three ducats more, they set forth on the march, against the custom of all soldiers especially of their nation, without any other pay than the hope of victory. They knew that it would be absolutely impossible for them to live without money if they found themselves in some place where it was difficult to obtain provisions, or if the enemy were close at hand.

The loyalty of these mercenaries towards their leader was, indeed, remarkable. But, in fact, they had little choice but to move onward. With every additional mile southward they had increased their stake, increased the difficulty of returning. At Bologna they were approximately at the point of no return, for it would have been as bloody a business to fight their way back home empty-handed, as it would have been to continue onwards with at least a hope of rich reward. It was at Bologna that the continent-wide diplomatic manoeuvrings, the years of battle, of marching and countermarching began suddenly to shape themselves into one single threat, a dagger pointed at the heart of Italy, at Rome. For it was at Bologna that, for the first time, the commanders lost control, and thereafter they became more and more the mere mouthpiece of the army.

Bourbon had tried to obtain a subsidy from the Duke of Ferrara. But beyond a few cartloads of food and four cannon, Alfonso d'Este could, or would, do nothing. Shrewdly, he realised that a too great display of generosity might be a dangerous gesture: 22,000 hungry men would be strongly tempted to forget they were allies. Instead, he urged Bourbon to take the road to Rome, a tactic which would simultaneously rid his state of these dangerous allies and strike a blow at the hated Medici pope. The weather was as vile as ever with continuous heavy rain exacerbating tempers that were already badly frayed. An argument or riot seems to have broken out and a sergeant-major who tried to quell it was killed. The soldiers, like sharks, that had hitherto been quiescent, were excited into a frenzy by the scent of spilt blood. Demanding pay, a mixed group of Germans and Spaniards besieged Bourbon. On this occasion he managed to maintain his ascendancy. The French gossip Brantôme recorded that:

> He addressed them all and pointed out that his necessities were as great as theirs . . . that they must have a little patience for he had no intention of defrauding them of the just payment for their services and sufferings. To show his sympathy he would divide amongst them all the silver vessels in his tent and all the rings and jewels, furnishings and clothes in his coffers. He would only reserve for himself the clothes he had on and the surcoat of silver cloth which he wore above his armour.

Brantôme was writing in France and from hearsay, but his sources were usually good; the incidental touch of verisimilitude regarding the 'surcoat of silver' bears testimony to this. Bourbon always wore the surcoat in battle, the softly gleaming stuff contrasting with his battered armour and easily distinguished in the turmoil of a battle-field; he would, naturally, not have wished to part with it. Brantôme's concluding remark that Bourbon's generosity so delighted the soldiers that they swore to follow him even to the devil was also, probably, accurate enough: though remote with members of his own class, Bourbon was capable of inspiring loyalty and even affection among his followers.

The final explosion was sparked off by Spaniards, however, for, of the three national groups which formed the army, they had the least motive to suffer: they had no potential goal. The Germans at least had the luxury of religious fanaticism to compensate for their empty stomachs; the Italians could entertain hopes of solid advantages in the form of land and titles. The Spaniards regarded themselves simply as professional soldiers – mercenaries, not crusaders – and not only were they receiving no pay, they were in actual physical want.

The army commanders had organised a species of flying column to forage for provisions ahead and to one side of the army's advance. The peasants and small farmers in the country through which they were passing had had centuries of experience in hiding food from marauders; but these foragers were not only skilled but desperate men who knew just where a peasant would hide a clutch of eggs, a batch of bread, or a keg of wine; or, failing that, who knew what pressures would bring him to disclose its hiding place. The foragers left behind them a trail of destruction and terror: burnt barns, smashed cottages; dead householders, screaming children. But with each foray they had to go a little further afield, and from each foray they returned with a little less. This was the dead season of the year, the season which all army commanders dreaded, for the peasants' stocks of winter provisions were running low and the first of the spring crops had not yet arrived. The small undefended villages and isolated farms were scraped bare of food.

There was food in plenty in the dozens of walled towns, but the 'imperials' had only four small cannon and they would starve to death long before a breach was made in the most modest city wall. So desperate was their state, however, that Bourbon decided to try the effect of a threat, at least. A trumpeter was sent to sound defiance outside the walls of Bologna, demanding provisions. Not surprisingly, the Bolognese simply ignored him and the trumpeter returned disconsolate to the main force. And always the rain fell, a pitiless, icy deluge which turned the line of march into a morass: men turned in at night in wet clothes, arose in wet clothes. marched in wet clothes. Hunger – actual, savage hunger – began to gnaw them.

A well-founded rumour swept through the camp that Pope and Emperor had signed yet another treaty and the march on Rome was to be discontinued. In return, they were to receive a beggarly 60,000 ducats – less than three ducats a man after nearly three months' painful marching and skirmishing. On the night of 11 March the Spaniards exploded. Yelling, they advanced upon Bourbon's tent, demanding money. He was a brave man, but also a sensible one, and only a fool would have dreamed of trying to parley with men in their hysterical condition. Ignominiously, he fled to the German lines: their discipline, at least, was better. The Spaniards promptly plundered Bourbon's tent of what few items of value remained: somebody found and carried off his famous silver surcoat but it was discovered in a ditch the following morning (presumably it was too distinctive an object to be sold) and was eventually returned to the Duke.

But if Bourbon hoped that the discipline of Frundsburg's troops still held, he was doomed to be disappointed. This was the hour when, in a well-found army, the campfires would be blazing merrily and the cooking pots would be sending out their savoury odours. But few fires could survive in this endless downpour, and the only food was a few hoarded cold scraps. Cold, wet, hungry, the landsknechts were roused from their apathy by the yells of the Spanish and the Spanish rage spread like a contagion. Grasping their own weapons, the landsknechts poured out of their soggy tents, advancing threateningly on their commander's tent. Frundsburg rose magnificently to the occasion. Towering above even the tallest of his men, his booming voice rolling out over the crash of drums, yells, and trumpet blasts, he strove to restore order. He called them his children: reminded them of their sacred duty to their Kaiser and to him, their father and their prince. Let them but return to their tents and this would all be forgotten. Soon money would be coming and all this would seem like a bad dream.

But even a German's tribal loyalty could not withstand the tearing pangs of hunger and, below them, the dull despair, the growing conviction that his lot was to be a muddy grave somewhere in Central Italy. One of the men lowered a halberd at the old man: instinctively he responded, reaching for his great sword. That, in turn, appears to have triggered off a sudden, personal hostility, for more men menaced him with their weapons. He tried to speak, struggling with rage and humiliation and then, subjected to such unprecedented emotional pressures, he was seized by an apoplectic fit. Choking, he lost consciousness and fell upon a drum.

The old man's collapse brought the incipient mutiny to a sudden end, for his men had genuinely loved him. They picked him up, remorsefully, and when the rough and ready camp doctors declared their inability to do anything for him, was carried by stretcher the long and weary way back to Ferrara, the only city which would give him shelter and where skilled doctors were in attendance. But he never recovered. Still in a state of stroke he was carried back through Lombardy, back through the Alps, and brought at last to his home, the castle of Mindelheim. And there he died in his eighty-second year, a victim not of sword thrust or arquebus, but of a broken heart.

Frundsburg's death gave Bourbon a breathing space, but no more than that. The entire burden of the imperial advance now lay upon his shoulders but, from this point onwards, bold and skilful soldier though he was, he was in no real sense the leader of the host. The Germans barely tolerated him: after Frundsburg's departure they elected a council from among themselves, a council which looked after the German interest with only a nod towards the commander-in-chief. Bourbon was able to relieve the immediate financial position with a tiny loan of 6,000 ducats from d'Este in Ferrara. The soldiers accepted the pittance only on his direct promise that there would be no more dawdling, no more debates: they would march directly upon Florence, the richest city in their path, and recompense themselves for their sufferings from the limitless coffers of her merchants and priests.

The decision had scarcely been made when an imperial envoy, Cesare Ferramosca, arrived at the camp waving the latest imperial-papal treaty: the Pope promised to pay them 60,000 ducats but they were to leave Italy right away. Bourbon listened, scarcely believing his ears: yet again, diplomats in their comfortable chambers had drawn up a wholly meaningless document, treating the 22,000 hungry, angry men as so many pawns who could be removed by the stroke of a pen. Vehemently, he pointed out to Ferramosca that the sum represented less than a fortnight's pay for men, some of whom had not been paid for three months. Ferramosca insisted that it would deeply embarrass the Emperor if the treaty were not honoured and Bourbon shrugged and summoned his captains: Ferramosca could have the task of convincing them.

The imperial envoy did his best. Wisely, he refrained from appealing to their loyalty to a distant emperor who had done signally little to display his loyalty to them. Instead, he outlined the problems before them. Did they really think they could march through hundreds of miles of enemy country, ill-equipped and badly provisioned? Did they really think they could batter down the walls of some of Europe's most formidable cities with the four small cannon that represented their artillery? But though Ferramosca was an intelligent man, he was an outsider, a diplomat with a comfortable home to return to and a regular salary and a good cellar and he could not comprehend the sheer desperation of the gaunt, ill-smelling, ill-clad men who faced him in Bourbon's lodgings. They did not even trouble to debate the proposition: the Spaniards merely remarked ironically that it was necessary to go to Rome in order to get absolution for their sins, while the Germans turned on their heels and stalked out.

By the time Ferramosca came to take his leave of Bourbon the common soldiers had learned of his presence and mission and, in a rage, wanted to kill him. He only just managed to escape, galloping to Ferrara where he wrote to his Emperor that the mailed arm of Caesar was now, for all practical purposes, outside his control: 'When I arrived with the peace, they were as furious as lions', he remarked feelingly. Bourbon, too, occupied himself with writing despatches, first to the imperial Viceroy, Lannoy, telling him that the army was completely out of his control and that he was little more than guide and spokesman. Then he wrote to Clement, not threatening, but simply explaining that a payment of 200,000 ducats was the very least that would halt the army. When Guicciardini heard of this, bleakly he told Giberti in Rome: 'It seems to me that you have to choose out of only three solutions: yield everything in a fresh treaty; fly; or defend yourself to the death. The most honourable is to perish like a hero.' Giberti, reflecting that Guicciardini was safe in Bologna, doubtless felt that it was easier for him to utter such warlike sentiments from a distance.

On 31 March 1527 the force once known as the Imperial Army broke camp, burned what they could not carry and began the southward march through the green of an Italian spring. They would not make permanent camp again until they reached Rome.

In Rome itself, Pope Clement passed successively from confidence to bewilderment to indignation and, finally, to fear. As far as he was concerned, the mere act of signing a treaty automatically disposed of the problems that had made it necessary, and Ferramosca's journey to the enemy camp had been only a formality, a courtesy. So confident had Clement been, that he had promptly dismissed a sizeable proportion of the papal army: the war was over now and he was entirely in agreement with Armellino that money should not be wasted feeding idle soldiers. Then had come the news that the ungrateful mercenaries had rejected his offer of 60,000 golden ducats, that the imperial envoy himself had scarcely escaped with his life, and that the mercenary army was again on the march. Terrified, Clement urged the Viceroy to go in person and Lannoy, hardly less worried about the prospect of this masterless army continuing its threatening march, agreed to go northward and meet Bourbon. Clement agreed, reluctantly, that the price would have to be raised – but Florence would have to pay, for, after all, it was Florence who was now directly menaced. In Florence, Lannoy met Bourbon's friend and envoy, La Motte, one of the Frenchmen who had steadfastly remained with the exiled duke, and after hard bargaining Lannoy, La Motte and the Florentine representatives agreed that the ransome – for such it was – should be raised to 150,000 ducats, to be payable in five instalments. Florence would raise the down payment of 80,000 ducats and the army would begin to withdraw within five days of receiving this sum. The news of the agreement was passed to Rome where, even before it was ratified, Clement celebrated it by dismissing the Bande Nere who had been hastily summoned to Rome after the last threat. Virtually no troops now defended the city and, for those who could see, the pattern of future events was suddenly terribly clear. Some thought that Clement had actually gone mad, and that through his madness a divine plan was being worked for the chastisement and eventual reformation of the Church. 'The whole world is astonished at his conduct', the Mantuan ambassador wrote to his master. 'It has undoubtedly been ordained by the will of God in order to ruin the Church and its ruler.' In Mantua, the Marquis studied the despatch with dismay, then wrote to his mother Isabella, urging her to leave Rome at once. The indomitable woman refused to do so, for she had not yet obtained the cardinal's hat for her other son, the whole reason for her presence in the city.

Clement was certainly not mad in any clinical sense: he was to survive and reign for another seven years, administering the complex affairs of the Papacy efficiently enough. But neither is there any doubt that, during the early months of 1527, he had lost contact with reality. For over two years this quiet, studious man had been subjected to quite unprecedented pressures; every decision he had made had worked to his disadvantage; every day had seen the closer approach, by an inexorable mile or so, of a once distant and nebulous threat. The disintegration of his personality proceeded by geometric progression: as his options were reduced so the penalties for making an error grew proportionately greater. He found refuge, at last, from the intolerable need to make decisions in pretending that the problem was abstract – a natural means of escape for one of his intellectual bent. He had been told clearly and unequivocally by both his advisers and the Emperor's, that the steadily advancing army in the north was now responsible to no power but itself. And yet he acted as though the mere signing of a document could, like some magical spell, totally dissolve the threat.

The Viceroy Lannoy and the Duke of Bourbon met in a little town in the foothills of the Appenines on 20 April. The two men had not seen each other since they had left Spain nearly a year before and there was a distinct coolness between them. Their staffs put this coolness down to the fact that Bourbon had bitterly resented Lannoy's action in snatching the captive King François from his care and taking him to Spain to receive the personal congratulation of the Emperor. Bourbon certainly felt aggrieved by Lannoy's action; but a more basic cause for their mutual dislike and distrust was their relative positions. Lannoy despised Bourbon as a traitor even while he envied him his influence with the Emperor: it had been the traitorous Bourbon, not the loyal Lannoy, who had been offered the dukedom of Milan and who had even been considered as husband for the Emperor's sister. Bourbon, for his part, felt that he could well do without such empty honours: he saw himself with justice as a catspaw being used to pull some very hot chestnuts out of the fire for an ally who kept well away from the heat. He received Lannoy courteously, then told him bluntly that the 150,000 florins to which they had agreed was not enough: the army now demanded at least 240,000 before they would consent to abandon their march.

Lannoy's reaction was curious. He was the Emperor's highest representative in Italy – in legal metaphysics, indeed, he *was* the Emperor in Italy. And yet, when one of the Emperor's officers coolly tore up in front of him the agreement he, the Viceroy, had signed with the Pope and the Florentines, he did nothing and said nothing. He remained in the camp for the next three days, but made no attempt whatsoever to persuade the men to honour a treaty drawn up on behalf of the Emperor who was still, legally, their master. It may be that he had a lively respect for his own skin: Ferramosca's account of how he had to run for his life from these same men lost nothing in the telling. But he could have retired from the camp and then despatched a protest to Bourbon, making it clear that the Duke was going against the Emperor's wishes. Instead, he merely informed Clement that the ransome demand had been nearly doubled to the incredible sum of a quarter of a million ducats and then withdrew to Siena, to await developments.

Lannoy's silence, his almost casual acceptance of the mercenaries' new demands, casts the strongest possible doubt on the later claims by the Emperor's defenders that he did not will the march on Rome, and that he was therefore not responsible for the Sack. As early as 26 January, when the army was still in Lombardy, Charles heard from one of his agents in Rome that 'Bourbon will not be able to give his troops any pay other than the sack of Rome and Florence'. He was kept regularly informed of the speed and direction of the army's march and, by early April, must have been perfectly well aware that its final goal could only be Rome. There are grounds for suspecting, indeed, that he deliberately reduced or cut off the supply of money and provisions to Bourbon, so acting on the principle of starving a lion before releasing it in the arena. Lannoy, who was closely in Charles' confidence, must also have known that Clement would refuse to pay the increased demands and that, as a result, the army would march that much closer to Rome. Lannoy and his master were almost certainly playing a game of calculated risk. They wanted to detach Clement, finally, from the web of anti-imperial alliances that had been built up. Again and again, he had wriggled out of his promises: now they planned to pin him down at last, by threat of direct assault. Doubtless they had no intention that the landsknechts and their allies should ever enter the sacred city: it was Rome's misfortune that they miscalculated not only the speed of Bourbon's advance but also the degree of ineptitude of those responsible for Rome's defence.

Bourbon struck camp on 26 April: thereafter, nothing would turn him aside. Skilfully, he chose his route so that it appeared as though the main assault was to be directed against Florence. The Holy League hastened to send troops to defend the League's treasure-house, and it was not until the army was crossing the Arno near Arezzo that they realised they had been tricked. Bourbon's own troops also were deceived by the manouevre, and when it became evident that they were by-passing this fat and apparently defenceless prize, a deputation of furious mercenaries waited upon him. Surely he did not seriously intend to attack the great city of Rome, the city that had been built by the greatest fighting race the world had ever known and that was manned by descendants of those fighters, when the ripe plum of Florence hung there for the plucking? Appearances were more than deceptive, he replied. It seemed as though Pope Clement feared more to put his native city at risk, than the city over which he ruled. The walls of Florence had been put into first-class condition: Niccolo

Machiavelli had been personally charged with that task by Clement. The garrison there was in good heart, backed up by an excellent militia, and with the stiffening now of several thousand men drawn from the ranks of the League, it was almost impregnable. Rome, on the other hand – why, the circuit of walls alone was nearly three times that of Florence, while the population to defend them was far smaller. Nothing lay between them and this great prize but some hundreds of miles of weary road: let them take heart, and march.

They took heart, and marched. The end of their long odyssey was as bitter as the beginning: then they had shivered in icy wind and rain, now they sweated in an unusually early summer. But shivering or sweating, still they starved. They had rejected great sums of gold in the hope of securing even greater and so they had no cash to buy food. Bourbon insisted that they should keep upon the swiftest line of march in order to reach Rome before the League: they even abandoned what cannon they had and it would be dangerous folly to slow down the march in order to hunt for food. His orders made sense and grimly the mercenaries obeyed, filling their stomachs with what food they could snatch en route: unripe almonds and figs, bean and pea plants boiled up in a kind of purée.

The road between Arezzo and Rome runs through tracts of land that more closely resembles North Africa than Italy: parched, arid, hostile, dotted with depressed villages. The Spaniards took it in their stride. It disconcerted the Germans, particularly those young men – little more than lads – who, having seen the frozen face of Italy, were ill-prepared for the torrid; but they swept across the badlands at the same fierce pace. At Centino, the swollen river Paglia would have checked the advance of any other group of men. They could not halt, nor turn back, nor turn aside: so they crossed. The cavalry acted as a kind of breakwater upstream. The mass of the troops struggled across by interlacing arms, and downstream the tallest and strongest landsknechts formed a cordon to snatch from death their weaker comrades who had been swept away. The burning sun dried them. A torrential rain soaked them but they attacked and sacked Montefiascone even in this deluge, grabbing food and drink as they smashed through.

On 4 May they camped at Veii, the ancient Etruscan city that had been brutally destroyed by Rome. Their final goal lay three hours' march ahead: the country was empty alike of friends and enemies.

Section Three

THE TRAGEDY

Chapter X

The City Prepares

Holy Thursday fell on 18 April that year. It was a warm, still day, heady with the scent of the blossoms that covered the scores of green places within the city walls. The Forum was like a meadow; the Colosseum hid its bloody secrets under a tapestry of moss and violets; the gaunt ruins of the vast baths of Caracall and Diocletian were clothed and softened with a myriad of plants whose perfume drifted even into the dark and noisome alleys at the city's heart. The Romans were out in their thousands, devoutly following the final stages of the busiest and most sacred cycle of the Church's year, but drawn abroad, too, by the beautiful weather. The Roman ever preferred to live his life on the public stage of street and piazza, rather than in the dark hovel he called home, and now was the perfect time for doing so with the long, cold wet winter in the past and the enervating, dusty heat of summer in the future.

By late morning, some ten thousand citizens had made their way to the vast square in front of St Peter's basilica. Before them were two churches, one behind the other – or, rather, the remains of one church and the half-completed façade of another. In the distance was the titanic new church, still without its dome but looming above the patched, battered millenial-old basilica which it was replacing. The old church still possessed its loggia and it was here that Pope Clement emerged to give his pontifical blessing. The crowd, as Romans, might have very mixed feelings about Clement as Clement; but the crowd, as faithful Catholics, were at this moment the humble and utterly devoted children of the Holy Father. As his hand swept up in the age-old and graceful gesture of benediction, so the thousands sank to their knees; and as the rustling of their garments and scrape of their feet ended, so an immense silence fell upon the square.

It was broken violently, obscenely, by a scream of rage and hatred: 'Thou bastard of Sodom!' In that enormous square it was some moments before the source of the scream could be detected: a figure was clinging to the statue of St Paul in front of the basilica, mouthing his hatred to the white-clad pope who was standing in front and below him. 'Thou bastard of Sodom! For thy sins Rome shall be destroyed! Repent and turn thee! If thou wilt not believe me, in fourteen days thou shalt see it.' Soldiers of the papal guard sprang forward and dragged the figure down. Most people in the crowd recognised him, for he was well-known in Rome and was certainly distinctive, dressed only in a leather apron, his body emaciated, his filthy, knotted hair growing down to his shoulders, his eyes blazing with prophetic fervour.

He was known as Brandano, born Bartolomeo Carosi, and had given up his worldly name and sinful way of life, having been granted a vision of the doom to come. Thereafter he had first led the life of a hermit, and had then begun preaching through the towns and villages until he came to Rome. Holding a cross of wood in one hand and a polished human skull in the other, he gave the Romans the kind of hell-fire sermons in which they delighted. Some thought him a madman; quite a few venerated him as a saint and swore they knew of miracles he had performed; all regarded him as a special person under the protection of Rome itself. It was, perhaps, his awareness of Brandano's curious popularity that led Clement to be lenient with him. The naked fanatic was admonished and then released. Two days later he was again attacking the Pope publicly: 'He has robbed the Mother of God to adorn his harlot, or rather his friend', was the somewhat oblique accusation, and then 'Rome! Do penance. They shall deal with thee as God dealt with Sodom.' On this occasion Brandano found himself in a prison cell, but was released soon afterwards and promptly resumed his career of prophet of doom as soon as he was outside the gates.

The bizarre episode touched Rome on the raw. Later, hindsight was to marvel at the apparent precision of Brandano's warning. Fourteen days was the time he had given in which the divine vengeance would fall on Rome; the invaders broke through exactly eighteen days later – close enough to impress the miracle-mongers. But now Brandano's was only the most recent, if the most dramatic, of a series of omens and prophecies of doom: posters warning that Rome would suffer the doom of Nineveh had mysteriously appeared on walls; a thunderbolt had struck the Vatican; houses had been destroyed by lightning from a clear sky. A thrill of superstitious horror sped through the city when news came that Bourbon's army was encamped on the ruins of Veii, for one of the innumerable prophecies of Rome's destruction had declared that it would be launched from this city that Rome had so wantonly destroyed.

Now, belatedly, Clement turned to his own people. When a courier had galloped into Rome, bringing warning from Florence that the mercenaries' goal was indubitably Rome, Clement had reacted in his now normal way, tearing up the treaty he had only just signed with Lannoy, appealing to France, England, anybody for funds, soldiers, help. But even if the monarchs of France and England felt disposed to help the Italian weathercock, they were hundreds of miles distant, whereas Bourbon's army was here, now, decreasing the distance between itself and Rome with every hour. On the last occasion when an invading force had attacked Rome, the citizens had stood by idly while their Bishop had been humiliated. Would they do the same again, or could they be persuaded that their cause and the cause of Pope Clement were the same? Clement determined to find out: he would ride out into the streets of Rome, personally.

It was a courageous decision, not so much because of the physical danger Clement was accepting, but because of the violence it meant he had to do to his own character. He was not a bonhominous man: all his working life had been spent among people like himself – lawyers and scholars, sober, discreet, low-voiced people who conducted their affairs with reason and logic, mistrusting demagoguery. For years, his only contact with the common people had been ceremonial: they consisted of a massed blur seen in passing through the streets, or from the altar or the loggia. But now this hesitant, diffident, but frequently irascible man would have to find spontaneous words and develop the patience of a politician listening to the complaints of a fishwife, the boasts of a cobbler, the maudlin sentiments of a baker.

Having made the decision, Clement stuck to it. There was even talk of moving the entire papal court from the remote halls of the Vatican on the distant side of the river, to the Palazzo Venezia at the foot of the Capitol Hill in the very heart of the city. That came to nothing, probably due to resistance from the papal bureaucracy; but where Clement could make his own decisions, he kept his word. He remained in Rome to the end.

His personal tour of the city seemed to be effective, the Romans responding warmly to their Bishop's unwonted warmth. Let the Holy Father be of good heart: his flock would not abandon him. They were, after all, Romans, descendants of those who had ruled the world for centuries, and more than capable of dealing with a scarecrow army of barbarians. There was no garrison? They would be their own garrison. In theory, there were some 14,000 Romans capable of bearing arms, and in the rush of warlike enthusiasm, several thousand of these came forward. Romans were ever addicted to the cult that later generations were to describe as *la bella figura*, a virtually untranslateable phrase which combines the ideas of 'cutting a dash', 'face' and 'swank'. Appearance was all important in the cult of *la bella figura* and the citizen soldiers indulged themselves to the full with their martial display of plumes and feathers and glittering swords and armour. Compared with the ragged landsknechts, they were indeed a brave sight; but most of the swords had not been used for a generation and more, except in street brawls, there were no firearms – even if these armchair soldiers had known how to use them; and after the stirring review, the 'soldiers' simply went home, hung up their military finery and returned to normal life.

Clement had chosen Renzo da Ceri as military commander of Rome. Renzo was a member of the traditionally pro-papal house of Orsini and was also a military envoy of the King of France, two qualifications which would attract Clement to him. He was an amiable, reasonably loyal but quite undistinguished soldier whose main claim to fame was his defence of Marseilles two years earlier, and his appointment was Clement's last and most disastrous mistake. Whatever his limitations, Renzo was a professional soldier and must have known from the beginning that Rome's defences were woefully inadequate. Indeed, rumour had it that when Clement had decided to dismiss the Bande Nere, Renzo had literally gone on his knees trying to dissuade the Pope from such a suicidal action. But it seems as though thereafter he was affected by the lotus-eaters of Rome and, rendered thereby optimistic, contributed to the unreal atmosphere by his own optimism.

There was, admittedly, little that Renzo or anybody else could do about the state of dilapidation of Rome's first line of defence, her great walls. Begun by Aurelian in the year AD 271, they had taken nearly ten years to complete. Sixty feet high, twelve feet thick and nearly thirteen miles in circumference, they had been repaired and repaired again and again over the centuries, this being the first charge on the purse of every ruler of Rome. But in late years they had become increasingly dilapidated. Even the warlike Pope Julius II, of whom it was said that he had thrown St Peter's Keys into the Tiber in order better to wield the sword of St Paul and whose preferred costume was a suit of armour, had not troubled over-much about the condition of Rome's shield. One of the features of the walls was the internal passageway which allowed the garrison to move swiftly and under cover from one point to another, available manpower thereby being used to the maximum effect. But long sections of the passageway were now choked up and, as in many areas buildings now appeared along the wall itself, the garrison was forced to make quite considerable detours when moving from one section to another. The overall effective height had also been reduced, partly by dilapidation from the top, but partly, too, by the natural accretion of spoil at the base outside.

If the condition of the walls could not be blamed upon Renzo, the extraordinary blind optimism which prevailed regarding the quality of the defending troops was, however, entirely his fault. At the beginning of his commission he had built up the troops in a sensible, workmanlike manner, scouring the city and surrounding country for unemployed veterans. Two thousand of the Bande Nere had remained in Rome: professional soldiers themselves, they had calculated the speed and force of Bourbon's advance and, confident of again finding employment, had been content, during the close season of winter, to spend their time and money on the delectable joys of Rome. In addition to this small but formidable Italian force, there were another 2,000 soldiers of the Swiss Guard on whom Renzo could count – men who had sworn personal loyalty to the Pope and who could be depended upon to wield their halberds and enormous swords to the death. Another five or six thousand professionals of varying quality came forward on news that Renzo was recruiting. These were not soldiers of the highest quality, being, for the most part, men who had come to Rome with one or other of the endless succession of mercenary armies and decided to pick up a living among the fleshpots. A very high proportion were suspected of being little more than bandits, but they were soldiers, knowing how to handle weapons, and aware that in battle their lives depended upon discipline, and that courage was no substitute for skill.

Ten thousand men: this was perhaps the total strength which Renzo really had with which to oppose that force of 22,000 men now five days' march away. Even the sanguine Renzo was aware of a discrepancy of numbers; but he thought that soldiers, like any other commodity, could be obtained for money. There was, however, no more money available, Armellino said firmly, and the Pope backed him up. It was precisely for this reason, he said querulously, that he had dismissed the Bande Nere four months before. Renzo turned to the civil governor, Girolamo Rossi, a man who had almost as bad a reputation as Armellino for the rapacious gathering of taxes. But they had squeezed that particular sponge dry, Rossi declared; they dared not risk a repetition of the previous September when the citizens of Rome had passively supported the Colonna raid because they believed they were overtaxed. However, Rossi went on, they could perhaps raise a voluntary sum from the richest citizens: they stood to lose the most and, in any case, invariably paid the least in taxation. He therefore undertook to arrange a meeting of the heads of the richest families in the city.

There was perhaps no greater indication of the sheer wealth of Rome than the size of the crowd which thronged into the governor's palace on the Capitoline Hill. Over three thousand were present, and the crush was so great that the meeting was moved to the vast church of Ara Coeli which stood upon the other spur of the Hill. For all his miserly habits and avaricious ways, Rossi was a fluent speaker. He mounted the pulpit and, looking down upon the sea of faces, he began to speak. He told how Clement had actually considered withdrawing from Rome: France had offered him asylum and there, though in exile, he would be free of the intolerable pressures placed upon him in Italy. But he had decided that his place lay here, with his children. And should filial love fail to move these rich men, Rossi went on to point out the fate that would befall them all, should Rome fall to the barbarians. Surely it was better to give a little now, than to risk losing all – losing all under singularly terrible circumstances? Therefore, let the citizens open their purses, confident that they were defending not only the Vicar of Christ but also their own hearths and homes.

At the end of his eloquent speech, Rossi must have been much heartened by the identity of the first man who came forward. He was Domenico Massimi, reputed to be the richest man in Rome, and who could have undoubtedly paid out of his own pocket for the entire garrison, for as long as it was needed, and still been scarcely incommoded. This man, whose handsome new palace contained a fortune in works of art, whose personal staff numbered more than 500, who had parted with thousands of ducats for his daughters' dowries, now came solemnly forward and handed over 100 ducats, a sum he might have given in casual largesse. Others followed, and a sensible if woefully delayed attempt to finance Rome's defence ended in farce.

The action of those rich men in the Ara Coeli showed not only the degree to which the Curia had become alienated from the city, but how the citizens themselves had become alienated from reality. Presumably, Massimi and his wealthy followers thought that Clement was only pretending to be bankrupt, and that Rossi's action was simply a manouevre designed to make them pay for something which they felt was the Pope's responsibility. They certainly went to remarkable lengths to humiliate Rossi, the civil representative of the Curia, for it was unlikely that Massimi's action was spontaneous. But it never seems to have crossed their minds that, whether or no the plea was genuine, there was a very real and terrible danger now approaching Rome like a thunderbolt.

Nobody troubled to find out: each went to his home, and, doubtless, there regaled his chuckling family and friends with the story of the latest discomfiture suffered by Pope Clement VII.

The rich men had failed Rome in her hour of need but that, after all, was to be expected of rich men who believed that their money-bags could pave a way for them out of all dangers and difficulties. Renzo turned now to the true strength of Rome, the people itself, specifically to the militia of the Regions. It had been the great Emperor Augustus himself who had first divided the city into *rioni* and they had survived the vicissitudes of fifteen hundred years, bearing testimony to the city's resilience and resistance to change. There were fourteen Regions all told, each with its own captain (the *caporione*), its own badge and banner, and even its own customs. Watchmen patrolled the borders of each, jealously guarding its rights, and prepared to call out the militia on any sign of an infringement of those rights by the neighbouring Regions. During the long, dark centuries when the popes had been absent or too feeble to control the city, the regional councils and the regional militia had been the only vestiges of civic authority to oppose the ruthless violence of the barons. But over the past century, as the papal Curia had exercised an ever greater degree of control over every aspect of life in the city, so the Regions' need for self-defence had declined. They had turned their energies towards ceremonies and festivals and games. During the great horse races, which were one of the sights of Rome, when riderless horses thundered down the Corso to the Palazzo Venezia, the Regions occupied cherished places along the route, each decorated in its appropriate colours and symbols, to cheer on their fancy. In the great festivals of the Church, and on such special occasions as a papal coronation, representatives of the regions, massed behind their banners, were given pride of place along with representatives of the great, the ambassadors and orators and agents of foreign powers. Tournaments had taken the place of street battles; and the caporioni might now spend as much time debating whether, or how much, a particular young girl should be dowered, or discussing the quality of the provisions in the regional market, as once they had spent, perhaps, debating whether to attack or join an enemy.

However, although their social functions had changed, the Regions remained unchanged in structure. Built into that structure was the statutory compulsion that, should the Lord of Rome have need of military assistance, the caporioni must call out the militia. The Lord of Rome was indubitably in need of military assistance and the call therefore went out to the caporioni. In theory, the caporioni should have then sent out their drummers to summon all ablebodied men to the largest square in the Region. The drummers went out: through the dark and narrow alleys they swaggered, rattling their urgent summons which should have brought out at least 14,000 men, tumbling over each other to rush to the designated square and there await their Lord's orders. In fact, only six of the fourteen Regions mustered.

The mockery of the rich men in Ara Coeli, and the lethargy of the poor men in a thousand unknown alleyways, had the same cause. Rich and poor, common and noble had alike been debilitated by the enervating atmosphere of Rome. As the popes had usurped more and more of the Regions' powers, a calm had been brought, it was true, to the notoriously violent city of Rome – but this was at the cost of virtually disenfranchising the inhabitants. The rich man had the power which naturally comes from gold but, excluded from the machinery of government (since that machinery was now almost wholly operated by ecclesiastics), he had no responsibility to any person outside his immediate family. The common man had neither responsibility nor power. Because of Rome's peculiar, indeed, unique social structure, the majority of the common people had no regular work, subsisting, for the most part, as parasites upon the Curia, upon those drawn to Rome – or worse.

The Venetian ambassador Mocenigo noted in one of his despatches that 'Almost all the native inhabitants of Rome are without a trade, whence almost all live in poverty – for which reason the women mostly sell their honour very easily and also that of their young daughters. This dishonour is, for the most part, the result of need . . .'. Mocenigo might have been exaggerating, but he was merely repeating the opinion of the Romans themselves. Judging by the words of Roman chroniclers like Infessura, the reader might be forgiven for believing that not only Rome's major trade, but its only trade, was prostitution and its auxiliaries. There were reputed to be some 30,000 prostitutes in the city in 1524 – an obviously impossible total, for, with a population of under 80,000, it implied that every female between the ages of 10 and 70 sold her sexual favours.

Cardinal Armellino, scenting another source of taxation, had organised a census, sorting out the professionals from the casuals, and thereby not only provided statistics for the profession in Rome, but also incidentally gave a statistical explanation for the plight of the ordinary Roman citizen. Out of 1,411 prostitutes only 198 were Romans: the rest came from other Italian cities and from all over Europe: from Spain, Poland, Greece, France, England, and one solitary girl from Turkey.

If, when he said that all the 'native inhabitants of Rome' were without a trade, Mocenigo meant Roman-born, he was talking of only 16% of the city's population: perhaps 13,000 people in all. The plum jobs in Rome very rarely indeed went to Romans. It was a commonplace that the artists who were busily turning the city into one of the great showpieces of the world almost invariably came from outside the city: from Florence, Siena, Perugia, Venice, Mantua. But also at the humdrum level of trade and commerce, foreigners dominated the city, with the vital banking trade that fuelled all entirely in Florentine hands. Mocenigo certainly exaggerated when he declared that most Romans had no trade: the craft guilds were relatively powerful in the city. But these were, for the most part, service industries: bakers, cobblers, taverners, in their turn heavily dependent upon the foreigners who overwhelmingly formed the bulk of the population. Most of these foreigners would, in time, regard themselves as Roman but until they were assimilated their loyalties and interests lay elsewhere.

Small wonder, therefore, that the 'militia' responded as sluggishly to the call to arms as their social superiors had responded contemptuously to the call for money. Rome's predicament was no concern of theirs: for the 'foreign' resident, the city was merely a place to be exploited, while the 'native' Roman had been so long accustomed to having all civic decisions made for him, that he could see no particular reason now to put his body at risk in order to defend yet another remote and incomprehensible principle.

But Renzo da Ceri, who certainly did not lack optimism, was not yet defeated. There were the servants of the vast domestic apparatus which served the Curia, the cooks and grooms and butlers and butchers who swarmed in their hundreds in the great palaces. There were even, for that matter, the artists and, by a typical quirk of the military mind, Renzo decided that sculptors were best employed in serving the guns – a decision which was to bring the swaggering genius Benvenuto Cellini into the very front line of defence. These improbable recruits were dragged out of their kitchens and stables and studios, and weapons were thrust into their hands. They were to prove worse than useless, for, when the time came for them to exercise their martial arts, scores of them deserted to the invaders, preferring to join in the pillage rather than place themselves at risk.

But while Renzo was optimistically drilling his scullions and stablelads, the military machine they were supposed to oppose was advancing inexorably southward. On 2 May it was reported passing Viterbo, less than fifty miles to the north and, for the first time, Clement appears to have become aware of his imminent, personal peril. Until now, his fears had been fears for his offices. Abruptly, there was substituted for the abstract picture of Emperor dominating Pope, the very real picture of the body of Pope Clement VII dangling from one of the battlements of Sant' Angelo. Clement had never really appreciated the force of anti-clerical, anti-papal feeling that had suddenly found vivid expression through Martin Luther. How could he? All his life had been spent as an administrator dealing with other administrators. Heresy was an aberration which could be dealt with through the normal channels – until now, when it appeared like a ravening wolf at the very gates of Rome. The motivation of the Spanish mercenaries and Lutheran landsknechts was cash, not conscience: but Clement, too, had heard of Frundsburg's halter, and it would have taken an unimaginative man not to fear the worst. A messenger was sent off to the Duke of Urbino, at that moment leisurely making his way through Tuscany, urging him to hasten to the aid of Rome, but Clement seems to have had but little hope. Du Bellay, the French ambassador, had an audience with him on that morning. 'I spent an hour with the Pope', he noted in his despatch. 'It is difficult to express the terror he is in but I tried to inspire him with a little courage. He wants Renzo to collect 1,000 men but it was impossible to raise as many ducats.'

Du Bellay, the foreigner, seems to have been better acquainted with the true state of the papal treasury than the native Romans. So, too, was the English ambassador, Gregorio Casale: he and du Bellay, after assessing the situation, actually decided to pawn their personal belongings and lend the few thousand ducats so raised to Clement. The Pope was, indeed, in desperate straits for money. Before that awful month was over he would be reduced to breaking up the great ceremonial tiara in order to sell the jewels in it; but now he limited himself to selling cardinals' hats. It was a measure that again and again had been urged upon him by his advisers and his allies, the Venetian ambassador contemptuously remarking that he made more fuss over selling a few red bonnets than others had made over disposing of entire kingdoms. Creating cardinals for cash was an established custom which many a pope had been glad to adopt when hard pressed for money, for cardinal was a political, not a religious appointment. However, while this practice did not qualify as simony, it offended Clement's personal sense of honour. He had no choice but to follow it now, and with bitter reluctance he assented to the transaction; six new cardinals received their broad-brimmed, tasselled, crimson hats for 40,000 florins apiece.

Among them was the hat intended for Isabella d'Este's son, Ercole, the hat for which she had come to Rome four months before, stubbornly refusing to leave until she had received it. Two days after the transaction the hat was delivered to her personally at her residence in the Colonna Palace, but by then it was too late for her to leave, for Bourbon's army was in sight of the city. She was probably safer in a place where her nephew and sons knew her exact whereabouts than travelling in her conspicuous coach across a Campagna crowded with refugees and the bandits preying upon them. But even if she had had the chance of leaving, she probably would not have availed herself of it and so lost a front seat as the curtain went up on the drama.

Clement had, as usual, made his decision too late. The 240,000 florins raised by the sale of the cardinals' hats was exactly the sum that Bourbon had demanded three months earlier; if the transaction had taken place then, and the money had been promptly paid over, then there is little doubt but that the march on Rome would have lost its impetus, indeed, its major object. Even now, there might have been time to halt the army with the colossal ransome, if the actual gold had been available. But it was not available: during the past few days the cannier merchants and bankers had been hastening out of the city, hiring or buying up every possible means of transport to remove their precious bodies, goods and gold. The new cardinals or their representatives were eagerly prepared to write promissory notes for the ransome, but it would have been as much use waving a promissory note before a hungry mercenary as before a hungry bear. Clement had compromised with his conscience to no purpose whatsoever.

However, Renzo da Ceri looked upon his motley band of defenders and saw that they were good. Of all the mistakes and miscalculations that led up to the Sack of Rome, none is more bizarre or mysterious than this optimism of Renzo da Ceri which led directly and inexorably to the destruction of the city. He was not a great soldier, but he was an experienced one: he must have been perfectly well aware that a scullion was not turned into a fighter by having a sword put into his hand. By the most optimistic calculation, Renzo's professional soldiers were outnumbered two to one; the mob who made up the rest of the garrison were scarcely of value, even as auxiliaries. Yet on 4 May Renzo was not only able to write to Giberti saying that 'Rome is well defended', he also urged that the military aid requested by Clement just two days earlier should be cancelled.

On receiving Clement's anguished plea, the Duke of Urbino had detached the condottiere Guido Rangone, at the head of 8,000 infantry and 500 horse, and sent them hastening ahead; not to have done so would have appeared as a brand of treachery which even Urbino could not commit without lasting shame. By forced marches, Rangone and his men had almost caught up with Bourbon, arriving at Viterbo the day after the mercenaries had left. A messenger had arrived in Rome from Rangone only that morning, bearing what he fondly thought was good news. But they were no longer needed, Renzo insisted: they should rejoin the main body in preparation for one single, massive blow in Bourbon's rear. All that was required were the cavalry and the 500 arquebusiers. Giberti, the administrator, reasonably enough accepted the recommendations of Renzo da Ceri, the professional soldier. The Romans were in good heart, he wrote to Rangone. 'Apart from the confidence which our Holy Father reposes in his people, he has made excellent provisions for defence. There is no need to have any fear whatsoever.'

One scents treachery, seemingly the only possible explanation for Renzo's quite ludicrous optimism, and particularly in view of the fact that he was among the first to run after the enemy broke through. But there is no evidence that he gained anything through his fatal counsel. His own son, in fact, was killed in the first few hours of the assault. Renzo was simply a working soldier, competent enough in a subordinate role but quite useless as a commander in a crisis, for he lacked the essential quality for military greatness: the ability to put himself in the enemy's shoes. He had done his sums correctly and honestly enough: he knew the enemy had no artillery, nor did they have the reserves of food to permit a siege. There was a wall between Rome and the mercenaries, and a garrison which, though small, was quite large enough to stop hungry men scrambling up a sheer wall more than thirty feet high. Therefore. . . . But he had omitted to take into account the very degree of desperation of these men and, more subtly, the degree of corruption and indifference of the defenders. 'He was little obeyed or trusted', Marcello Alberini remembered, but he did not wholly blame him, for the Romans lacked all will to defend themselves. 'And I think it was the will of God that they should have been so deprived of judgement and courage.'

Alberini was just an ordinary citizen, striving to recall the details that led up to those terrible May days, and was possibly prone to see the hand of God everywhere. But many other, and more seasoned observers were tempted to see the working out of fate in all this. Remarking on Renzo's optimism, Guicciardini wrote that 'it was no less wonderful – if it be a wonder that men know not how, or are unable, to resist fate – that the Pontiff, who used to despise Renzo da Ceri above all other generals, should now throw himself wholly into his arms and repose an entire confidence in his judgement'.

Not the least remarkable thing which struck both the sixteen-year-old Roman and the fifty-year-old Florentine statesman was Clement's own sudden fortitude. 'The confidence and benignity which he demonstrated seemed miraculous to everybody', was Alberini's opinion, unwittingly echoed by

Guicciardini years later: 'Whereas he was usually timorous and daunted at lesser dangers, and had been several times inclined to abandon Rome, now, on the contrary, in so great a danger, divested of his nature, he had the constancy to stay in the city with such great hopes of defending himself as if he had taken upon him to be an agent for his enemies.' The barometer of Clement's spirits rose and fell dizzyingly during these last few days, responding instantaneously to the smallest stimulus. Thus, barely a day after du Bellay had found him in a state of terror at news of the imminence of the enemy's arrival, the success of a trivial skirmish sent his confidence soaring again. A handful of Bourbon's advance guard had attempted to cross the Tiber by boat, had been pounced upon by a greatly superior mounted patrol and, after a short, sharp action the survivors had been brought into Rome in triumph.

But the people were as volatile as their Lord. It was on the Friday – 3 May – that Clement, on his tour through the city, received the enthusiastic applause of the citizens. And yet, on that same day the great gates of the city had to be closed – not so much to keep the enemy out, as to keep the citizens in. Over the past week there had been an ever-increasing exodus, by road and river. Most of the refugees were 'foreigners', merchants from other cities who saw no particular reason why they should go down with the Romans. The river route was particularly popular: a merchant could step with all his goods and servants and, above all, his gold from the stone quay of the Ripetto on to a boat, and from there be wafted swiftly, comfortably, safely to Ostia on the coast twenty miles away. And from Ostia one could take ship to the wide world. The craziest bark could be sold over and over again: watermen who had considered themselves lucky if they picked up as much as a ducat for a week's grinding work now had bags of clinking metal thrust eagerly at them. And when the press on the quay became too great, or the price of a passage just too usurious, there were the great consular roads, whose great basalt blocks had survived the neglect of a millenium.

The via Cassia was closed: that was the road down which Bourbon's army would come tramping, for it led directly from Viterbo to the bridge crossing the Tiber to the Porta Milvio. But there were the via Flaminia offering safety in the hills beyond Terni: the via Appia arrowing southward by the Alban Hills; the via Nomentana going eastward; and the via Casilina going south-west. Hourly the caravans passed through the city gates; men huddled together for protection, facing an immediate uncertainty but travelling towards safety. And those who had to remain watched them sullenly or jeeringly, and there was a restlessness through the city that belied the brave words and gestures. And Clement forbade any further flights, under pain of confiscation of goods and imprisonment of person, and though the 'foreigners' protested, he was adamant.

Because Rome was the capital of Christendom, there were living here many members of the 'enemy' nations: Spanish and Germans and Ghibelline Italians attached to the court of Rome. These people became immensely popular suddenly, as Italians with goods to hide or loved ones to protect implored their protection against their compatriots. So it was that Isabella d'Este found shelter in the palace of that Colonna family who, more than anybody, had brought the disaster to Rome; and young Marcello Alberini found himself in the beautiful Cancelleria, the palace of the Chancery, that belonged to Pompeo Colonna in his office of Vice-Chancellor of the Roman Church.

By Saturday, 4 May, Renzo da Ceri had done what he could to make Rome ready. He had concentrated the best of his garrison to the north-west and west of the city and his calculations in this case were correct. It would, indeed, have been difficult to make a mistake in this matter. An enemy travelling south from Viterbo had no choice but to travel down the western bank of the Tiber. The bulk of Rome was built on the eastern bank, and so the green, swiftly flowing Tiber formed the best possible defence of the city. In fairness to Renzo, it must be said that at an early stage of his preparations he had planned to have the bridges destroyed. But, according to the French ambassador du Bellay, there was an uproar 'because the bridges were too beautiful to be destroyed' – or more likely, because the inhabitants of the suburbs on the western bank had a lively objection to being cut off.

The Emperor Aurelius had continued the line of his walls along the river's western bank. The Aurelian walls ran along the upper slopes of the Janiculum, just below the crest of the hill, enclosing the area which was to become known as Trastevere (Rome-over-the-water). Aurelius did not continue his walls to the Vatican Hill: the area had no particular significance for him, as there was little there in his day apart from a burial ground and the Circus of Nero. It was not until the ninth century that Pope Leo IV walled in the Vatican City which had developed there (incidentally giving it his own name as the Leonine City), and included as part of its fortifications the tomb of the Emperor Hadrian now known as the Castello Sant' Angelo.

Forty feet high and more than ten feet wide in places, crowned with a score of towers, the walls of the Vatican City formed a vast peninsula of reddish-brown brick jutting out from the main mass of Rome. Bourbon's army would have to march past it to get at the soft underbelly represented by Trastevere, although even here the ancient Aurelian walls would have proved a formidable barrier had they been kept in reasonable repair. At this point, however, the walls ran through the vineyards of Cardinals Armellino and Cessi who had treated the city's defences as though they were private property. A small house had been built against the wall at one point, its projections offering both shelter and foothold to any determined assailant. In his report to his government the Venetian ambassador Domenico Venier noted with amazement that there was actually a gap in the wall running through Cessi's garden. Repair work was in progress and neither Renzo, nor Giuliano Leni, the inspector of the walls, had done anything to reinforce the gap. Ironically, a great deal of trouble had been taken to dig a ditch in the Belvedere Court in the Vatican – inside the massive Vatican walls. It gave the enemy a laugh, Giovio noted sourly, 'but we felt more like crying'.

Renzo divided his defence into semi-independent sections, using his professionals as a core to stiffen the amateurs. Lucantonio Tomassino, lieutenant of the late Giovanni de' Medici, together with the remaining 2,000 of the Bande Nere defended the vulnerable section where the Vatican walls joined the Aurelian. He had under his command, as gunners, the painter Lorenzotto and the sculptor Raffaello da Montelupo: the region of Parione, which supplied the auxiliaries for this section, was a favourite residential area of artists of one kind or another. Among those who guarded the Porta Settimiana, the southernmost gate on the west bank, was Renzo's own son, Giovanni Paolo, and Ranuccio Farnese, of the great Roman family. Ranuccio had been among those who took part in a harassing operation on Bourbon's troops near Viterbo and was to give a good account of himself in Rome.

Renzo placed his second-in-command, Orazio Baglione, and Antonio Santa Croce, the captain-general of artillery, on the east bank. If Bourbon decided to cross the river by the first bridge upstream, the Ponte Milvio, the main attack would fall upon the ancient heart of the city; and a huge section of the wall there had been torn down by citizens seeking building material. Santa Croce had done an excellent job siting his guns not only to cover this vulnerable point but also throughout the city, wherever they would be most effective: on the walls, on the crests of hills, on the bridges, commanding the entrances to the streets on the left bank. He had done what he could to cover that fatal gap on the west bank, and backed the first line of defences with well-sited emplacements leading towards the bridges: it was not his fault that the central control of defence collapsed with such suddenness as to render his whole elaborate system useless.

On Saturday evening, shortly before sunset, a mounted trumpeter appeared outside the walls. Protected by his sacred office as herald, he was left unmolested as he shrilled his ritual defiance and then rode forward to pass over a letter at the gatehouse. The letter was short and to the point: Bourbon demanded a ransome of 300,000 ducats, payable immediately, or else. . . . No reply was made and the trumpeter, once more shrilling defiance, wheeled his horse around and galloped back to the army, encamped now at Isola Farnese some twelve miles from Rome.

Bourbon was not surprised by the reception given to his trumpeter. The man's fruitless mission had been undertaken simply to satisfy the tender conscience of Bartolomeo Gattinara, Bourbon's Spanish adviser. Gattinara, Regent of Naples, and brother of the Emperor's powerful chancellor, Mercurino Gattinara, appears to have regarded himself as keeper of the imperial conscience. During Saturday, 4 May, Gattinara took Bourbon on one side. Did he really intend to go ahead with the mad scheme? Was he really going to attack Rome? It was madness, Gattinara insisted, and could have only one of two outcomes. If the attack was successful, the troops would be uncontrollable and their rape of the mother city of Christendom would plunge all concerned into eternal infamy and that included his Emperor. But if the attack was repulsed, what then? The soldiers would drift southward like a horde of locusts and the only worthwhile goal south of Rome was – the Spanish Kingdom of Naples.

Considering that Gattinara had left his plea until they were scarcely two hours from Rome, it looked very much as though his main object was formally to disassociate his Emperor from what was about to happen. Bourbon evidently thought so, and it was with more than a touch of irony that he agreed to send one last demand to Pope Clement. And yet, it was not wholly an empty gesture. Bourbon, like most of those involved, just could not credit that the treasury of St Peter's could not yield the 300,000 ducats' ransome in cash. He, too, had heard of the sale of cardinals' hats and the sum he demanded had been calculated on that knowledge. It was a large, but not impossible sum. It would give each of his men some 15 ducats apiece, and with that amount clinking in their wallets, a ravening army of mercenaries would have been turned into relatively docile visitors all eager to spend their money in the fabulous city. Rome would have got back a large part of the money within hours via her shopkeepers and taverners and prostitutes. And afterwards? Bourbon would probably have taken his men on southward, once they had been sated with food and drink and women. Like Gattinara, he was perfectly well aware that the next major goal south of Rome was Naples; unlike Gattinara, he felt no particular urge to protect this outpost of the Spanish kingdom. The crown of Naples had changed hands many times in the past and there was no reason now why it should not be placed on the head of the Duke of Bourbon. As a collateral descendant of the Angevines who had once ruled in Naples, he had as much right to that crown as the Emperor, a descendant of the house of Aragon who had wrested it from the Angevines.

But all that was in the future. The immediate need was to rally his troops and complete the last few miles to Rome. Gattinara, on learning of the failure of his suggested mission, shrugged and contented himself with writing a long report to the Emperor. No other attempt was made, at any level, to deflect or divert the assault. Bourbon had chosen to halt at Isola Farnese in order to gather his men into a compact mass. Despite the urgency of their march, the men had become scattered over a relatively wide area in their endless search for food, and it was no simple task to get them assembled in a central area that offered no particular advantages in terms of food or shelter. All through the mild spring night the trumpets shrilled, the drums rattled, the torches flared as, company by company, the army assembled according to its national groups: 14,000 Germans, 5,000 Spaniards – and 3,000 Italians. Here was demonstrated the enduring tragedy of Italy: a substantial part of the force about to hurl itself upon Italy's prime city for purposes of booty were themselves Italians, many bearing the same name as those defenders behind the wall. There was a Sciarra Colonna here, and a Stefano Colonna standing at the head of his troops outside the basilica of St Peter's. There was a Pier Luigi Farnese here, and a Ranuccio Farnese just inside the Porta Setiimania. Here, too, was Luigi Gonzaga, while in Rome his mother Isabella d'Este was admiring the hat she had just obtained for his brother. So the correspondences could be extended, family by family, demonstrating yet again that the worst enemy of the Italians was ever the Italians.

An army of 22,000 men, without artillery and with very little in the way of baggage and camp followers, covers perhaps a mile of ground, when in line of march, and takes a correspondingly lengthy time to assemble. The vanguard was able to snatch a brief rest while they waited for their comrades behind to find their places but the last company had scarcely fallen in behind its standard bearer when the trumpets sounded the advance and the long snake began to move down the road to Rome. There was no real reason why the men should not have had a good night's rest before the battle, completing the march the following day. But there was little food or drink to tempt them to linger and both leaders and led were too keyed up to rest. They had been seven months upon this journey and their feverish desire to end it and to stand at last before the walls of Rome impelled them on in the early hours. They moved in an eerie relative silence, for the heavy boots of most had long since disintegrated and they shuffled rather than marched in makeshift sandals. But their swords were honed, their lances sharpened, their arquebuses oiled. They could still kill.

By the time they came in sight of Rome the early morning sun was shining in their faces, creating that reflection upon their armour which the watchers in Rome saw as a river of light approaching their city.

Chapter XI

The Attack

Dotted with pine and plane trees, the Janiculum looms above the western region of Rome like an immense green bastion. Halfway up its steep slope the pious monks of the Hiernymite Order had built a hermitage a century earlier, dedicating it to the Egyptian hermit St Onophrius. The exotic nature of S. Onofrio was only in its origins: the church itself was a beautifully austere building with a simple cloister. Here Bourbon made his headquarters. He had not chosen the hermitage for its beauty, or even because it could offer reasonably comfortable accommodation; he had no intention of staying there for more than a single night. Its main attraction was that from the little plateau in front of the church it was possible to gain a panorama of Rome, from the Pincian Hill in the north to the Porta Latina in the south. The view from the Janiculum was one of the sights of Rome: generations of tourists, visitors and pilgrims had puffed their way up to the crest and there breathlessly marvelled at the golden city spread below their feet.

Bourbon would have been less than human had he not marvelled too, for this was his first, and probably his last, visit to the mother city of Europe. Rome had a significance for him, half Italian himself, which was denied to the Germans and Spaniards under his command. The spectacle of the vast basilica to his left, rising above the bones of the Apostle, had an additional stimulus for him, wholly Catholic, and it was rendered all the more poignant and bitter by the fact that his Holy Father, the Bishop of Rome, had formally excommunicated him the day before.

Charles de Montpensier, Duke of Bourbon, aged thirty-seven, widowed, ruined, exiled, standing outside his staff quarters at the end of his long odyssey is a figure of tragic dignity. Yet that remoteness which was his dominant characteristic obscures his essential nature, his true motives, from posterity. His soldiers might indeed have followed him 'to the devil', but no man apparently ever got close enough to him to probe his inmost thoughts – certainly, no man with the ability to record those thoughts in writing. Bourbon had arrived at the end of his journey: in a little over eighteen hours he would be dead; and the only words directly attributed to him during that period are the six words uttered at the moment of his death. It is understandable that contemporary historians, looking back at that enigmatic figure, striving to understand the motives that brought him here, at the last, to the green hill of the Janiculum, should have put words into his mouth. Even the great German writer Gregorovius over three centuries later could not resist the temptation of giving meaning to Bourbon's wasted life and suicidal end by imputing to him a final speech of noble sentiments:

> From the Janiculum Frundsburg's landsknechts gazed with savage hatred on the Vatican, formerly the goal of the longings and pilgrimages of their ancestors, to them nothing but the awful seat of Antichrist. With justice their leader might have told them that there below was the great manufactory of those artificial politics by which peoples and kings were perplexed and entangled, and driven into bloody wars in order to give the Pope dominion of the world. There, almost within range of their muskets, trembled the enemy of the Emperor . . . they themselves appeared as the avengers of the long prevailing wrong which their fatherland had suffered at the hands of the Roman priesthood . . .

But here Gregorovius allowed his sympathies as a German and a Lutheran to overcome his objectivity as the historian of Rome. The Germans who may, or may not, have seen themselves as the avengers of 'the wrong which their fatherland had suffered at the hands of the Roman priesthood' formed little more than half the host that now threatened Rome. The remainder were good Catholics, as was Bourbon himself. There is no clearer evidence of the desperate condition in which this army had existed for months than that there had been no sectarian violence among them, the sheer problem of survival absorbing all their enemies.

Luigi Guicciardini, brother of the historian Francesco, gave a far more realistic picture of Bourbon appealing to his men's cupidity, underlining their likely fate should they fail. 'He reminded them of their hardships – the intolerable hunger and total lack of money – throughout their march to the walls of Rome. But now, if they would only show that fire which he was certain was in them, within a few hours they would be rich and safe and able without difficulty to enjoy the incredible riches of many prelates.' Luigi Guicciardini probably had the speech from one of those who heard it, and certainly his version describes a sentiment that sounds more likely to appeal to a mercenary, whatever his nationality or religion, than any high-flown notions of defending the purity of Christianity or chastising the enemy of their Emperor.

Bourbon had divided his force into two. Upstream, a detachment under his cousin and loyal follower, Philibert, Prince of Orange, was to launch a feint upon the Ponte Milvio. Bourbon was far too good a soldier to commit a substantial body to one river crossing, but a vigorous action by young Philibert would draw off a disproportionate number of the defenders. And there was need for such a diversion. From his position on the Janiculum Bourbon could see that he had not one, but three cities to attack. On the west bank the Leonine, or Vatican City and Trastevere formed two separate walled enclaves: both would have to be taken in order to defend his rear as the army advanced across the Tiber bridges. Even when, or if, these bridges were captured, his men would still have to fight their way on to the east bank in the face of point-blank fire from Santa Croce's guns.

The attack would have to take place within twenty-four hours, for his men now had provisions for only that length of time, and he would have to stake everything on that first assault. There would be no time to regroup, to have second thoughts, to try another tactic. Almost hourly, he expected to hear that Rangone had arrived as vanguard of the main body under Urbino. Rangone had only 6,000 men but they could harass the besiegers, slowing down the action, clinging to them like a terrier clinging to a badger until its master arrives for the kill. Bourbon, indeed, would have liked to have launched the attack the moment the men were in a favourable position but they were exhausted after that last rapid march from Isola Farnese. The afternoon was passed in the deceptive calm of pre-battle, the army briefly becoming 22,000 individuals each pursuing what seemed to him the most important or useful activity before putting his life at hazard.

It was then that Bourbon showed himself as a great soldier in the classical tradition. 'Fully armoured and wearing his white surcoat he was seen everywhere, riding now here, now there among the troops, comforting and encouraging them, reminding the Spanish of their deeds in Milan, telling the Italians that they must not be shown up by the Oltremontani – the foreigners, encouraging the Germans with hopes of booty.' Such was Luigi Guicciardini's memory of the Duke of Bourbon, his admiration for the man showing through his stilted words. Mounted on his great charger and dressed in that gleaming silver surcoat, Bourbon could be distinguished very clearly from the walls. But the defenders, too, seemed to have drifted into the pre-battle trance, and were waiting passively for the enemy to take the initiative; and so Bourbon went about his work unmolested although many times he was well within range of arquebus.

Bourbon himself seems to have been quite calm and relaxed during these last few hours of his life. With the absence of hope, perhaps, there was a compensating absence of fear, his unhappy spirit achieving a private equil-ibrium after three tormented years. Certainly, he was calm enough to enjoy a profound if brief sleep during the early hours of the evening, being awakened around midnight by the tremendous clatter of the bells of Rome ringing *a stormo*. He ordered the drummers to sound the stand-to, the combined roar of the drums ascending to the defenders on the wall as a response to the challenge of the bells. He then made his confession to his chaplain, Michele Fortin, and confided his will to him: if he was killed, all should go to the Emperor. This was largely a formal gesture, however, for the Duke of Bourbon who once could challenge the might of the King of France and match any magnate in the land ducat for ducat, possessed now only what was on his back and in his tent. He was as dependent as the meanest, humblest footsoldier on the outcome of this battle for the very necessities of life.

The mood of his soldiers was, like his own, fatalistic and was admirably summed up in a letter which one of the officers, Sigismondo della Torre, wrote to the Marquis Gonzaga of Mantua five days later. Tersely, Sigismondo described their long and painful march southward, telling how the Spaniards had nearly mutinied on discovering that they were going to attack Rome, not Florence; how they had ridden 'through such terrible days, by such strange roads, in such vile weather, with such great perils that one can scarce describe it'. They had arrived outside Rome on 5 May and camped 'on the side of the Belvedere and Trastevere. And having found ourselves in such a poverty-stricken, starving place, with Rome and the Tiber before us and a great army behind us, there was nothing for us to do but take fortune by the forelock. . . . So on the 6, which was last Monday, a little before dawn, that poor fellow Monsignore de Bourbon led an attack upon the walls above the Porta San Pancarzio and all the camp went to the battle, shoulder to shoulder.'

The ideal place to have launched an attack would have been on the western wall of the Vatican, for the vast bulk of the new St Peters' and the Vatican Palace itself would have protected the attackers from the guns of Sant' Angelo. But they had no artillery with which to make a breach and therefore were obliged to attack the lower, more ruinous walls of the city itself. As they approached the wall, they should have moved into a curtain of artillery fire; but the extraordinary mist that arose at dawn covered them. It was an act of God, Reissner thought: 'Clearly God manifested himself for them: at the moment they advanced to the attack, there fell a thick mist which covered and protected them so that the papalists could not see from where the attack was coming.' Reissner was recording the scene from outside the walls, but a friar from the convent of S. Pietro in Vincolo, within the city itself, confirmed the devastating result of the mist. Telling his story to the Doge of Venice after he had escaped from Rome, the friar reported: 'When the enemy entered Rome there was the thickest mist around them that was ever seen.' He said that, although he stood on a balcony near the wall, he could see nothing. Under cover of this natural protection, the besiegers were able to advance to the very foot of the wall and prop up their makeshift ladders. All night long the defenders had been puzzled by the sounds of seemingly random movement in the vineyards that bordered the walls, and only when the ladders appeared did they realise that Bourbon's men had been uprooting the trellises to make their flimsy siege equipment.

But the defenders were in good heart and, with every advantage on their side, succeeded in repelling that first desperate wave by the simple expedient of throwing down the ladders. The attackers retreated in disorder and it was almost an even chance that the retreat might be a rout when Bourbon spurred his great horse forward, dismounted, and with a shout of encouragement, began to climb one of the ladders, his silver surcoat dulled with mist but still distinctive.

Meanwhile, on the wall immediately above him Benvenuto Cellini had arrived with two other young men, armed with an arquebus.

On reaching the walls we could see that famous army which was making every effort to enter the town. Upon the ramparts where we took our station, several young men were lying killed by the besiegers. The battle raged there desperately and there was the densest fog imaginable. I turned to Alessandro and said: 'Let us go home as soon as we can for there is nothing to do here: you see the enemies are mounting and our men are in flight.' Alessandro in a panic said: 'Would to God we had never come here', and turned in maddest haste to fly. I took him up somewhat sharply with these words: 'Since you have brought me here I must perform some action worthy of a man', and directing my arquebus where I saw the thickest and most serried troops of fighting men, I aimed exactly at one whom I remarked to be higher than the rest: the fog prevented me from being certain whether he was on horseback or foot. Then I turned to Alessandro and Cecchino and bade them discharge their arquebuses showing them how to avoid being hit by the besiegers. When we had fired two rounds apiece I crept cautiously up to the wall and observing among the enemy a most extraordinary confusion, I discovered afterwards that one of our shots had killed the Constable of Bourbon: and from what I subsequently learned, he was the man whom I had first noticed above the heads of the rest.

Cellini was dictating his story to an amanuensis years after and there were few details that were not improved in the telling, but his claim to be responsible for the death of Bourbon is by no means inherently improbable. Bourbon was actually on the ladder and not on foot or on horseback, but that might be due to a simple confusion of memory on Cellini's part. Bourbon was, indeed, killed by a shot from an arquebus, the same diabolical weapon that had despatched the knightly Bayard and Giovanni della Bande Nere. The shot struck Bourbon in the groin, severing an artery, hurling him from the ladder to lie in a widening pool of blood. 'Ah, Notre Dame! Je suis mort' were his last coherent words. He survived for a little over half an hour, but in a delirium, believing that he was still on that nightmare march, calling out 'A Rome! À Rome!' until he died.

Bourbon's death marked a turning point in the battle. It should have been the moment when the besiegers lost heart and withdrew. Instead, it was the besieged who left the walls. They were not running away, but carrying the wonderful news into the city that the terrible Bourbon was dead and the battle over. When they found they were wrong and that the fury of the landsknechts was redoubled, they lost their nerve; and what had begun as a frivolous dereliction of duty rapidly developed into a precipitate flight towards the safety of the bridges and the east bank. In vain the captains tried to stem the flight with violence. 'The generals Renzo da Ceri and Orazio Baglioni were wounding and slaughtering everybody who abandoned the defence of the walls', Cellini remembered, while the Frenchman du Bellay saw Renzo forcing men to mount the walls by beating them with a stick, 'but as soon as he had moved on they descended and ran away'.

The first of the besiegers gained the walls. According to some sources, the first was a Spaniard, Don Giovanni de Avalos who successfully climbed up Bourbon's ill-fated ladder, and gained the wall but was shot dead as he scrambled over. The Germans, naturally, gave the honour to one of their own number. Nicolas Seidenstücker, a giant of a man, survived long enough to create a beach-head for his comrades. Yet even now, the attackers could have been halted. They had been forced to concentrate their numbers in this one relatively small area, and the bulk of the defenders, too, could be concentrated upon them as they scrambled up their makeshift ladders. What doomed Rome was the presence of two small gaps in the walls.

Sigismondo della Torre entered through one of these gaps – the same, probably, that the Venetian ambassador Venier had noted. 'It was made with a pick-axe in the wall by the gate into the Belvedere. This was the first entrance and it was so badly defended that, despite the fact that we could pass through only one at a time, the cowardly defenders fled and the victory was simple.' The other gap was actually through the little house that was built against the wall. As Luigi Guicciardini described it, almost certainly from his own observation, the house had a small window at ground-floor level outside the city wall. This gave access to a cellar – apparently used as a cantina – but had been disused for so long that it was covered with a heap of earth and manure. However, though hidden, it was an appallingly vulnerable point in the wall, 'and one cannot deny that it was a great and most grave mistake to leave it so and it is not possible to excuse either Signor Renzo or those captains who had the duty to inspect the walls'. The little window was discovered, a few bold souls wriggled through, opened the street door on the other side, and found themselves in Rome. They were Spaniards and, according to Guicciardini, it was Renzo who discovered them. It could not have been more unfortunate. The commander-in-chief of the Roman defences seems totally to have lost his head. Gazing at them in horrified disbelief, he did not even attempt to draw his sword but then, as they advanced upon him, he turned and fled crying out at the top of his voice that everything was lost and that every man should save himself. He did not stop running until he had gained the Capitoline Hill on the other side of the river.

The defence collapsed. Sigismondo della Torre estimated that in the fighting in the suburbs 3,000 of the defenders were killed for the loss of only 60 or 70 of the attackers – evidence enough of a mass of tough professionals slicing into a large mass of bewildered amateurs. So swiftly did the defence collapse in his area that Sigismondo later calculated that the battle had lasted barely an hour and a half there, whereas fierce fighting continued, in fact, on the west bank until 1 p.m., some eight hours after the attack had commenced.

Not all the defenders that day were cowards: many remained behind to save the honour of the name of Rome and died at their posts. The militia from Parione suffered nearly 90% losses from their contingent; the company of the artillery commander Antonio Santa Croce, was totally wiped out; so, too, were the Bande Nere and the Swiss Guard, who fell fighting in and around St Peter's Square, guarding their last charge, the Vatican Palace. But these last could save only honour, not the city. The numbers of the invaders snowballed, each group which scrambled over the wall, or squeezed through a gap, hastening to reinforce their comrades inside to capture a gate or another stretch of wall and so bring in yet more.

Throughout the morning Clement had been in his private chapel, saying mass after mass, 'harvesting prayers' in Giovio's sardonic words. To his normal fears and uncertainties was added the sheer frustration created by the thick mist: again and again he hastened to his balcony, and strove to peer through that thick natural curtain to determine the course of the battle. But if he could not see, he could hear as closer and closer came the screams of pain and fear, the savage cries of triumph, the rattle of arquebus fire. And when the Swiss Guard fell in front of the basilica it was obvious that the Vatican itself must soon fall. His masses and prayers proving useless, Pope Clement again prepared to abandon his palace for the shelter of Sant' Angelo, so joining the hundreds who were streaming towards this one sure refuge in Rome.

He and his immediate entourage were luckier than most: instead of having to find their way through those crowded, veiled and murderous streets, they could walk safely overhead along that passageway that had been constructed precisely for this purpose. Clement was wearing the white robes and skullcap of his office, a dangerous distinction if one of the invaders should look up while he was scurrying along the walkway. Giovio took off his own purple cape and hood, and threw it over the Pope, symbolically extinguishing his God-given distinction, perhaps, but hiding him, too, from any sharpshooter.

The flight towards Sant' Angelo became a rout: 3,000 people had poured into the castle before the castellan, acting on his own initiative, let the portcullis drop, injuring and killing some of the poor wretches who happened to be passing through at that moment, and cutting off the only hope of safety to a panic-stricken crowd. Among them was Cardinal Armellino: he had had the indescribable anguish of witnessing the attackers tearing up his vineyard and now he was to be abandoned to them. He worked his way away from the mass of people, calling up to those in safety on the walkway high above him. Someone spotted his crimson garments and lowered a basket down to him, and he was drawn up the dizzy height like a load of groceries.

Cellini was among those who managed to reach Sant' Angelo in time.

On the instant that I entered, the captain Pallone de' Medici claimed me as being of the papal household, and forced me to abandon Alessandro which I did much against my will. I ascended to the keep and at the same moment Pope Clement came through the corridor into the castle. Having got into the castle in this way I attached myself to certain pieces of artillery under the command of a bombardier called Giuliano Fiorentino. Leaning there against the battlements, the unhappy man could see his house being sacked and his wife and children outraged. Fearing to strike his own folk, he dared not discharge the cannon, and flinging the burning fuse upon the ground, he wept as though his heart would break, and tore his cheeks with both his hands. Some of the other bombardiers were behaving in a like manner: seeing which, I took one of the matches, and got the assistance of a few men who were not overcome by their emotions. I aimed some swivels and falconets at points where I saw it would be useful and killed with them a good number of the enemy. Had it not been for this, the troops who poured into Rome that morning, and were marching straight upon the castle, might possibly have entered it with ease, because the artillery was doing them no damage.

Cellini's fellow artist and fellow gunner, the sculptor Raffaello da Montelup, had also been impressed into the artillery of Sant' Angelo and substantially supported Cellini's description.

> We stood there and looked on all that passed as if we had been spectators at a festa. It was impossible to fire for had we done so, we should have killed more of our own people than of the enemy. Between the Church of St Mary Transpontina and the gate of the castle there were four to five thousand people crowded together and, as far as we could see, hardly fifty landsknechts behind them. Two standardbearers of the latter forced their way through the turmoil with uplifted banners as far as the great gate of the castle, but were shot down at the head of the bridge.

The artists of Rome seem to have given a better account of themselves than many of the supposed soldiers: the goldsmith Bernardino Passeri killed many of the enemy and captured a standard before being cut down near the church of S. Spirito.

By mid-day the Borgo and the Leonine City were in the hands of the invaders and, as the hard core of defenders was wittled away, the tempo began to change from one of battle to one of massacre. Later, it was assumed that the death of Bourbon had been the worst possible thing that could have happened to Rome, as the troops had thereby lost the only man who could have controlled them. Nevertheless, even without Bourbon, a remarkably high level of discipline was maintained during the first few vital hours after entry had been forced. A mercenary army was known to be at its most vulnerable at the very moment of victory, for that was the moment when the soldiers were tempted to scatter in order to reap the booty that formed the major purpose of their existence as mercenaries. And during that critical period the defenders who kept their head could turn the tables. Philibert, Prince of Orange, who had succeeded to Bourbon's command, had ordered that no plundering was to take place until Rome had been secured. Soldiers in the first wave of the attackers had even been ordered to kill any draught animals they found, so that those who followed them would not be tempted to load the beasts with loot and slip away. Remarkably, the orders had been obeyed even though Orange quite lacked Bourbon's charisma. Here was another example of the quite unprecedented singleness of purpose that for many months had welded this heterogeneous mass of soldiers into a deadly fighting unit.

The plundering, malicious slaughter, and rape that did now begin to take place in the Borgo was therefore mostly the work of camp followers, the human hyenas that tagged behind all armies, and, as often as not, of citizens who had a grudge to settle. And yet it was a first, sinister herald of what was to come, the first unqualified indication that what had happened was not simply a diplomatic reversal, but a total military defeat which put some 90,000 people at the very slender mercy of their conquerors. The Leonina was, for the moment, spared the full impact of that fact for the guns of Sant' Angelo commanded both the main streets and the only bridge that led out of the area. Most of the gunners resembled Cellini rather than Raffaello being perfectly prepared to mow down their own as long as they also mowed down the enemy, and the bridge was interdicted. Temporarily baulked, the attackers turned their attention to the softer option of Trastevere. The Germans had already broken through by scaling the wall and now, with the mass of the attackers hurling themselves upon this second city and using the defenders' own artillery from the walls, the suburb fell within the hour.

By 1 p.m. fighting had died down on the west bank. There was a brief lull as the attackers regrouped, scoured the area for food and drink – for their first decent, if hurried, meal in days – and considered their next objective. They do not seem to have appreciated, even now, the full extent of their victory and certainly, in purely military terms, their situation was anything but ideal. On their flank was the vast mass of Sant' Angelo, well defended by determined gunners; behind them was the army of the Duke of Urbino which must surely be hastening to Rome's rescue; in front of them was the fast-flowing Tiber and the Ponte Sisto. Every man in that army knew the story of Horatio, for every man of that army was an heir of the Rome he was bent on destroying. Was there, at this moment, a latter-day Horatio preparing to hold off the enemy while his comrades destroyed the bridge?

There is little doubt but that, if the bridges of Rome had been destroyed, the Sack of Rome would have ended on that afternoon, the invaders contenting themselves with the suburbs and the Leonine City. The controversy regarding the responsibility for not taking this obvious action was afterwards long and bitter. A month later, an apologist for Clement explained that the Pope 'had continually agitated for the destruction of the bridges but Signor Renzo had refused to do so because of the houses in Trastevere, saying that if ever the enemy entered Rome His Holiness could take his head from his shoulders.' But by then Renzo da Ceri was the natural scapegoat for every aspect of the disaster and the fact that it was he who had initially wanted to destroy the bridges, and had been over-ruled on behalf of the Trasteverines, was conveniently overlooked. Nevertheless, he could and should have prepared defences at the bridgeheads; but, as part of the pattern of spineless optimism, nothing was done.

Yet it was at the Ponte Sisto that there was displayed the last flicker of the self-sacrificing courage that had given Rome a world. Young Marcello Alberini saw it all from the balcony of the Cancelleria on the other side of the river. 'With the simplicity of my years [he was then just sixteen] I went on to the balcony of the palace to watch the bold assault of the enemy, and the brief fighting and little courage of our defenders.' It was between six and seven o'clock in the evening, and it was with the casual magnificence of the Roman sunset as background that the last brief battle for Rome began. The Ponte Sisto was almost blocked by terrified refugees, but holding the bridgehead were two or three hundred Roman knights who had spontaneously taken upon themselves the task of organising this last fragile defence. Among them young Alberino spotted Pier Paulo Tebaldi, 'a noble and valorous man who that day performed deeds more memorable even than Horatio against the Etruscans'. There was Giulio Vallati, only a year or so older than Alberini himself, proudly bearing a great banner inscribed in gold: 'Pro Fide et Patria.' There were the three Orsini brothers, Gianantonio, Camillo, and Valerio, shoulder to shoulder with Tibaldi's brother Simeono and Ranuccio Farnese. Even Renzo da Ceri made his way back accompanied by his son Gianpaolo; for Renzo lacked sense, not courage. These were some of the handful of men who proposed to hold the bridge against several thousand blood-maddened enemies. There was a brief stir of excitement on the east bank as a deputation of city fathers made their way to the bridge. They were led by the young Margrave of Brandenburg who believed that he had some influence with his compatriots on the west bank. He was wrong and nearly lost his life as a result of his error. The refugees parted to let the stately procession through, but they were only halfway across the bridge when the enemy launched the last attack. The line of defenders wavered and then, like a sandcastle before the incoming tide, it collapsed. A few escaped, Renzo amongst them; most died where they stood. The deputation took one terrified glance at the incoming wave, then turned and fled.

All this Alberini saw from his vantage point. Years later, he was to place a plaque on the scene of the action commemorating the death of Tibaldi. 'Now was this city lost, as much through our negligence and disgrace as from the anger of the heavens.' Why was this? he asked himself. How could a great city collapse in hours under pressure from a starving, ill-equipped enemy? And in a few bitter sentences the young strategist gave the answers with which posterity was to agree. There was no central command; the defenders, instead of being concentrated in the area under assault, were spread thinly along the entire circuit of walls; the supply system was virtually non-existent with ammunition failing at critical moments and men going without food and drink for hours on end, and even abandoning their posts to go foraging; the death of Bourbon gave a dangerous false encouragement to the defenders. But the all-encompassing reason, Alberini thought, was that the city was corrupt and ready to fall, 'for the defenders were more used to the battle of Venus than the battle of Mars', and by far preferred to swagger up and down in martial display than to actually risk themselves in battle. Rome, in short, carried within itself the seeds of its own decay.

The crowd of refugees from the west bank surged down the via Papalis, past Alberino's refuge, the Cancelleria, and went to ground in the numerous alleys and courtyards of the city. Behind them thundered the enemy, cavalry and foot driving the citizens before them like wolves after sheep. 'All were doomed to certain death who were found in the streets of the city; the same fate was meted out to all – young or old, woman or man, priest or monk. Everywhere rang the cry: Empire! Spain! Victory!' Smoke and flames began to rise from sacked houses, the badge of a defeated city, ascending into the tranquil spring sky to tell the far-off watchers that Rome was about to enter its agony.

But Rome's hour was not yet quite come. Both citizens and invaders alike were still hourly expecting the arrival of the army of the Holy League. Rangone with his 6,000 horse had, in fact, got as close as Monterotondo, some five miles away 'and from there it would have been easy to have entered Rome by the Porta del Popolo and impeded the enemy and given heart to the army of the League, which was still on the way. And why they did not do this I leave to the reader to judge', Luigi Guicciardini wrote bitterly. Guido Rangone, an experienced soldier, had, presumably, calculated his chances in attacking an enemy now ensconced within the walled city and decided that the odds were too high. The enemy did not know this, and throughout that night they waited for the attack.

They had separated into their national groups. The Italians under Ferrante Gonzaga were camped near Castel Sant' Angelo, the only point in the city that still held out. The Spaniards were camped on the Piazza Navona and, a few hundred yards away on the other side of the via Papalis, the Germans were camped on the Campo de' Fiori. Back in Trastevere, the camp followers were beginning to plunder, although they found little enough of value in this predominantly working-class suburb. But the professionals held their ranks all through the night, knowing full well that their lives could be at stake. There would be time enough for plunder on the morrow; during the dark hours they contented themselves with searching the neighbouring houses for food and any booty that might have been left by the fleeing families. Those who were not required to stand guard dropped where they were. Most had been without sleep for two successive nights. They had marched twelve miles, attacked a great city in the face of artillery fire, engaged in hand-to-hand fighting for the better part of a day, and were now utterly exhausted. Rangone's 6,000 fresh, well-fed men might have turned the scales had they come down that road towards which all thoughts were turning during the short night. But nothing happened.

And at dawn on Tuesday, 7 May, exactly twenty-four hours since they had launched the attack upon the walls, some 20,000 soldiers began to seek for what they wanted in one of the wealthiest and most luxurioous cities of the world.

Chapter XII

Tuesday, 7 May

Shortly after dusk on the Monday night, Camilla Gonzaga was sitting looking out of the window of her aunt Isabella's palace on the Piazza Colonna. The young girl was one of hundreds of women who had taken shelter under the protection of Isabella d'Este and she was drawn now to the window, like many others, by the indescribable confusion in the square below. Here the refugees running from the advancing imperialists encountered those who were abandoning their homes in and around the square. Entire families were making the agonising decision whether to go or to stay and, if going, what to leave and what to carry. Counterpoint to the cries and shrieks was the dull booming of the guns of Sant' Angelo, and the sharper crack of arquebus fire coming rapidly closer.

The scene in the square resembled nothing so much as a disturbed ant-heap; but one familiar figure among those scurrying hundreds caught Camilla's attention. He was on foot but wore in his helmet the black, red and white colours of the imperial cavalry; he was heavily bearded and, ragged, travel and battle-stained though he was, Camilla recognised her brother Alessandro, one of the staff officers of the late Duke of Bourbon. The girl called out the news to those inside but no attempt was made to open the great street doors: if they had done so, the palace would have been swamped by the terrified inhabitants of the neighbouring warrens. Instead, a rope was lowered from the window and, in that unceremonial manner, Alessandro Gonzaga entered his aunt's refuge.

For the first time she, and those under her protection, heard for certain what had until now been only an appalling rumour. Alessandro told her about the attack upon the walls; of how her nephew the Duke of Bourbon had been killed in the first moments of the assault, and that his body lay in state in the captured Sistine Chapel. The Pope and many of his cardinals were safe in Sant' Angelo but were besieged there. There was no news of the army that was supposed to be marching to the relief of Rome and it was best, now, to prepare for the worst. Isabella's son, Ferrante, was encamped outside Sant' Angelo: it was his duty, as captain of artillery in the imperial army, to deploy the captured guns against the castle. He would join his mother as soon as possible, and meanwhile had sent Alessandro to reassure her.

Shortly afterwards another imperial soldier was hauled up by rope, a

Spaniard, Don Alonso da Cordova, whose words were those of a courtier but whose eyes were those of a bailiff. He was an ally of Isabella's son, the Marquis of Mantua. Some of the wealthiest people in Rome had crowded into Isabella's palace and Cordova's presence there was a grim reminder that they, and all they possessed, were at the disposal of the conqueror.

It was past midnight before Ferrante Gonzaga arrived. Later he wrote apologetically to his brother, the Marquis, explaining why he had not been able to come earlier to comfort and protect their mother: 'I was with the battalion guarding Sant' Angelo and could not, for my honour's sake, leave before midnight.' Isabella was delighted to see him, though dismayed by his appearance. Three years had passed since he had left to go to the court of the Emperor: in place of the dashing young prince who had ridden out of Mantua to see the world there was a gaunt and haggard man smelling of gunpowder and blood and stale sweat, and seeming more a Spaniard than an Italian.

After the family greetings there began, in that gloomy shuttered palace, a most curious conference between the three newcomers and Isabella. She was the mother of one of these young men, the aunt of another and the third was the ally of her son, the Marquis. She was, nevertheless, a spoil of war. Or, to be exact, she was a spoil of war of their men. As Ferrante explained the situation to his brother: 'It was difficult to effect Madama's escape, for report in the camp said that more than two millions' worth of valuables were concealed in this palace, and this was solely owing to Madama's compassion, for she had given shelter to more than 1200 noble women of Rome and 1000 men.' Ferrante's men had followed him, just as all the other men had followed their captains, for one over-riding pupose: loot, whether in the form of immediately portable valuables or negotiable ransome. Isabella d'Este represented a fortune to these men: the fact that she was also their captain's mother was unfortunate but quite irrelevant. She was resident in a captured city and the rules of war placed her, her property, and those under her protection at the mercy of the captors. Both Alessandro and Alonso da Cordova made this very clear to Ferrante: whether or not they found it embarrassing, their men would expect them to assess the ransomes available and exact them. Failure to do that would mean simply that the place was turned over to the soldiery. Ferrante bowed to the logic of the argument: a guard of Spaniards was placed at the main gate and throughout the night the work of assessing ransomes went on.

Ferrante had underestimated the number of people sheltering in the palace: there were, in fact, at least 3,000, including the ambassadors of Ferrara, Urbino and Venice, and Domenico Massimi, that rich man who had derisively sought to pay for his protection with 100 ducats and who would soon be called upon to pay with all that he had. Matteo Casale, the Ferrarese ambassador, wrote to his master from the palace early on the Tuesday morning:

It has pleased God that the Imperial army should storm and enter the city at noon. At the first attack my lord of Bourbon was killed with a shot and the said army pillaged the unfortunate city all that evening and night, and it is still going on. Oh! wretched, miserable city! What grief and what sorrows! I, with others, have found refuge with the illustrious Madama, who has safeguarded the house and all within. I think that the house and all it shelters will continue to be safe since Don Ferrante, her son, and Count Alessandro and a Spanish captain, Signor Alfonso di Cordova, are here. I have lost everything I had: horses, clothes, everything. The Pope is besieged in the Castle along with the greater part of the cardinals. They say that the Viceroy [Lannoy] has been sent for: the Colonna have not yet arrived. The world is in commotion. I shall be glad if I come off alive. Madama, illustrissima, notwithstanding the preparations, is now dead with fear.

Casale was ambassador of the Duke of Ferrara, that same Duke who had given timely aid to the landsknechts when they were starving in Lombardy. Nevertheless, he was not exempt. Nobody was exempt. But it was all done legally, precisely, with a kind of lunatic pedantry. Every ransomed person was assessed according to his property: thus the Venetian envoy, Venier, had to pay a ransome of 5,000 ducats – a huge sum for a private individual; but his noble compatriot, Giustininian, who had come to Rome in search of a cardinal's hat, was assessed at 10,000 ducats. The name of each person was duly recorded and notarised, and from this one palace, whose mistress was related by blood to the leaders of the conquering army, a sum approaching one-third of the entire ransome initially demanded by Bourbon was extracted on this first harvesting. Ferrante Gonzaga, contemplating that harvest of gold wrung from his mother and those under her protection, and mindful of his honour, forcefully declared: 'I did not receive so much as a quattrino of all this.' Nevertheless, when Francesco Guicciardini came to write up the story for his monumental *History* he pilloried the unfortunate Ferrante for all time with his casual remark: 'It is said that Don Ferrando, the marchesana's son, had 10,000 ducats for his share.'

The refugees in Isabella's palace were fortunate: as Casale assumed, the presence of Cordoba and the Gonzaga cousins gave them some guarantee against physical assault. But others paid in both blood and gold. The great palaces of the city were the natural first target of the enemy's fury, for they were obvious depositories of wealth. Most of them were situated within a stone's throw of each other in and around the handsome new thoroughfare, the via Papalis, which ran through the heart of the Renaissance city, and the first of these to fall was the home of a redoubtable Roman matron, known simply as the Signora Lomellini.

Her palace was under the shadow of the Pantheon, that indestructible monument from Rome's great past, and she, a worthy descendant of the iron men who had made Rome great, had made excellent provision to defend it against these yelling barbarians. She had hired seventy mercenaries, seen that they were plentifully supplied with powder and ammunition and that the palace itself was well-provisioned, and was prepared to ride out the storm. The attackers were taken utterly by surprise. Expecting the timid or non-existent resistance which they had come to associate with Romans, they advanced boldly and openly upon the palace – and were greeted with a murderous blast of arquebus fire which dropped at least a dozen of them.

But what the Signora Lomellini had not reckoned upon was that, during these first few hours, the bloodlust of the invaders was at least as great as their lust for booty or even women. It was as though they wished to purge themselves of, and be revenged for, the long months of privation and humiliation; and resistance tended to heighten their fury. So, now, reinforcements from other groups came forward to take the place of those that had fallen and, under cover of their own arquebusiers, a dozen men wielded a beam like a battering-ram, smashing against the great street door of the palace until it gave way. The Signora got good value for her money, unlike so many employers of mercenaries: her guard fought literally every inch of the way as they were forced back across the vestibule and then slowly up the stairs to the piano nobile, the first floor where the family lived. The defenders fought well, but there were only seventy of them, whereas for every attacker who fell there were a dozen eager to leap into his place, convinced that a house that was so well defended must be studded with treasure.

It had become obvious that the battle was lost and Signora Lomellini, correctly deducing that she could expect little mercy from these bloodstained wolves, escaped by sliding down a rope into the inner courtyard. Or, at least, that was her intention. The rope snapped, dropping her some fifteen feet onto marble, so that she broke a leg. There must have been some especial quality about the Signora to make her servants and hired bravoes risk their lives for her: one of her servants, seeing her accident made his way into the courtyard, helped her to her feet and they began to half walk, half run across the wide, exposed expanse, making for the garden behind. From there, it would have been possible to obtain access to a neighbouring convent. But servant and mistress never made it. The invaders had gained the first floor while the two were still making their way across the courtyard and an arquebusier, spotting them from one of the windows, dropped the Signora with one shot. A moment later one of his companions did the same for the servant. By that time the defending force had been wiped out and the invaders began their search for booty.

Not far from the Signora's palace was the home of a goldsmith. It was not, perhaps, as splendid as the palazzo Lomellini but it was the decent solid home of a decent solid citizen and he, like his social superior, had obstinately decided that he was not yielding up all that he had worked for without a fight. His family, like all Roman families, was extensive, cousins, uncles, brothers, sisters, aunts living in a tight social network a few yards from each other. During the Monday evening, before the massacres started but after it had become certain that Rome would fall, the goldsmith and his relatives had decided to make their own defence. They were able to get hold of two or three arquebuses and, putting these together with their traditional weapons, they prepared for a siege. At this stage, few people had any concept of the nature of the disaster and appeared to believe that it would be necessary to hold out only for a few hours, or a day or so at the most. But even this limited objective was to prove an illusory hope for the valiant goldsmith and his equally valiant relatives.

As with the defenders at the Lomellini palace, their determined resistance at first took the attackers by surprise and a good handful of landsknechts fell, shot by arquebus or crossbow fire. The neighbouring houses, however, fell easily, the men, women and children in them being cut down on the spot. Using these houses as cover, the landsknechts poured in volley after volley, swamping the defence while some of their number forced the street door. Within the narrow confines of the house the defenders temporarily had the advantage, but again the sheer weight of numbers told: more and more men poured in from outside and the defence at last broke. The goldsmith – never identified – escaped with a handful of relatives, scrambling over the roofs to safety. Those who remained were slaughtered.

On the Campo de' Firori the Florentine merchant Francesco Vettori defended his house and possessions with true Florentine acumen. He could not, or would not abandon his house stuffed full with valuables and, fortunately for himself, he was physically incapable of bearing arms. When he heard that the enemy had crossed the Ponte Sisto, he put his plan into action. It was simplicity itself: he ordered his servant to trace, on the streetdoor, the sign indicating that there was plague within. By chance, he had a boil on his leg and this he tinted reddish and took to his bed. His plan nearly failed through the ignorance of the enemy: it was not Spaniards or Italians who came hammering on his door but Germans, slow-witted men who had never seen this sign before and had no idea what it signified. Vettori's German-speaking servant enlightened them: his master had lost wife and four children and now himself was dying. The Germans accepted the explanation, chalked their own sign on the door to warn their fellows and went plundering in a safer area. But, in an episode like the twist at the end of one of those macabre tales so popular in their homeland, they encountered one of their companions who had had considerable experience as a grave-digger and they prevailed upon him to examine the patient. Alberini, who tells the story, does not make it clear why the Germans should have gone to this trouble, for at no stage do they seem to have suspected the deception. The probability is that the lust for gold overcame even the scruples of self-protection – a sequence which became ever more apparent over the ensuing weeks.

The grave-digger inspected the 'invalid' and solemnly confirmed the diagnosis: yes, he did have the plague – but he was getting better. The landsknechts left the grave digger on guard, departed on another plundering expedition, and then, apparently fearing that he might cheat them, hastened back. Vettori was forcibly tumbled out of bed and a ransome demanded. He pleaded to be allowed to send his servant to Tivoli to raise the money – an excuse which would have been accepted by no one except Germans, for Tivoli was at least twenty miles distant. However, the landsknechts waited while the servant raised 300 ducats from a source Vettori had hidden in Rome itself and returned within the hour. But Vettori's elaborate plan failed in the end: the landsknechts, having scented money, refused to move on, but camped down for the night; and the Florentine was glad to be able to escape through a window when fatigue relaxed their vigilance.

'In the whole city, there was not a soul above the age of three years who had not to purchase his safety.' The writer scarcely exaggerated, for neither age, nor sex, nor class nor even political affiliation inhibited in the slightest the soldiers' demand for ransome. The Portuguese ambassador was a relative of the Emperor's, but that did not prevent the Germans from making demands for heavy payments from the rich bankers and merchants who had crowded into his palace. The embassy was in the part of Rome that had been taken over by the Spaniards and, annoyed at the Germans' trespass, they offered 'protection' to the ambassador – at a price. Under pressure from the merchants, the ambassador accepted, and then incontinently baulked at the demand that he should run up the Spanish flag. The only flag that would fly over the Portuguese embassy was the Portuguese flag, he said stubbornly, and nothing the terrified merchants could do would persuade him to abandon his national pride, displayed at so inopportune a moment.

The Spanish thereon, indifferent as to whether they received their booty in the form of loot or protection money, launched a massive attack upon the embassy. Under their savage onslaught, the defence crumbled and the soldiers found booty that exceeded even their fevered hopes. Not only were the refugees who had crowded into the palace bankers, but also they had reasonably enough assumed that such a place would be sacrosanct and accordingly had transported thither the bulk of their possessions. The ambassador, Don Martino, was robbed personally of 14,000 ducats, but it was later calculated that the entire haul amounted to around half a million ducats, shared by a few hundred Spaniards.

Yet even that immense haul did not satisfy them. A Florentine banker, Bernado Bracci, pleaded that all his cash was deposited in the Bank of the Foreigners on the other side of the city: he was promptly hauled thither by a band of soldiers and forced to pay out the curiously precise sum of 8,206 ducats at which he had been 'assessed'. Even then his troubles were not over, for on crossing the Ponte Sisto on his way back into the city he had the misfortune to meet La Motte, Bourbon's aide who had been appointed military governor of the city. And the aristocratic La Motte did not disdain to enter the scramble for ransome. Grasping the wretched Bracci by the throat, he threatened to pitch him into the Tiber then and there unless he paid up. He received 600 ducats.

The anti-imperialist cardinals had sensibly fled into the castle Sant' Angelo along with Clement. The pro-imperialist cardinals foolishly stayed in their palaces, counting upon their status with the Emperor to protect them from the Emperor's troops. Their privileged status lasted for exactly eight days. That period, perhaps, is the measure of time between the capture and the total social disintegration of Rome. During the first few days – in particular, those three days which became known as the 'days of violence' – the soldiers' fury was directed against those who could (if with some stretch of the imagination) be identified as legitimate military targets, being the aiders and comforters of the Emperor's enemies. But with the collapse of a human society, all distinctions were lost: all men became enemies or objects of plunder, even those men who had been comrades-in-arms. That stage was not reached until relatively late in the Sack – until, in fact, the men had become sated with loot, but faced plague and famine. However, the point of disintegration was marked on 14 May with the attack on the palaces of the pro-imperial cardinals, Piccolomini, Cesarini, Valle, Enkevoirt, and even Colonna.

The palaces had been placed under the protection of Spanish officers and Spanish bodyguards. Their owners had been spared physical assault but, even so, had been obliged to pay heavily for the indemnity, the officers protesting that it was not their will or desire but that of their troops. The assessing, levying and distributing of the ransomes proceeded in that orderly, indeed, pedantic manner which was one of the characteristics of the Sack, contrasting so strongly with the bestial indulgences of the troopers. At first, a round sum of 100,000 ducats had been demanded from each cardinal but later this was reduced to 45,000 from Cesarini, 40,000 from Enkevoirt and 35,000 each from Valle and Piccolomini. The men wanted cash, not jewels or tapestries or other precious but bulky objects; they wanted the solid gold coins, each of 24-carat, known as the *ducat di camera*. Each coin was scrutinised, weighed and added carefully to the growing pile, a slow process which probably sufficiently accounts for the protection granted to the cardinals. For the end of protection, and the end of the accounting, coincided closely in time. The Spaniards, having garnered their gold, told their clients with a shrug that, alas, they were unable to restrain their German comrades any further; they withdrew with their kilograms of gold, and the landsknechts rushed in. In vain, the cardinals protested that they had already paid. They must pay again, the Germans informed them, for the money had gone to line Spanish, not German pockets. Cardinal Piccolomini was unwise enough to order his servants to resist: the Germans sacked his palace, beat him up until he produced another 5,000 ducats, then dragged him off in captivity. His three fellow imperialists abandoned everything and fled to the Colonna palace. The Germans then systematically set about 'taxing' everybody in the palaces. Even under normal circumstances some 180 people lived in the Piccolomini Palace, 275 in Cesarini's and 130 in Valle's. These numbers had been vastly swollen by the refugees who, too, had thought that their protectors' pro-imperial sympathies would act as a shield. In the palazzo Valle alone there were now over 390 people who between them yielded up another 34,455 ducats in addition to the 35,000 that the Spaniards had earlier extracted.

Even the palace of Cardinal Pompeo Colonna was not safe, as the Alberini family found. Marcello's father was seized by eight soldiers and dragged out into the streets, 'and for many days we bewailed his death, for from the window we saw, lying among the many dead bodies in the street, someone who resembled him closely'. Alberini senior survived after paying a ramsome of 400 ducats. Others were not so fortunate. The elderly Cardinal Ponzetti died from the injuries he received – and he had paid a ransome of 20,000 ducats. Cardinal Numai had the terrifying experience of being present at his own funeral. He was lying ill in bed when the landsknechts burst in and, with a macabre sense of humour, decided to use mental torture as a change from the usual physical torments, and so staged a mock funeral. Chanting a dirge, they carried him on a bier through the streets to a church. There, a slab was raised and a shallow grave scratched out in the bone-filled soil. With howls of laughter and obscene parodies of the mass for the dead, the landsknechts lowered the wretched man into his grave and prepared to drop the slab on top. Already robbed of all he had, Numai was quite unable to ransome himself and would very probably have suffered burial alive had he not been able to persuade his tormentors that his friends would stand surety for him. He was carried away, still on the bier, to a friendly house where his freedom was obtained in exchange for his friends' signatures on a promissory note.

The cardinals' palaces were the first to be attacked, but it was not long before the soldiery stumbled upon another rich source of wealth – the convents. Thousands of women who had fled to these as the most natural and obvious source of protection found that they had entered the most deadly of traps. Sister Orsola Formicini, one of the nuns of Santa Cosimata in Trastevere, left one of the few accounts of the destruction of the city to be written by a woman: a restrained, laconic but poignant description of the desecration and rape of her own convent.

Trastevere, the first area to fall wholly into the hands of the invaders, was the first to feel the full fury of their lust for booty, and women. They were disappointed in the first. Most of those who lived in this suburb were simple artisans, the least successful of their class. The jewellers and carpenters and upholsterers and drapers who were growing rich through the patronage of the wealthy upper classes lived, for the most part, on the other side of the river near the Campo de' Fiori within call of their wealthy and usually impatient clients. The artisans of Trastevere supplied the needs of their own class, or those immediately above them, and their way of life was correspondingly frugal: the few cups and plates in their houses were made of wood or pottery, not precious metals; the little money in their purses was copper, not gold. And their daughters, though beautiful, were unavailable, believing themselves safe in the convents. It may have been simple, if savage disappointment at the meagreness of their booty that turned the soldiers' attention to the convents, first to the monastery of Santa Rufina and then to Sister Orsola's house not far distant.

Santa Rufina, with its beautiful twelfth-century romanesque campanile, stood at the end of a short, narrow alleyway. The attackers took no particular precautions, and were taken completely by surprise by the violence of the resistance. There were few men, and therefore few conventional weapons in the convent, but the determined defenders turned to devastating effect the weapons procured from the kitchen of a large establishment. Boiling water and boiling oil formed the first line of defence: tipped out from first floor windows, or down the steep stairwell the boiling liquid caused fearful injuries to the first, unsuspecting invaders. And even when hand-to-hand fighting started, the invaders discovered that the tigerish Roman woman defending her honour was considerably more deadly than her menfolk defending even their gold. Neither did the wearing of a nun's habit extinguish her ferocity. Grasping cleavers, spits, skewers, any metal object that could be wielded to cut or bludgeon or pierce, the women fought back until overwhelmed by sheer brute force.

Comparatively few survived here, and those who did not were the fortunate ones.

Santa Rufina provided good booty, for the women had brought with them their personal jewellery and the more valuable of their household's portable articles. Santa Cosimata, sister Orsola's house, was the next to fall before the wave, but warned in time, the sisters and their temporary guests had fled under cover of darkness. 'These poor handmaids of the Lord left the convent full of every treasure', Sister Orsola lamented, detailing those treasures with house-wifely sorrow:

> There was the statue of the Madonna dressed in a robe of huge pearls and on the high altar there was a hanging of Cremonese velvet – the very first time that it had been put on show. . . . The sacristy was full of treasures because all those illustrious gentlemen who became monks left all their valuables there. . . . There was a cross of the finest gold covered with pearls and precious stones which was of great value – all was left, nothing was saved.

And yet, because they had had warning of the attack, they were able to save the most precious possession of all:

> Everything was lost, but because honour was not lost one can say that nothing was lost.

The sisters from Santa Cosimata fled blindly to the other side of the river. They had no plan, beyond the intention of putting as much space as possible between themselves and the despoilers of their home: they had no real hope, except to live for another five minutes, ten minutes, quarter of an hour. Their survival was due entirely to the caprice of fortune, as unpredictable as the bomb blast which tears one person to pieces and leaves his neighbour untouched. At the church of San Lorenzo in Panisperna, they fell into the hands of a group of Germans: robbery, followed by rape of the young and attractive and murder of all, might reasonably have been expected to be their fate. Instead, the Lutheran landsknechts took these Catholic nuns under their protection, defending them not only against fellow Lutherans but also against Spanish and Italian Catholics.

Sister Orsola's experience was unusual but not unique. Of the three races, the Germans were marginally the more human. 'In the destruction of Rome the Germans showed themselves to be bad enough, the Italians were worse, but worst of all were the Spaniards', a citizen of Narni reported of his scarifying adventures in Rome. But others were prepared to give the Germans their due: 'It was observed in some cases that the Lutheran Germans showed more pity, being prepared to defend the virtue of women', an observer remarked, although he could not resist adding, caustically: 'It was enough for them to lay their hands on booty.' He agreed with the man from Narni that the Spaniards were worst of all, 'practising unheard-of tortures to force their victims to disclose where they had hidden their money'.

The one class of persons who suffered more than any others during the first few hours were the younger, poorer women. These were the women whose homes offered only flimsy protection, whose husbands or fathers could find only a few silver or even only copper pieces as ransome, and whose bodies, therefore, fell prey to the invaders. But these unfortunates were soon joined by their wealthier sisters. Rape and booty had always been the traditional wages of soldiers, the main motive for putting their lives at stake. Traditionally, the commanders of a conquering army allowed their soldiers unrestricted opportunity to satiate their lusts for a brief period – usually up to a maximum of three days. It was reckoned that the psychic tension created by battle would dissipate itself within that period and that afterwards discipline could again be applied. La Motte, the military governor, did indeed attempt to follow this traditional custom; on the third day after the fall of the Borgo he promulgated a decree that all further acts of violence, particularly that of rape, should end. He was totally and contemptuously ignored and what had been a casual, random and virtually accepted pattern of violence suddenly became a delirious orgy of cruelty conducted on a systematic basis.

Turning from the daughters and wives of the poor, the soldiers sated themselves with those women who, normally, they would have lusted for in vain, since the class barrier was unscaleable. Delicately nurtured girls whose entire life had been spent within the safety and comfort of their fathers' strong walls, whose contact with the lower classes was limited to the service provided by servants, found themselves seized, stripped and subjected to the uttermost indignities by evil-smelling, fantastically dressed creatures who must have appeared to them as devils out of some unimaginable hell. The Spaniards were particularly adept at refining cruelties, at inventing new variations of obscenity whose object was less to satisfy the physical lust of the soldier than to break the spirit, totally, of the woman. Mothers were forced to assist, not merely witness, the ravishment of their daughters, and daughters that of their mothers.

Those who were murdered at the climax of lust were perhaps the fortunate ones: others were raped again and again by new gangs until they died of shock, or were dragged away to be sold at mock auctions. The men who resisted were killed casually, out of hand. Some, in their desperation, adopted their ancestors' code: 'a Roman gentleman, not having the time to save his two virgin daughters, killed them both with his own hands'. The aristocratic Domenico Massimi, the same who had mockingly contributed 100 ducats to Rome's defence, was forced to watch while his daughters were raped in front of his burning home. Convents were turned into brothels where the famous courtesans of Rome now plied their trade, and were reinforced by recruits from the upper classes. This forcible prostitution aroused the ungallant mirth of the Sieur de Brantôme, the courtly chronicler of gallant deeds: 'Marchionesses, countesses and baronesses served the unruly troops and for long afterwards the patrician women of the city were known as "the relics of the Sack of Rome".' And regarding those noble women who were supposed to have killed themselves rather than suffer dishonour, he added spitefully: 'of such Lucrezias it is not possible to mention even one by name'.

So wrote the Frenchman, comfortably distant from Rome. Grolier, a Frenchman who was actually in Rome, was less light-hearted. He was reasonably safe in the house of a Spanish bishop and from the roof looked into what seemed a version of hell: 'Everywhere cries, the clash of arms and the shrieks of women and children, the crackling of fire and the crash of falling roofs. We were numb with fear and held our ears, as if we alone were preserved by fate to look on the ruin of our country.'

Sacrilege, like rape, went far beyond the casual explosion of energy from pent-up men. Even though for two of the three races involved this was the Holy City of Christendom, it was pursued with a dedicated single-mindedness that would have been more appropriate to a religious war. 'Burned is the great chapel of St Peter and of Sixtus: burned is the Holy Face of St Veronica:... the heads of the Apostles are stolen . . . the Sacrament thrown into the mud . . . reliquaries trampled under foot. . . . I shudder to contemplate this for Christians are doing what even the Turks never did', Cardinal Salviati later wrote to Baldassare Castiglione in Madrid. 'Surely the Catholic Emperor will have great displeasure at this news.' But whether or not the Catholic Emperor took great displeasure at the news, there was no power on earth that now could halt the depredations of his Catholic troops. They seem, indeed, to have been the worst in the matter of sacrilege. It was Spanish troops who broke open the tomb of the great Pope Julius II, dragging the corpse out of its fourteen-year grave in order to plunder it. The more naïve Germans were taken in by the claims of the papists they affected to despise: Sebastian Schertlin got hold of the rope, 'thick enough for the neck of a Polyphemous', with which Judas was supposed to have hanged himself and, despite all financial offers, insisted on taking it home with him. Nearly a hundred years later it was still in the church of Schorndorf with a label proudly announcing its origins.

Salviati was wrong in declaring that the Handkerchief of St Veronica had been burnt. It was later reported as being passed from hand to hand through all the taverns of Rome, one such report declaring that it was in rags. But if this was so, the Handkerchief's miraculous origins preserved it, for it was later back in its wonted shrine, unharmed. Likewise, the heads of St Andrew and St John: after being casually kicked around the city, they – or something like them – in due course found their way back to their shrines. The great golden cross of Constantine, that had lain in the basilica of St Peter's for over 1,200 years, disappeared and was never recovered, it being conjectured that it was broken into pieces for the ease of transport. The Holy Lance of Longinus, that had been given to Pope Innocent VIII by Sultan Bajacet himself just over thirty years before, was fastened to a pike and derisively trailed about the city by a landsknecht. The Lance, too, seemed to have the miraculous property of reproducing itself, for it was later to turn up in Vienna while still remaining in Rome.

As great as the loss of precious objects was the loss of books and documents, both those belonging to the city itself – its statutes, histories, laws – and those so enthusiastically collected by humanist popes and cardinals. Sebastian Schertlin described the barbarians' hatred of letters which is curiously at variance with his own laborious, stilted, but earnest attempts to record, in letters, his own and his comrades' treatment of Rome: 'In the year 1527, on 6

May, we took Rome by storm, put over 6,000 men to the sword, seized all that
we could find in the churches and elsewhere, burned down a great part of the
city, tearing and destroying all copyists' work, all registers, letters and state
documents', he stated baldly.

The already priceless Vatican Library would never have seen its centenary
had it not been for the Prince of Orange. He had taken up his residence in the
Vatican Palace and made the most strenuous exertions to save its treasures
from the marauders. He was not even safe from his own troops: 'Monsieur le
prince was robbed by landsknechts in the porch of Saint Mark', his secretary
recorded. However, his presence in the Palace was sufficient to deter men for
whom there was much easier prey elsewhere. Posterity has another, overwhelming reason to be grateful to this young man, for it was the guards he
posted about the Palace who certainly saved the Stanze of Raphael and,
probably, the Sistine Chapel. The murals in the Stanze had been completed
only a little over ten years before: in their pristine freshness and only a little
above eye-height in the small chambers they would have been the natural target
of casual vandalism. In the Sistine Chapel, the presence of Bourbon's body
gave, of itself, a measure of protection. He lay in state upon his bier in front of
the High Altar beneath Michelangelo's glowing ceiling, the sightless eyes
peering up at the charged figure of God energising the slack figure of Adam. It
was perhaps appropriate that the honour-guard of the man who had brought
about the destruction of the city should be in part instrumental in saving this
jewel-box of art. There was little enough to tempt marauders, however, for the
murals were too high for all except the most dedicated vandal, there was very
little combustible material, and the few portable articles of value were on the
High Altar.

Elsewhere, the soldiers were interested only in articles of intrinsic value: the
scores of works of art in marble and bronze that decorated the Vatican, many of
them only recently brought back to light after centuries of burial, might be
damaged in passing but they remained in situ. There was no wholesale
destruction of such works, as had taken place in that last Sack of Rome a
thousand years before when the defenders had smashed the marble statues on
Hadrian's tomb to make missiles to use against the besieging Goths.
Significantly, this time, it was the Italians who stole works of art made of non-
precious materials, for they, unlike their fellows, were sophisticated enough to
realise their true value: Sigismondo Ferrarese admitted to removing certain
antique heads of marble. Spaniards and Germans were satisfied with objects
made of gold, silver or precious gems; they were attracted by the glittering
metal and stones, indifferent to the form in which they were cast. The tiara of
Nicholas V, heavily decorated with gems, and the beautiful Golden Rose
presented by Martin V, to mark the healing of the grievous Schism, almost
certainly suffered the fate of Constantine's Cross. They were never seen again
and were probably broken up – the fate suffered by most of the jewellery that
was carried off.

'They divided pearls with shovels: the poorest soldier acquired three to four
thousand ducats.' Men threw priceless brocades and velvets and cloth of gold

and silver over their stinking rags, wove pearls and precious stones into their beards, forced their muscular fingers into massive rings intended for plumper, softer hands. They staggered about, laden with kilograms of gold and silver in specie or ornament, dispensing it with lordly hands: vast sums changed hands on the fall of dice; the camp followers who were accustomed to coupling for the price of a drink and a few coppers now received gold in exchange for their services. These women were dressed like queens in the most splendid garments that a fashion-conscious city could yield, while the late owners of those garments were dragged half-naked through the streets or lay butchered in their own homes.

In Rome, during the two or three days following the breakthrough, there was enacted for perhaps the last time in history the conflict between triumphant barbarism and defeated civilisation. There were to be other sacks of other cities: the Spanish Fury which hit Antwerp in 1576 was on a comparable scale, and the long agony of the Thirty Years War brought proportionate suffering to many a little town and city. But these were products of war between equals, to be excused or apologised for or rationalised by those responsible, whereas in Rome, during those early May days, was displayed the goblin grin of the forces that all societies usually keep at bay. Feasting on unaccustomed delicacies in the splendid halls of princes, flanked by their screaming lemans and waited upon by their terrified social superiors, the soldiers played the ancient role of the Lord of Misrule, in a world turned upside down, the hunter snatching up the carefully garnered harvests of the toiling farmer.

Money, jewels, costume, plate poured out in a stream of unheard-of wealth, but still the soldiers were not satisfied. About the third day, after the more easily accessible treasures had been harvested, there arose the headiest rumour of all, the belief in hidden treasure. Every soldier was convinced that every adult citizen of Rome had hidden away a fortune in specie and there began a systematic campaign of extortion which, like those of sacrilege and rape, went far beyond the satisfying of a casual greed or lust. In his eyewitness account of the martyrdom of Rome Luigi Guicciardini recited a catalogue of horrors:

> Many were suspended for hours by the arms; many were cruelly bound by the private parts; many were suspended by the feet high above the road, or over water, while their tormentors threatened to cut the cord. Some were half buried in the cellars; others were nailed up in casks while many were villainously beaten and wounded; not a few were cut all over their persons with redhot irons. Some were tortured by extreme thirst, others by insupportable noise and many were cruelly tortured by having their good teeth brutally drawn. Others again were forced to eat their own ears, or nose, or their roasted testicles and yet more were subjected to strange, unheard-of martyrdoms that move me too much even to think of, much less describe.

The Spaniards' lust for cruelty here paid them dividends for they were not only to devise, but to maintain tortures at which even the Italians baulked. A Venetian, Giovanni Barozzi, had the misfortune to fall into the hands of a group of these demons. 'I am a prisoner of the Spaniards', he wrote to his brother:

> They have fixed my ransome at 1,000 ducats on the pretext that I am an official. They have tortured me twice, and finished by lighting a fire under the soles of my feet. For six days I had only a little bread and water. Dear brother, do not let me perish thus miserably. Get the ransome money together by begging. For God's sake do not abandon me. If I do not pay the ransome in twenty-six days they will hack me to pieces. For the love of God and the blessed Virgin help me. All the Romans are prisoners, and if a man does not pay his ransome he is killed. The sack of Genoa and Rhodes was child's play to this. Help me, dear Antonio, help me for God's sake and that as quickly as possible.

The torturers did not always have it all their own way. Guicciardini admiringly tells the story of a Florentine or Genoese merchant, Giovanni Ansaldo, who was put to the usual tortures until he agreed to pay 1,000 ducats. He appears to have been a successful merchant dealing in items of small intrinsic value, for he had sufficient money hidden in his house to pay the very large ransome. The money, however, was in silver, not gold. The soldiers refused to be burdened with such an immense weight of metal and promptly put him to the torture again, convinced that this time he would produce gold. They had gone too far, however: Ansaldo's reason snapped and, with it, his fear. Drawing a dagger he hurled himself upon his tormentors and killed at least one before he was himself despatched.

Not the least remarkable aspect of the Sack was precisely this sort of fanatical courage, displayed both by natives and visitors in defence of their money. In some cases, the victims quite evidently suffered death rather than disclose the hiding place of their treasure: in 1705 there was discovered the enormous sum of 70,000 ducats hidden beneath the palazzo Verospi, and other, smaller troves were continually being unearthed during the years following the Sack. In many cases, these caches would have been the belongings of people who had hidden them before fleeing, intending to return, but who had been killed before they could do so. But the survival of many other treasure troves was due to a lethal miscalculation on the part both of the victim and of his torturer, the one believing he could hold out, the other applying just too much violence at a critical moment.

The corpse of Pope Julius II was not the only one to suffer the indignity of being exhumed and the tomb robbed: in church after church the more important-looking tombs were broken into, a macabre indifference being shown to the state of the contents. The jewellery was removed, the corpses stripped of their garments, if these were of precious stuffs, and the remains casually tossed back and left to rot uncovered – one of the sources of the plague which later decimated the city.

Another source of disease was the sewers and cesspits that now became the object of search. Some of the wilier or more desperate Romans had thought that human excrement formed the ideal hiding-place for precious metal and jewels:

the valuables would not themselves be affected, and the most dedicated treasure-hunter might hesitate before stirring up the noisome deposits on speculation. They had, however, under-estimated the powerful lure of treasure, even buried under such circumstances, and they had overlooked the fact that they were entirely in the power of the treasure-hunters. Forcing a Roman nobleman, his haughty wife and elegant daughters to grope in ancient cesspits exactly appealed to the robust sense of humour of all three races of soldiers. Again, it was not enough simply to disturb the contents: anxious that they should not be cheated, the soldiers insisted that the semi-liquid matter should be scooped out and, after being examined, it was left, exuding a visible miasma which, according to one disgusted report, could also actually be tasted.

The remarkable amity which had prevailed between Spaniards, Italians and Germans throughout the long weary months of the march dissolved now at the moment of triumph. 'The Spaniards and Italians have decided to cut the landsknechts to pieces and the said landsknechts, having heard this, are on their guard' was the gist of a hopeful report smuggled out of Rome on 12 May. The Italo-Spanish alignment was purely temporary, the usual pattern being a three-way tussle, and the Romans benefited not at all. The most common ground for dissension was the rivalry for ransome: the Spanish tortured more and killed less than did their rivals, and therefore they gained far more. The Germans, in particular, were prone to lose their temper and kill their victim out of hand, and while this may have gratified their bloodlust, in the later totting up their gains were seen to be very much inferior to those of their Latin rivals.

One of the episodes which Luigi Guicciardini recounts has an element of pure farce. A group of Spaniards broke open a shop and discovered, to their delight, what seemed to be a sackful of freshly minted gold coins. Fearing to be robbed of their stolen gains, they made haste to barricade the door before settling down to count the booty. A passing band of Germans saw them shutting the door, guessed the reason, and started banging lustily upon it, bellowing that they did all the fighting while the Spaniards got all the booty. The Spaniards refusing to share their find, their late comrades tried to break the door down and, failing in that, succeeded in setting the house alight. All the Spaniards were burnt to death. The triumphant Germans pounced upon the blackened pile of coins – and found that they were not, in fact, gold but copper coins of the lowest possible value.

'The gates of Rome are wide open and whoever wishes to may go in and out', a Franciscan reported to the Venetian Serenissima on 20 May. He had escaped from Rome on 12 May and other observers reported that, by this date, the invaders no longer formed an army. Gathering together all these reports, as well as interviewing such eyewitnesses as his brother Luigi, Francesco Guicciardini came to the judicious opinion afterwards that even such a small force as Guido Rangone's 8,000 could have recaptured Rome at this period:

> For the imperialists . . . were dispersed all over the city, being all very intent upon so rich a prey, some in stripping the houses, others in searching out concealed treasures or in making prisoners and securing them. They had no

settled quarters, did not rally to their colours and paid no obedience to their commanders. Hence many were of the opinion that, if the troops which were with Count Rangone had been speedily conducted into Rome, they would not only have procured the deliverance of the Pontiff but would also have had the opportunity of performing a most glorious exploit. The Enemies were so busy about their prey that it would have been difficult to get any considerable number together and on some occasions when, by order of the generals or on some emergency, an alarm was given, not one soldier appeared under his colours.

But why was the recapture not attempted? Because we are wise through hindsight, was Guicciardini's cautious explanation: 'Men often persuade themselves that if a thing had been done or not done, there would have succeeded a certain effect whereas if the experiment might be tried, such judgements would sometimes be found fallible.' If Francesco Guicciardini had found himself in Hell he would have rationalised the situation, giving Satan himself the benefit of the doubt.

Cardinal Pompeo Colonna rode into Rome at the head of a thousand men on 7 May. His admiring biographer, Giovio, represents him as an angel of deliverance. Affectingly, Giovio describes how the cardinal wept bitter tears at the misery of his naked city, lamented the stern decrees of heaven and threw his palace open to the outraged women of Rome. He may very well have wept: if any man should have wept tears of remorse that man was Cardinal Pompeo Colonna. He did, indeed, extend his protection to some 500 nuns and women of the better sort but, like the army commanders, he found that the soldiery paid not the slightest attention to his orders or presence. The Alberini family appealed to him to arrange the release of Alberini senior and, to do Colonna justice, he made the attempt. 'He sent the lord Sciarra [a relative] to plead with those soldiers for my father', Marcello recorded, 'but all that happened was that they carried him to the Borgo where for days we had no news'. And even though Cardinal Colonna might have been overflowing with benignity and pity, his followers threw themselves upon the city like wolves upon fat and stricken sheep.

The contemporary chroniclers of the Sack echo each other again and again: the Colonna troops were worse than the imperials; they were worse than the Turks. 'They were peasants, dying of hunger, and they sacked and robbed that which the other soldiers had not deigned to harvest', said the Cardinal of Como. The Franciscan who had escaped to Venice also conveyed that impression of desperate men scavenging what they could: 'they carried away even the ironwork of the houses'; and a correspondent of the Duchess of Urbino's described in a vivid phrase how they 'raked together' the chattles of the poor. These armed peasants – they were certainly not soldiers – at least had the justification of need. Their social superiors seem to have acted virtually out of a delight in pure evil. 'They went to a convent of most saintly ladies and sacked it brutally, and amongst them was a nephew of the Cardinal's who laughed greatly at all that happened', the Venetian Sanuto recorded. Such a remark may, perhaps, have been born of hearsay, and may have exaggerated or distorted a possibly innocent fact. But there was ample proof of the astonishingly callous action of Pier Luigi Farnese, the bastard son of the future Pope Paul III. Coming to Rome in the entourage of the Colonna, after all danger of fighting had passed, he picked up 25,000 ducats in ransome in a whirlwind tour of the city and then hurried away, heading north to the Campana Romagna where he planned to hide his plunder in one of the Farnese castles. Outside Rome, however, he was attacked by peasants who robbed him of every ducat – one of the few totally satisfying events of the Sack of Rome.

Colonna's entry into Rome marked the end of the first stage of the Sack, the three days during which the majority of the deaths through violence (as opposed to disease and famine) took place. No one knew then, or later, how many died in those first days. 'They say 12,000 have been killed and the bodies lie unburied', the Franciscan friar told the Venetian senate. He probably did not exaggerate. The grave-diggers were paid for disposing of 9,800 bodies, and the riparian Regions of Rome eased their problem by throwing corpses into the Tiber. In the Borgo and Trastevere generally over 2,000 bodies were disposed of by this method. And over the city there hung the spectres of those two other Horsemen – plague and famine – who would take their thousands before the summer was ended. Well might Pope Clement lift up his hands in lamentation as he looked out over the burning city from that tomb of a long-dead emperor which was now his sole asylum.

Chapter XIII

The Cruxifixion of Pope Clement

When the Emperor Hadrian had built his enormous circular mausoleum on the west bank of the Tiber, he had caused a vast pile of earth to be heaped up in the form of a cone on its flat upper surface. Turfed and planted with pine trees, it resembled an artificial hill, crowned by a statue of the Emperor in scale with everything else in the undertaking. The statue rested upon a species of tower which formed a core to the mound of earth, and whose chambers were used for the sarcophagi of lesser members of the imperial family.

In the course of centuries, the earth was removed, leaving the core or *mastio* standing isolated; and the statue of the Emperor was replaced by a statue of the Archangel Michael from whom the structure now took its name. No further changes of any magnitude were made to the castle, as it had now become, until some thirty years before the reign of Pope Clement when first the Borgia pope, Alexander, and then his successor Julius II, had begun to build upon the flat drum. They carved out dungeons and store-rooms in the solid heart of the drum, and on its surface erected halls and residential buildings. Between them they created a kind of aerial city, a tiny, cool, charming – but above all, safe – little city high above the dusty streets of Rome. An unimpeded walkway ran the whole circuit of the drum and from this it was possible to obtain a dramatic view of the entire city eastward beyond the river, and of the pine-covered hills to the west beyond the walls.

It was here, according to a vivid description of Luigi Guicciardini's, that Pope Clement stood, looking down into the tormented city and then, with streaming eyes, raising his hands towards heaven, intoning the lament: 'Quare de vulva eduxisti me.' And it was from this walkway that Benvenuto Cellini, 'who had always taken pleasure in extraordinary sights', witnessed the tumult in the streets of the Borgo on the afternoon following the imperial break-through.

The speed with which the residents of the Vatican had retreated to the Castle Sant' Angelo had baulked the attackers. Indeed, so precipitate had that retreat been that, when the portcullis was slammed down because there was no room left for any more inside, not only had one person been killed, but also as influential a man as Cardinal Armellino had found himself shut out and had been forced to make that humiliating ascent in a basket. The castle was almost as badly provisioned as it had been nine months earlier during the Colonna raid. The great stone jars which Alexander Borgia had installed and which could hold many months' supply of grain and oil, were almost all empty. The only meat available was that of asses, and even that was in such short supply that it was reserved as a delicacy for the Pope and his eleven cardinals. There were three thousand non-combatants – priests, diplomats, scholars and servants – but fewer than 500 soldiers – some 400 Italians and the ninety survivors of the Swiss Guard. As a result of his brief, enforced sojourn in the Castle during the Colonna raid, Clement had decreed that a bath should be installed in his private quarters: that – with one outstanding exception – seems to have been the sole result of that lesson taught so painfully by Cardinal Pompeo Colonna.

The one exception regarding the unpreparedness of Sant' Angelo was the artillery. This was under the command of the efficient Santa Croce and, from the first, had given so excellent an account of itself that the bulk of the enemy force had remained across the river, dug in behind a line of trenches and hastily thrown-up fortifications. Benvenuto Cellini was a bombardier under Santa Croce's command and from the pen of this bragging, fluent writer posterity receives a most vivid picture of the siege in its first days. None of the stories which Cellini tells loses anything in the telling, particularly not those in which he figures as hero – and they are the majority. But the impression he conveys overall is not that he has invented, but simply that he has exaggerated detail. It was his task to light the three beacons and discharge the three cannon shots each evening at sunset which told the outside world that the Castello Sant' Angelo was still holding out. He revelled in the dramatic task and, so he claims, became a special favourite of the Pope's:

On one occasion the Pope was walking round the circular keep when he observed a Spanish Colonel in the Prata: he recognised the man who had formerly been in his service, and while he was talking about him, kept his eyes fixed on him. I, above, by the Angel, knew nothing of all this but spied a fellow down there busying himself about the trenches with a javelin in his hand. He was dressed entirely in rose colour and so, studying the worst that I could do, I selected a gerfalcon that I had at hand – it is a piece of ordnance larger and longer than a swivel and about the size of a demi-culverin. This I emptied, and loaded again with a good charge of fine powder mixed with the coarser sort: then I aimed exactly at the man in red, elevating prodigiously, because a piece of that calibre could hardly be expected to carry true for that distance. I fired, and hit my man exactly in the middle. He had trussed his sword in front for swagger, after the way these Spaniards have, and my ball, when it struck home, broke upon the blade and one could see the fellow cut in two fair halves. The Pope, who was expecting nothing of this kind, derived great pleasure and amazement from the sight, both because it seemed to him impossible that one should aim and hit the mark at such a distance, and also because the man was cut in two and he could not comprehend how this could

happen. He sent for me and asked me about it. I explained all the devices I
used in firing, but told him that why the man had been cut in halves neither
he nor I could know. Upon my bended knees I then besought him to give me
the pardon of his blessing for that homicide . . . thereat the Pope raising his
hand, and making a large open sign of the cross upon my face, told me that he
blessed me, and that he gave me pardon for all the murders I had ever
perpetrated, or should ever perpetrate, in the service of the Apostolic
Church.

Considering that Cellini's path was strewn with homicides for which he had
felt no overwhelming urge to obtain absolution, his petition here seems
somewhat disingenuous. But a pardon for crimes not yet committed probably
seemed well worth having.

A gallantly conceived, but ineptly executed attempt to rescue the Pope
succeeded only in tightening the cordon around the Castle. The Spanish were
in charge of this blockade and carried out their task with their usual
indifference to the age or sex of their victims. Some small children were
discovered at the foot of the Castle, tying food to ropes for the men above. They
were shot out of hand. Later an old, dim-witted woman was arrested as she was
making her way to the Castle 'with a lettuce for His Holiness' and she was
publicly hanged, her body left dangling to warn any others who thought of
bringing aid and comfort to the besieged.

Hourly the defenders peered out to the north whence their deliverance
should come: at each night, as the flames of Cellini's beacon lit up the statue of
the Angel, despairing eyes were turned again to the north, waiting for the
answering flame of hope. On the third night there was a stir of hope: on the crest
of Monte Mario there burned what appeared to be a beacon but rapidly the
orange glare spread, the smoke rolled down in great black billows. It was no
beacon that was burning but Clement's favourite villa.

And meanwhile, the great army of the League that was supposed to be
marching to the relief of the city was idling down the peninsula as though
bound for a tournament, occasionally halting altogether while the commanders
squabbled among themselves, occasionally even turning aside to take part in
some local feud. Urbino and his fellow commanders were perfectly well aware
of the course of events in and around Rome, for almost every day brought yet
another weary messenger, spurring his lathered horse into the camp to deliver
the latest bulletin of disaster. Like messengers in a Greek drama recording the
development of the tragedy off-stage, they charted the course of the imperialist
march on Rome, the attack, the fall. On 6 May, that bright May Sunday which
saw the imperialists assembling on the Janiculum, a messenger arrived at
Urbino's camp at Arezzo, imploring him to hurry because the landsknechts
were at Viterbo. On the 8, the day when the advance force under Rangone
actually came in sight of the city and then turned back, Urbino was comfortably
at Cortona over 100 miles away, listening to a soldier who had managed to
escape from the city. And on the same day he received the most urgent, most
unequivocal message of all. It was written in Viterbo, forty miles from Rome,

by the Bishop of Motula, Commissary to Clement:

> Illustrious generals of the League. Your Excellencies do not have a moment to lose, for as you will perceive from this letter the enemy have taken the Borgo by assault. Monseigneur Bourbon has been killed by a shot from an arquebus, and a man has just arrived here who was present at the removal of his body. More than 3,000 of the enemy have fallen: Your Excellencies must make haste since the enemy are in the greatest confusion. Quick. Quick, without loss of time.

Apart from its exaggeration of the numbers killed (the total of imperialists killed in action was to be measured in hundreds, not thousands), the Bishop's intelligence was as accurate as it was rapid, in particular his assessment of the enemy's indiscipline. A forced march would have brought the League army to Rome precisely at the moment when the enemy was at their most vulnerable. Instead, Urbino pounced upon the Bishop's statement that the Borgo had fallen: 'If the Borgo is taken, then is Rome in an evil case, even if the city holds out until our arrival!' Equivocal to the end, he did not openly state that the relief of Rome was impossible: he merely let it be assumed that this was the fact.

Francesco Guicciardini, the Pope's Lieutenant-Governor, was with Urbino at the time. Fuming and fretting at the delay, trying all that he knew to prod the enigmatic commander into action, he now virtually despaired of ever bringing succor to Rome. 'The end of it all is that the Pope has been left to his fate', he wrote to Salviati in Paris:

> I need not say whose the fault is. . . . I am no general and do not understand the art of war, but I may tell you what all the world is saying: if, when the news of the capture of Rome had reached us, we had pressed on to the relief of the Castello, we should have released the Pope and his Cardinals and might have crushed the enemy and saved the unhappy city. But all the world knows what our haste has been. You would really think that our object was not the deliverance of this unhappy pope, on whom we all depend, or the rescue of this great city in its death agony, but some trifling matter. So the Pope remains in the Castello, begging for help so earnestly that his entreaties would melt the very stones, and in so abject a state of misery that even the Turks are filled with pity.

At Orvieto, Guicciardini and Urbino had a violent quarrel. The papal governor of Orvieto had absolutely refused to provision the army unless he had assurance that it would march direct to the relief of Rome. Urbino believed – or affected to believe – that Guicciardini was responsible for the governor's refusal and he turned upon the unfortunate statesman, openly accusing him of trying to corner grain and wine in order to make a profit. Enraged, Guicciardini shouted that he was no merchant, that he would pay for provisions out of his own pocket to prove his good faith, and did so.

Slowly the army lumbered on southward. On 11 May Pietro Chiavaluce, one of the gentlemen in Clement's personal service, arrived at the camp. He had actually been confined in Sant' Angelo and had escaped, and was able to give, for the first time, a first-hand account of conditions in the Castle: Clement was being urged to surrender and soon he would have to; were the generals of Italy going to stand idly by while this ultimate shame was put on Italian arms? Two Italian soldiers were moved to make gallant but foolhardy gesture. Federigo Gonzaga, lord of Bozzoli and his friend Count Ugo Pepoli decided to make that ill-fated attempt to rescue Clement. Without consulting their supposed commander, they gathered together a number of like-minded patriots and galloped headlong for Rome, travelling by night. Gonzaga's horse fell, and he broke an arm and a leg. Pepoli and his companions penetrated as far as the Ponte Molle and sent four of their number to reconnoitre in the neighbourhood of Sant' Angelo. They were taken prisoner, Pepoli retreated, and the sole result of the rescue expedition was that the cordon was drawn even tighter around the Castle.

On 22 May, two weeks after Rome had fallen and nearly three weeks since it had left Florence, the army of the League arrived at Isola Farnese, the traditional springboard for an attack on Rome. But of the 25,000 troops who had set out from Florence scarcely 15,000 now mustered to their colours. The rest had deserted, some because they were hungry, some because they lacked all faith in their commanders and some, indeed, to take part in the sack of the city which they were being summoned to protect. Urbino held a council of war and the advice he received could have been but little to his liking. Most of his officers felt that they could still save Rome: their numbers were probably barely half those of the enemy, but they were an organised, compact fighting force whereas the imperialists were now simply a drunken mob. A few days earlier, less than a third of them had gathered to their colours when Rangone's light cavalry had gone skirmishing up to the city walls. They should march now: they should march fast and strike hard. Such was the unequivocal advice given by the officers of the army of the Holy League. And at last Francesco della Rovere, Duke of Urbino and Commander-in-Chief of the army of the Holy League made up his mind: they would retreat.

For the first time Francesco Guicciardini despaired totally, outrightly accusing Urbino of treachery. But there was nothing that an ageing scholar could do. Urbino had the confidence of Venice: without Venice, nothing could be achieved. Therefore, if Urbino said that Rome must be left to its fate, and with Rome its Bishop, there was nothing to be done. And in that manner ended the high and thrilling call to arms of a resurgent Italy. There was no battle, no honourable defeat, just a dreary anti-climax in which some thousands of armed soldiers turned on their heels and began trailing back to the north.

Deep in his heart Pope Clement must have been aware that this was how matters were likely to end. Two weeks before the Army withdrew he began his own tentative negotiation with Orange, the young leader of the imperialist forces. Orange grasped at the opportunity for none knew better than he just how fragile and precarious was the situation of the imperialists. The first signs of plague had appeared in the city and, with it, famine. Even after Rome had been given over to the Sack, peasants had continued to bring their produce into the city, either through stupidity or cupidity. But then the landsknechts had been unwise enough to attack, kill and plunder a caravan entering Rome, and thereafter the peasants of the Campagna had sensibly stayed at home. In Rome now an egg cost more than a human being; for a noblewoman could be bought from her captor for two giulio, but an egg cost six.

Suddenly, too, there was an incredible shortage of money. Hundreds of thousands of gold pieces had poured through the grasping hands of some 20,000 soldiers, but by the first week in June these same soldiers were clamouring for arrears of pay. The words of the fanatical prophet Brandano, who had been adopted as a mascot by the landsknechts, achieved an almost eerie accuracy: 'Dear comrades, now is the time to rob and take all you can', he had adjured them in the first days of the Sack. 'Remember, however, that whatever you take will be taken from you. The property of priests and the spoils of war go as they come.' Much of the booty had disappeared into the hands of the Jews who had their own, well-tried methods of keeping valuables away from greedy eyes and prying hands. Much had been taken out of the city by the cannier soldiers who, having plundered their drunken fellows in games of chance, sensibly took themselves out of Rome. Every part of Rome was squeezed dry – except the great castle of Sant' Angelo. And the soldiers gravitated towards it, telling each other that here was the true treasure house of Rome and that once it was in their power every man really would be rich for life – and have enough to eat now.

Throughout the occupation of the city, the gunners of Sant' Angelo had forced the enemy to keep a very respectable distance. On 31 May, while the Prince of Orange was riding around the trenches, a shot from the Castle killed his mule and wounded him. He was carried into an inn where, in some consternation, the remaining commanders of the army joined him. He had not been a particularly effectual commander but he was the only one they had and if he, too, should die, then their chances of getting out of Rome alive were very greatly diminished. According to Cellini, who naturally claimed to have fired the shot that wounded Orange, the Pope had witnessed the incident and had hastily given orders that every gun that could be brought to bear should immediately bombard the inn, thus killing off the entire command structure. Fortunately, Cardinal Orsini, who had served in arms before taking holy orders, heard of the matter. 'He began to expostulate with the Pope, protesting that the thing ought by no means to happen, seeing that they were on the point of concluding an accommodation and that if the generals were killed, the rabble of the troops without a leader would storm the Castle and complete their utter ruin.' Wearily Clement told Orsini to do as he thought best and the order was countermanded. Cellini, however, 'chafing at the leash' fired off his piece and a furious Cardinal Orsini demanded that he be immediately hanged. This Clement refused to do, less because he was quite so fond of Cellini as Cellini would have the world think, than because he had need of the goldsmith's special skill – for the breaking up of the papal tiara in order to use it for ransome.

The 'accommodation' to which Orsini referred was the negotiations begun, on behalf of the Prince of Orange, by Bartolomeo Gattinara. Despite his sanctimonious reproaches of Bourbon when, far too late to achieve anything, he had attempted to divert the army from Rome, Gattinara seems to have conducted himself more like a bandit than a representative of the Emperor. He received a slight flesh wound when entering the Castle, and Cellini later claimed that 'It was I who shot Iscatinaro when I saw him talking to Pope Clement without the slightest mark of reverence, nay, with the most revolting insolence, like the Lutheran and infidel that he was'. Gattinara was certainly no Lutheran, but he could not have treated Clement with greater disrespect if he had been. During the course of the interview, when Clement protested that he had no money to pay a ransome, the Spaniard actually grasped the Pope's hand and jeeringly drew attention to the enormous bishop's ring upon it.

The treaty which Clement signed on 5 June virtually brought to an end the thousand-year-old temporal power of the Roman papacy. Clement undertook to pay the army the colossal sum of 400,000 ducats in three payments, and gave high-ranking hostages to be held until the entire sum was found. The fact that there was not even a tenth of that sum available in specie was the least of his troubles. He agreed, in addition, to surrender huge tracts of those states of the Church which he and his predecessors had expended so much energy and blood and treasure to maintain. Ostia, Civita-Vecchia Modena, Parma, Piacenza: all were ceded to the enemy. And the Colonna, too, were generously recompensed. Clement had been prevailed upon to receive Cardinal Pompeo Colonna and on 1 June the Cardinal, whose high-vaulting ambition had acted as trigger to this avalanche, and the Pope, whose indecision had caused his city to be swamped by it, had met in a highly emotional interview. The courtly Giovio watched approvingly as his hero and the Holy Father embraced, Colonna lifting his voice in a lamentation as bitter as Clement's. The fact that his tears flowed again did not necessarily mean that he was acting. Colonna, after all, was a Roman, unlike Clement, and what he had seen in these past few weeks had genuinely appalled him. However, the wide-ranging concessions that the treaty of 5 June bestowed upon him went a long way to help dry his tears. Some 20,000 corpses had acted as useful rungs in the ladder of Cardinal Pompeo Colonna's career.

Two days after the treaty was signed, the papal garrison left the Castle. They had served their Holy Father well, these 500 men, the only soldiers to emerge with credit from the whole tragic affair. Cellini went with them to seek his fortune elsewhere. He, too, had served his temporary master honourably according to his lights, as both gunner and craftsman. Years later, indeed, he would suffer interrogation and imprisonment in this same Castle by Clement's successor the Farnese Pope Paul III who was convinced that the master-goldsmith had helped himself liberally to the papal treasure – an accusation which was, for once, unfair to him. As the papal garrison marched out a mixed detachment of Germans and Spaniards marched in. Sebastian Schertlin was among them. 'We found Pope Clement with twelve cardinals in a small room. We took him prisoner. They wept bitterly. We were all moved', Schertlin noted in his laconic style but added: 'Nevertheless, we all became rich.'

But the soldiers were only temporarily satisfied. By raising loans, melting down the papal regalia and stripping the churches of their remaining sacred vessels, Clement raised the first instalment of 100,000 ducats. But after that, it was impossible to raise any more. The governors of the papal cities refused to surrender them from a misguided sense of loyalty to the Pope, and brutal pressure began to be put on Clement. His nerve broke. 'For the love of God do not exact from me promises which, it must be known to all the world, are impossible. So great is my misfortune that the three Franciscans who are with me would be in want of their daily bread if they were not able to borrow money from some compassionate souls.' The hostages were dragged out and threatened with instant execution but there was nothing Clement could do but pray.

The treaty of 5 June, like all the other treaties that Clement had signed, did not affect the situation in the slightest. A few days after that total capitulation, a Spaniard recorded the appearance of an Eternal City that seemed to be little more than an open graveyard inhabited by monsters:

In Rome, the chief city of Christendom, no bells ring, no churches are open, no Masses are said, Sundays and feastdays have ceased. The rich shops of the merchants are turned into stables, the most splendid palaces are stripped bare; many houses are burnt to the ground; in others the doors and windows are broken and carried away; the streets are changed into dunghills. The stench of dead bodies is terrible; men and beasts have a common grave and in the churches I have seen corpses that dogs have gnawed. In the public places tables are set close together at which piles of ducats are gambled for. The air rings with blasphemies fit to make good men – if such there be – wish that they were deaf. I know nothing wherewith I can compare it, except it be the destruction of Jerusalem. I do not believe that if I lived for two hundred years I should see the like again. Now I recognise the justice of God, who forgets not, even if his coming tarries.

So concluded this Spanish moralist, comforting himself for the destruction wrought by his fellow countrymen with the thought that they were, in a way, merely instruments of divine vengeance. 'In Rome all sins are openly committed – sodomy, simony, idolatry, hypocrisy, fraud. Well may we believe, then, that what has come to pass has not been by chance but by the judgement of God.'

But the judgement of God had not yet finished either with his Vicar's city, or with her tormentors. With a certain macabre justice it was the bodies of Rome's citizens which enabled Rome to be revenged upon her conqueror. 'A most grave plague broke out because of the many dead bodies which lie both in the churches and the cardinals' palaces and the Romans' houses. No one has troubled to bury them and they are beyond counting. The stink of their putrefaction makes it impossible to enter the city and those who are in Rome get a mouthful.' The stench was so overpowering that when the wind blew from the city it was almost unbearable to stand on the battlements of Sant' Angelo. The death roll was heavy even in this relatively protected place, amongst the victims being Cardinal Armellino. In the city itself, the landsknechts suffered terribly. Plague was not new to them, but most came from small mountain villages where deaths would be counted on the fingers of one hand and where an energetic man could gain pure air after a few minutes' brisk scramble. They fell victim, too, to that scourge which always took its toll of northern soldiers: 'Many of our men died here of the plague', one of their captains wrote. 'The men drink heavily, become delirious and die – the wine here is very strong.'

Through sheer lust for destruction, the men had contributed to their own fate for they had destroyed the newly restored aqueducts and pure drinking water in Rome was as rare and as precious as vintage wine. Some 3,000 Germans had died by the end of July and at the peak period between July and August the death roll for the city as a whole was probably well in excess of 6,000 a week. In disorderly groups the soldiers withdrew from the city to prey upon the neighbouring communities. They were not sated with slaughter even now. Schertlin, with his brutal honesty, records how some 2,000 landsknechts attacked the little city of Narni: 'We took the town and castle without firing a shot, by God's grace, and then put to death about 1,000 men and women.'

That the attackers now feared disease had brought relief of a kind to the ordinary citizens of Rome. They now had to contend only with famine and bubonic plague and lack of water, troubled by those soldiers alone whose greed or stupidity kept them rummaging still in the city. Clement, however, was denied even this relief. He and his cardinals were quartered in the maschio, that central tower on the drum whose chambers had been built for dead people. A few small windows had been pierced into its walls but the rooms were still dark, airless: almost literally, the Pope and his court were entombed alive. Their captors established themselves in the airy suites of rooms built below the maschio on the surface of the drum. Here, in the halls designed by Sangallo, beneath Pinturicchio's frescoes, Spaniards and Germans caroused, high above the dying city. From his living tomb, Clement could hear the strident voices of the camp-followers, the roaring good-fellowship of their protectors and, not infrequently, sudden yells of anger and clash of arms. The Italians who formed a part of the imperial army were now less and less in evidence, having melted into the background of a country with which they were familiar. For the Spaniards and Germans, this was the end of the road, for they had little hope of making their way back up the peninsula without a resolute commander. The two races loathed each other and, cooped up here high on this stone platform, they released the tension of their boredom and underlying fear through ferocious quarrels which invariably ended in bloodshed.

But the real target of their hatred was the wretched Pope. It was his intransigence, they believed, which kept them all imprisoned in this pesthouse of a city: as soon as he had disgorged his ransome they could all leave for purer airs and happier places in which to spend their fortunes. They therefore put increasing pressure upon Clement. 'The Pope is treated as an actual prisoner', Francesco Guicciardini wrote. 'They have not left him ten scudi worth of property. He is beset daily with fresh demands, and not the slightest attention is shown to his wishes.' In vain Clement protested that he had scarcely money enough to buy food. They mocked him openly to his face, for did not the world know that the treasury of the Holy See was bottomless? And if His Holiness did not actually have the cash available, then let him appeal to his rich friends, the bankers of Venice and Genoa and Florence. The papal bankers managed to scrape together 195,000 ducats by recklessly pledging the income from yet more papal territories, but that was only sufficient to pay the second instalment of the ransome. The Genoese and Spanish bankers who provided that loan saw no reason why they should not make as much hay as possible while this particular sun shone so brilliantly, and they deducted nearly 25% of the loan in handling charges. Thereafter, the barrel was empty and the reluctance of bankers to advance loans to the occupant of Europe's oldest and most stable throne was the chilliest possible sign by which to assess the likelihood of his survival either as Pope or as man. The bankers would have been even more reluctant had they seen their client face to face. Pale, haggard, the cast in his eye ever more pronounced, the once smooth olive skin now drawn like discoloured parchment over stark bones, partly obscured by a grey beard, Clement at the age of forty-nine seemed an old and decrepit man. So alarmed did the imperialists become at his appearance that they offered to move him out to Gaeta but he refused. A wandering pope was no pope. He did, however, request and receive permission to send a special envoy to His Imperial Majesty.

The envoy chosen was Cardinal Alessandro Farnese, known to the irreverent as the Petticoat Cardinal because it had been his sister's adultery with the Borgia pope that had earned him a cardinal's hat. He had, too, an additional claim to fame of a sort, for it had been his son, Pier Luigi, who had made that blackmailing trip around Rome only to be robbed on his way home to the family castle. This was the man whom Clement, with his usual inspired bad judgement, now chose to be his advocate at the court of the Emperor. Farnese, not unnaturally, assented eagerly: each day that passed saw death coming that much nearer to the castle – death from starvation, from plague or from the hands of frustrated and frightened soldiers. Each high-ranking hostage represented a solid investment for them and it was unlikely that there would be a second chance for any of Clement's court. And so gratefully Cardinal Alessandro Farnese chose a mule, and picked a couple of servants and rode down the long, spiral ramp into the sweltering, stinking city and through the city gate and out into the clean, hot air of the Campagna. He headed northward, but got no further than Mantua, for survival was the first tenet in his creed, and he saw no overwhelming reason why he should change the charnel house of Rome for the lion's den of Madrid. Courteously he sent a note to Rome, saying that alas, considerations of health forbade him to continue further on his journey, and sat back to await the development of events. He was a skilled survivor, was Cardinal Farnese, for he managed to balance himself long enough on the tightrope to descend, in the fullness of time, as Pope Paul III.

And Clement, waiting like Noah for the return of his messenger, concluded wearily that yet again he had been betrayed, yet again abandoned, and set about choosing another. His choice fell upon Cardinal Salviati, for Salviati was in France and not having directly experienced the savagery of the Emperor's soldiers might be more disposed to travel to Spain. But Salviati, though an honest man, was also a prudent one and, like Farnese, saw no great attraction in venturing into that lion's den and he therefore wrote his emotional letter to Baldassare Castiglione, papal nuncio at the Imperial Court, putting the responsibility squarely upon that little man's shoulders. It was from Salviati's letter, dated from Paris on 8 June, that Castiglione first heard of the calamity which he had been half expecting for nearly a year.

Chapter XIV

The Throne of St Peter's

On 13 May, six days after Bourbon had met his death and the imperialists had broken into the city, Isabella d'Este slipped out of her palace accompanied by a handful of favoured refugees and hurried through the darkening city to the Tiber. The little party was under the protection of her son, Ferrante, the imperial commander of artillery, and had a strong bodyguard of Italian and Spanish soldiers but, even so, it was thought wisest that the refugees should be disguised. During that mile-long dash to safety Isabella witnessed sights which were to haunt her for the rest of her days. The peak of slaughter was past, but the streets, literally, were littered with corpses beginning to swell with putrefaction; the Roman sunset was killed by the mounting flames of burning houses; and from the darkened alleyways there came the indescribable cacophony that was the requiem for the dying city: the scream of women, some in agony, some in rage, some in diabolical enjoyment; the yells of men in bloodlust, or drunken good-fellowship, or fear and pain – 'the funeral of the city of Romulus'. The escort shouldered a way through the roaming mobs of armed men and brought the frightened little party at last to a landing stage where two galleys lay waiting. Here Ferrante kissed his mother's hand and guided her on board and, as soon as the vessels were safely in midstream, he turned back into the city.

The galleys arrived safely at Ostia at the mouth of the Tiber and there the refugees disembarked and made their way overland to Civita-Vecchia. They were joined there by others fleeing the doomed city. These were, in the main, wealthy and influential people, men and women who had been able to buy their lives and freedom or, at least, been able to persuade their captors to accept their promissory notes. Domenico Venier, the Venetian ambassador, was one of those who gained his freedom in this manner. He had been unable to pay the 5,000 ducats' ransome at which he had been assessed in Isabella's palace and it was only when she personally went bail for him that he was allowed to leave. He had escaped, disguised as a porter. The haughty Cardinal of Trani had considered himself lucky to get out disguised as a muleteer, for he at least had a mount to carry him: the Orsini princes, who accompanied him, made most of the journey on foot. The guise of muleteer was also adopted by the Venetian

nobleman, Marco Grimani. Cardinals, princes, diplomats, bishops, noble-
women, each with some terrible story to tell, flocked into the city that was the
only safe place within reach of Rome, for it was under the protection of the
formidable Genoese fleet. And there, too, came Niccolo Machiavelli despatched by his friend Guicciardini to find out how matters lay. Like Clement,
Machiavelli had aged in these last few weeks. In a little over a month's time he
would be dead and, as bitter prelude, he had to witness now the end of those
high hopes which, scarcely a year before, had seemed to promise a whole new
age for Italy.

From Civita-Vecchia the refugees dispersed to their homes. Burnt indelibly
into their minds was the memory of what they had seen, heard, smelt during
those terrible six days and it was from their accounts that the world first learned
of what had happened to the mother city of Christendom, their emotional
stories fleshing out the bald hastily written reports of professional observers.
The humanists and scholars and artists who had simultaneously created Rome
of the Renaissance and drawn upon it, mourned as for a personal friend. 'Come
here, I implore you, and leave the miserable corpse of our once beautiful
Rome', Pietro Bembo wrote to his friend, the poet Tebaldeo, from the safety
of Venice. Erasmus, that sardonic Dutchman who was not usually given to
emotional outbursts, wrote to his friend Sadoleto: 'Rome was not only the
shrine of Christian faith, the curse of noble souls, and the abode of the Muses,
but the mother of nations. To how many was she not dearer and sweeter, more
precious than their own native land? In truth this is not the ruin of one city but
of the world.' Sadoleto, comfortable in his bishopric of Carpentras, shook his
head sadly for Rome, for the days of Rome were also the days of his young
manhood when he and Bembo and Castiglione and the Lady Isabella and a
dozen other brilliant minds had walked in cool groves, talking and laughing and
building the world anew. 'Alas, those days are gone for ever and the cruel fate of
Rome has darkened all our joy.'

But there was another kind of reaction; a savage rejoicing that emanated not
only from Germanic Lutherans but also from Latin Catholics, particularly
Spanish Catholics. It was to be expected that the Lutherans should regard their
godly soldiers as instruments of divine vengeance: for over a decade now they
had been telling the world that Rome was Babylon, Sodom, the seat of
Antichrist, a sewer and place of evil. The world had taken little note, becoming
ever more accustomed to the baroque extravagance of puritan invective. But it
was a Catholic, Lopez de Soria, who wrote to his Emperor from Genoa: 'The
Sack of Rome must be regarded as a visitation from God who has allowed your
Majesty to become the instrument of his vengeance.' And even if it could be
argued that Soria was a veteran diplomat whose concept of good and evil was
based on expediency, and who was merely concerned to place his master's
action – or lack of action – in a favourable light, the same could not be said of
Alfonso Valdés. He, the Emperor's personal secretary, hastened to develop the
theme in a long and deadly anti-papal invective; and Valdés was no elderly,
cynical politician or drab sectarian but a warm and eager young man, very
susceptible to liberal ideas, yet also a good son of Holy Church. It was he who,

at the burning of Luther's writings in Worms, shook his head over the flames and said: 'This is the beginning, not the end of a tragedy.' The title of his invective now was unequivocal, and later brought him under the shadow of the Inquisition, but it showed how the young were thinking: 'A Dialogue between a Spanish Cavalier and an Archdeacon, showing how the events that took place in Rome in the year 1527 were for the Glory of God and the Universal Good of Christendom.'

News of the destruction of Rome did not reach Charles until 17 June, nearly five weeks after his leaderless army had clawed its way into the stricken city. He did not, at first, seem disposed to weep too many tears for Pope Clement. Life was very sweet for him, for he was not only basking in the honeymoon afterglow of his recent marriage, but his beautiful young wife had just presented him with an heir, the future Phillip of Spain. He was actually on the tilt-yard when the message was brought to him, and though he looked grave at the information that Clement was a prisoner and the imperial troops were on the rampage, he carried on with the tournament. News that was some five weeks old necessarily lost much of its impact.

But the Emperor's attitude had changed by the time Castiglione was granted an audience on the following day, for in the meantime the Spanish clergy had reacted violently. They might hold Giulio de' Medici and Italians generally in very low esteem but Medici was their high priest and they closed ranks firmly and persuaded the grandees to join them in their protest. Whatever might be his private opinion, Charles thought it best to adopt an expression of public sorrow, summoning the foreign ambassadors, declaring that the destruction of Rome had not been his will but a result of the incompetence of Bourbon and the insubordination of his troops. 'We all thought that he said this very heartily', Lee, the English ambassador, reported to Cardinal Wolsey in England. 'Even the Nuncio (Castiglione) with whom we condoled before seeing His Majesty is convinced of the Emperor's good faith.'

Throughout the critical period when the receipt of timely information might have allowed them to avert, or at least modify, the catastrophe, Castiglione had been starved of news. But now that it was too late, it seemed that every post brought news of a fresh tragedy. He learned that his friend, the gay young Cardinal Ercole Rangone, had died of the plague; Giberti, the Datary, was a hostage; Paolo Giovio was mourning the loss of his manuscripts; Fabio Calvi, the gentle, learned old man who had worked so happily and industriously with Castligione and Raphael on that epochal survey of ancient Rome, had been stripped and searched and left for dead, for he had no money for ransome. The endless succession of bad news shattered Castiglione, but fate had not yet finished with him. Sorrow for the loss of dear friends murdered was a commonplace: it was for Castiglione to experience the additional bitterness of ingratitude.

Throughout these beautiful days of early summer in Vallabolid he had worked himself almost to a breakdown, lobbying, arguing, cajoling, threatening, pleading with whomsoever would listen, on behalf of the Pope. It was very largely due to his efforts that the Emperor at last sent an embassy to Rome with the strictest instructions to obtain the Pope's immediate release from prison. Or so at least Castiglione understood, and he sent his own chaplain down that long weary road to Rome bearing a filial letter to the Holy Father, to tell him that all was in train for his deliverance; for the Emperor, more than any other Christian, was His Holiness's humble son and bitterly resented the humiliations that sacriligious hands had placed upon him. However, Castiglione, being himself predominantly a Christian gentleman, overlooked the fact that Charles of Habsburg was both Christian and Emperor, and that while the Christian might sincerely and deeply grieve the insults heaped upon the Vicar of Christ, the Emperor was only too glad to make as much capital as possible from it. Despite the Emperor's personal assurances to Castiglione that Clement's release was imminent, four more months were to pass before the Pope obtained even a limited freedom.

Buried in his living tomb, half-mad with frustration and fear and shame, and seeking the weak man's scapegoat, Clement turned upon the one man who had served him faithfully at great personal cost and who had never, ever, swerved in his loyalty. On 20 August a papal messenger left Rome, bearing a letter for Castiglione in which the Nuncio was viciously attacked. As Castiglione sadly noted, it was 'written in your Beatitude's own name and not, as is usually the case, in that of your secretary'. Clement, who had raised the practice of turncoat to a fine art, outrightly accused the Nuncio of having been bought by the Emperor, and complained that it was his bad advice that had brought about the tragedy, and that he had done nothing whatsoever to make amends. Castiglione rejected the accusation in a long, dutiful, but dignified letter and, in due course, Clement retracted it with grace. But the episode finished Castiglione, contributing in no small measure to his death a year later. The epitaph which Charles spontaneously bestowed upon the man he had admired so much and deceived so shamelessly would doubtless have pleased him more than any other accolade. 'I tell you', said the Emperor sadly, 'the greatest gentleman in the world is dead.'

Almost the same post that brought Charles news of the Sack of Rome brought him a letter which made a mockery of his claims that he regretted what had happened. The writer has never been identified but was certainly close in the Emperor's confidence. 'We expect that your Majesty will give us accurate instructions so that we may know how you intend governing Rome henceforward, and whether some form of Apostolic Chair is to remain or not.' The writer was doubtless only thinking aloud. Further on in his letter he stated politely but firmly: 'I will not conceal from Your Majesty the view of some of your servants who hold that the Sacred Chair in Rome should not be utterly and entirely abolished.' But the fact that he dared place such a subject upon paper argues forcefully that Charles' inner circle of advisers were perfectly well aware of the direction of their sovereign's thoughts.

To abolish the Sacred Chair . . . to dismantle that papal monarchy which for more than a thousand years had striven to dominate Europe and, with Europe, Europe's anointed emperor: this must have been a powerful and enduring temptation for Charles. It would have been so easy, too, to give this drastic political action the appearance of a purely altruistic, religious duty. Generation after generation of Italians had bewailed the existence of the papal monarch. 'It is now more than a thousand years since these territories were given to the priests, and their wars to maintain them have swallowed up more men than live in Italy right now', the Chronicler of Piacenza had written over two hundred years before. And if Italians would have applauded the divorcing once and for all of the spiritual from the temporal power, how much more so would the non-Italian races of Europe, the Germans and the English and the French and the Dutch and the rest, faithful children of Mother Church all of them, but indignant and resentful of the way in which the governance of Mother Church was so hopelessly, inextricably tangled with the affairs of an Italian princedom? Charles, as Holy Roman Emperor was the General of Christ, the Apostle's mailed arm, charged with the duty of protecting the Vicar of Christ – if necessary, from himself; and Charles must long have seen, in his mind's eye, the sword of St Paul descending to sever the chains that bound the Vicar to his corrupting earthly kingdom. But the sword never descended. For gradually there came into focus, in the shifting shapes of the possible political alliances, the portly figure of England's cardinal and the still shapely figure of England's king. Wolsey had almost fallen over himself to come to the aid of Clement, for here was a God-given opportunity to serve his king and bring his own head nearer to a papal tiara, if even a proxy one.

'The affairs of the Holy See are the common concern of all princes', Bluff King Hal trumpeted. 'The unheard-of outrages that See has undergone must be avenged.' Henry's championship was something less than disinterested: the wretched business of his divorce would become even more complicated if the Pope – the only man who could grant that divorce – were the captive of his wife's uncle. Wolsey left England in great splendour on 3 July to attend a great synod in France where the sole topic was the Pope's imprisonment. Forcefully the Englishman pointed out to his continental colleagues that they were in an impossible situation. Canon law placed them totally under the control of the Bishop of Rome, but if that Bishop were himself totally under the control of a Spanish monarch . . . So confident was he, that not merely did he advance the dangerous thesis that Clement should, in effect, abdicate, but also suggested that he, the Cardinal Legate of England, should take on the great burden of the Church during Clement's incapacity. Nobody was fooled for a moment, for Wolsey's soaring ambition was the talk of the hierarchy. Had he not, indeed, boldly put himself forward as a candidate in that election which had produced Giulio de' Medici as Pope Clement? And there were not wanting those who believed that the triple tiara might well sit upon the massive head of the butcher's son from Ipswich. Salviati plainly warned Castiglione of what was afoot in France: 'You know Wolsey's ambition and the bold assurance with which he asks Clement to make him his vice-regent. The French agree because he is useful to them.' This was the spectre which held Charles' sword-arm: if he deposed Clement then infallibly an antipope would come into being. And not just one antipope, but two, three, four, each produced by national need or pride. 'This victory – or rather this massacre of Rome – has been of very little use to the Emperor', Salviati observed sourly. 'On the contrary, it has aroused the princes to greater activity and it is poor Italy that must pay the bill.'

All through that summer Clement had been almost totally cut off from the outside world, his few visitors being closely vetted by his guards. Knight, the English ambassador charged with the little matter of Henry's divorce, found it impossible to obtain an audience. With great courage and no small skill, the Englishman had made his way to Rome and, living there in hourly danger of discovery, had sought fruitlessly for an entry into Sant' Angelo. In September, like some dreadful natural phenomenon, the landsknechts returned to Rome. They had spent their own version of a summer vacation away from the stifling heat and plague-ridden streets of Rome scouring the valley of the Tiber, taking town after town that seemed to be paralysed by their mere advance. It seemed incredible that Rome could yield anything further but, according to Schertlin's laconic account, the landsknechts harvested almost as much gold on this second occasion as on the first: 'In September we re-entered Rome, sacked the city well once more and now first found great treasures under the ground and lay there six months more.' The 'army' was now quite out of control. The command had been offered to the Duke of Ferrara but he had declined outright to be responsible for this 'gang of mutineers', and they ravaged unchecked. They were particularly incensed that the Pope had not yet paid the outstanding instalments of the ransome and demanded that the hostages be yielded up to them. The wretched men were confined like beasts in the Colonna palace of the Cancelleria and became the casual sport of the landsknechts. On three occasions they were dragged out, loaded with chains and, in their once rich costumes now ragged and filthy, forced to shamble behind their captors' horses to the Campo dei Fiori, the landsknechts' headquarters, where gallows had been erected. They endured this treatment throughout the autumn until, probably through the belated conscience of Cardinal Colonna, a plan was evolved for their escape. A number of 'friends' of the landsknechts guarding the hostages arranged for an orgiastic banquet to be held in the palace. Sodden with wine, the guards passed out while the hostages escaped. They avoided the prowling soldiery in the city by scrambling over the roofs and through attics, and at last gained the open country.

The escape of the hostages made matters just that little worse for Clement and those still remaining in Sant' Angelo. There had been a brief lifting of hearts when news had trickled to them that a French force under Lautrec was supposed to be marching south to their aid, but that hope proved illusory. There was such a force, and it was moving southward, charged personally by King François to rescue the Pope. But the French proved no more effective than the Italians. The chaotic condition of Italy made nonsense of any concerted plan of action. The French bypassed Rome to launch an attack upon Naples, the Spanish power-base in Italy, and the strategy was justified in the long run. But it was of little help to Clement in the autumn of 1527.

Lannoy, the imperial Viceroy, was dead of the plague and while Lannoy had not been a partisan of Pope Clement's, he had been a veteran diplomat, able to balance conflicting aims and aim for goals that were a little higher than immediate self-interest or parochial gain. The man who now took his place, Don Pedro de Veyre, was a narrow bigot who loathed Clement and all he stood for. Accompanied by that other Italophobe, Ugo Moncada, Veyre arrived at Rome in October and with relish presented a letter from the Emperor in which the very existence of the Pope was pointedly ignored. Charles simply addressed himself 'To the Romans', explaining how this whole regrettable affair could be traced back to the insensate avarice of the papacy, its lack of both honour and political commonsense. But now the arms of Spain and the Empire were stretched out to raise the recumbent figure of sacred and suffering Rome.

On 26 November Clement signed a peace treaty with the Emperor. It seemed, on the face of it, a remarkably generous offer: not only was Clement to be restored to liberty, but those papal cities and territories that had fallen to the imperialists as booty of war were to be returned to the papacy. In return, Clement merely had to swear to be neutral; and to pay off the outstanding ransome; and to agree to a Council for the reformation of the Church. It was this last clause more than any other that checked his wavering pen. A Council of the Church . . . laymen and subordinate priests setting themselves in authority above the Vicar of Christ . . . ordinary men daring to criticise the actions of he who had been chosen directly by the Holy Ghost . . .? This was intolerable. Yet he signed, for there was nothing else he could do, and in his heart he exculpated himself in anticipation for breaking an oath sworn under duress. Tacitly, he had allowed King François to break a similar oath and he was, surely, entitled to do the same.

More hostages were found for the unpaid ransome; more papal territories were mortgaged to raise something towards that impossible sum; Clement even created another clutch of cardinals – very unworthy men, Guicciardini recorded disapprovingly, 'men of smoke' who saw nothing shameful or incongruous in buying the hat of a prince of the Church under these circumstances; thousands more golden ducats were shovelled across the bankers' tables to disappear into the apparently bottomless pockets of the landsknechts. And Clement felt, reasonably, that he could now claim his freedom. He had been confined to Sant' Angelo since early May, for eight months of horror and privation. From that now claustrophobic platform in the sky even the corpse-strewn streets and charred buildings of Rome itself seemed desirable by contrast. But Moncada and Veyre objected, putting obstacles in the way. They claimed that they would be betraying their trust if they allowed him to depart before the rest of the ransome was paid. So patent was it, though, that the colossal sum still outstanding could not possibly be raised for months, that it was evident that the two men were playing their own personal game. The opportunity of having a pope under immediate and total control had perhaps gone to their heads, filling them with illusions of ever more splendid concessions that could be wrung from him, the spiritual lord of all Europe and the territorial lord of much of Italy.

But at this Luigi Gonzaga revolted. He had, throughout, played a curious, equivocal and unhappy role, epitomising himself the conflicting loyalties and hopes that were sundering the whole society of Italy. As captain of the imperial cavalry he had fought well for the Emperor; but then had found himself forced to levy a ransome on his own mother. He had taken part in the destruction of the papal power as a good Ghibelline should, but now he saw the reality that lay behind those high-sounding words: the reality of a sick and prematurely aged man, once handsome and vigorous, now seemingly palsied with trembling hands and staring eyes. Veyre and Moncada were apparently fully prepared to let the unhappy man rot the remainder of his life away in Sant' Angelo. Gonzaga took direct action to prevent it, arranging for Clement's escape on the night of 8 December.

An eyewitness described this last ignoble scene as Pope Clement VII, Servant of the Servants of God, Vicar of Christ on Earth, Successor of the Apostle, Pontifex Maximus and true inheritor of the mantle of Caesar, scuttled out of the tomb of a Caesar like a hermit crab, exchanging one borrowed shelter for another. It was midnight, very dark and bitterly cold – certainly cold enough to explain the threadbare but voluminous cloak and hood which Clement was wearing, and which effectively hid his straggly grey beard. 'In that ignoble dress he appeared to be a servant, for he carried a basket upon one arm and had an empty sack thrown over his shoulder. And he said to the guards that he had been sent ahead to prepare lodgings for the Pope and his cardinals as soon as they had been freed.' Considering that the guards must have seen Clement almost daily for weeks and perhaps months on end, it is curious that they did not recognise him through his very sketchy disguise. And it was perhaps even more curious that they did not trouble to enquire further as to why His Holiness should be sending a personal servant out at midnight in winter to prepare lodgings which he could not hope to occupy for the foreseeable future. But they let him through. He hurried through the sleeping city to the Vatican, the beautiful palace which he had left so precipitately on that May morning and which was now a forlorn, evil-smelling barracks. Skirting the palace, he made his way through the ruined garden and so to a secret gate in the city wall. Outside, in the so-called Meadows of Nero, Luigi Gonzaga was waiting with a small group of horsemen. They accompanied Clement to Viterbo, handing him over to the astonished garrison, and from Viterbo he made his way to Orvieto.

The Etruscan city of Orvieto, high upon its volcanic spur of rock, had time and again acted as refuge for some hard-pressed pope. Some had stayed only a few weeks, some had dragged out an entire pontificate there, leaving their memorials in painting and architecture and sculpture. Nicholas IV had built the great cathedral there nearly two centuries earlier and other popes had brought their favoured artists to dignify their place of temporary residence: Niccolo Pisano, Fra Angelico, Benozzo Gozzoli each in turn setting his indelible seal upon the place. Clement's contribution, like his contribution of a bathroom to Sant' Angelo, was strictly practical: the architect San Gallo was instructed to create not a palace or a church or even a chapel, but a well. This was a clear indication of Clement's preoccupation with security, his almost pathological need to ensure one refuge in a hostile world. The water-table lay

180 feet down and San Gallo, bringing his skill as architect to bear upon this humdrum domestic problem, created something unique: a well 48 feet wide with a double, winding, inclined plane so that oxen could descend to that great depth and bring up water in barrels. That, at least, was the plan; but San Gallo never finished it, for long before the water table was reached through the rock, famine drove Clement out of Orvieto to Viterbo.

Clement's freedom in Orvieto was only relative. He was again accorded the honours of his position, and the little hill city temporarily became the hub of Western Christianity as ambassadors made their way thither from all over Europe. But the caustic report of two of those ambassadors, Gardiner and Fox, shows plainly enough that, in terms of physical discomfort, Clement was probably worse off than he had been in Sant' Angelo. Prodded by an increasingly anxious Cardinal Wolsey, the two Englishmen had taken up the task entrusted to Knight and, following Clement to his wretched refuge, were trying to force from him a decision about Henry's divorce. They reported:

The pope lieth in an old palace of the bishops of the city, ruinous and decayed, where or we came to his privy chamber we pass three chambers, all naked and unhanged, the roofs fallen down and as one can guess, thirty persons – riffraff and others standing in the chambers for a garnishment. And as for the pope's bedchamber all the apparel in it is not worth twenty nobles.

That Orvieto was ill-provisioned was not really Clement's fault. Never, in his most nightmarish dreams, had he ever considered that he might one day be flying for his life from Rome and he had therefore given no instructions for this city, rather than any other, to be prepared to receive him. Orvieto lay on the main route from Florence to Rome, in the very heart of a countryside that had been preyed upon by two huge armies for over a year. It mattered little to the unfortunate inhabitants that one of the two armies was supposed to be defending them. Both were 'living off the land', the traditional euphemism for the taking of food by violence. The peasants had gone to earth, also in their traditional manner, and the supply of food to all the cities, including Orvieto, had accordingly dried up. All this was to be expected of a country at war; but the desolate picture that the Englishmen reported is that of a totally defeated man: a man with scarcely the will to live, much less to continue to uphold his terrible burden, drifting between one city and another, motivated by the availability of food for himself and his dwindling court, watching with a dull gaze the last act of the tragedy as it swept over Italy.

From the Alps to the Tyrrhenian the land was embroiled in war – but a war without form or frontier. Dominating the struggle were the giant forms of France and Spain, locked still in their combat, though it was evident now that France was buckling. Around their giant feet were played out the feuds of lesser folk, smaller in scale but no less vicious in intensity, for the always precarious equilibrium of Italy had been pushed just too far out of balance, and would not re-establish itself in the lifetime of any of those now engaged in fratricidal battle. Family against family, village against village, city against city, Guelph against Ghibelline; so the ancient curse of Italy was reactivated. Some took the opportunity of setting old scores or making a last desperate bid for freedom: so Florence twitched off, for the last time, the cautiously descending bridle of the Medici, chasing the family into exile, joyously establishing a genuine republic. That stirred Pope Clement at least – deeply, bitterly: there was nothing he could do about it now but he marked his native city down for later attention and vengeance. Spaniards, Germans, French, Italians marched and counter-marched across the face of the distracted land. No man knew where an enemy might appear, or when an ally might suddenly turn and rend for the sake of temporary advantage.   But out of this chaos and agony came Rome's deliverance. The French hurled themselves against Naples, the imperialist stronghold, and the order went out to the imperialists in Rome to march south. Other orders had gone out to the imperialist soldiers in Rome time and again without noticeable effect, but on this occasion they were obeyed. There was really nothing else to be wrung out of the city now, and to speed the parting guests Clement, in Viterbo, somehow found 40,000 ducats. Bitterly Lautrec accused the Pope of financing an attack upon him and it was, in essence, true. Yet Clement, for once, made an effective decision: those 40,000 ducats were just enough to tip the scale for men who were already hankering for wider horizons and fuller purses and cleaner air.

On 17 February 1528, ten months after capturing the city, the 'imperialists' began to withdraw. Of the 22,000 who had smashed their way in on that May morning, there were scarcely 12,000 left – Spaniards and Germans for the most part. The rest were dead, of plague or brawling; or had deserted; or were fighting elsewhere in Italy. The 12,000 men had been sufficient to act as gaolers of one of the great cities of the world, for they had been guarding, in effect, little more than a corpse. Rome's population, on this bright, cold February morning was less than a third of what it had been a year ago: at least 30,000 people had died of hunger, or plague, or violence and almost as many again had fled into exile.

And as the soldiers began to march off, company by company, so, like famished wolves, the Romans began to creep out of their hiding places to slake their long thirst for vengeance. Over the ten months they had learned to live with the impossible, burrowing deeper and deeper into their ancient city, making their homes in the long-buried halls of imperial Rome. Those soldiers who were foolhardy or greedy enough to try and follow them into this subterranean city were cut down, for armour and military weapons were of little value in these dark and winding passages. Thereafter the survivors were left to get on with their own lives. They now emerged like troglodytes to pounce upon a tardy soldier, cut his throat, rifle his pack and away. And even now the soldiers lingered, not really believing their reign was over.

In a merchant's house in the fashionable quarter near the tomb of Augustus there was enacted one of many curious scenes of farewell. The owner of the house, a rich merchant in grain and vegetables, prepared a farewell meal for seven landsknechts who had been billeted upon him. It seems to have been a merry occasion with the merchant congratulating himself on his approaching freedom and plying his 'guests' with wine and the landsknechts planning their own surprise. At the end of the meal they arose, then, drawing their swords, demanded that their host should disclose the treasure which all these months he had kept hidden. In vain he protested that this was an ill way to return his hospitality. They threatened him and he gave way. He had buried a chest of ducats on Monte Testaccio, that extraordinary artificial hill of broken shards that rose from the Tiber near the Ostian Gate, and his son would show them where it was. The lad and his captors embarked in one of the few remaining boats and they swept down the Tiber towards their goal. The moment they were in midstream and in the grip of the Tiber's powerful current, the boy dropped the oars, hurled himself into the river and left the helpless men to be carried to certain death in the downstream whirlpool.

Rather similar was the fate of three landsknechts who had been billeted upon another merchant, Girolamo Baratti. He, too, had prepared a supper to speed the parting guests; he too was menaced by the ungrateful men. In his case, however, there was a genuine treasure, a valuable collection of silver plate stored in a chest and dropped in a well in the courtyard of his house. The landsknechts enthusiastically set about torturing him but obstinately he refused to disclose the existence of the treasure. 'Are you mad?' his wife cried. 'We are young and can collect more – what's the good of being killed now? Tell them it's in the well.' Fuddled with wine, the landsknechts listened owlishly to her instructions and then two of them descended by rope while the third stood guard. He fell, an easy victim, his body being tumbled down into the well to strike his compatriots struggling in the water far below.

Many such stories were to go the rounds after the soldiers had withdrawn. There is a curious consistency, almost that of a folk or fairy tale, about them. Invariably, they concern a group of landsknechts – never Spaniards or Italians – who were inveigled to look for treasure in a particular place and then fell victim to their late victims. There was the baker who enticed his tormentors into his huge oven and then slammed the great iron door upon them after tossing in live sulphur. There was the harlot who persuaded her interrogators to stand upon a rickety table placed over a cesspit – a story straight out of Boccaccio polished up anew for the occasion. Some of the tales might have had foundations in reality but the probability is that the majority were simply devices to save the Roman face. Certainly, if the Romans had displayed a tithe of such ingenuity during the occupation, the soldiery would have been reluctant to return and even more reluctant to stay. But the Romans were ever more prepared to expend ingenuity on the maintenance of appearances, *la bella figura*, than on the reality behind them.

Epilogue

The Return

The evening of 6 October 1528 was unseasonable, cold and dark, with the first rain squalls of autumn spattering the black cobbles. A large, silent crowd had gathered at the open Porta del Popolo, and were peering through the gloom up the Roman road that led to the north. It was still light when the vanguard of horsemen breasted the rise about half a mile from the city wall – light enough to see that the colours they sported were not the cheerful red and yellow of the papal guards but the sombre black and gold of the imperial. Behind them came a handful of the Swiss and in their centre rode Clement, returning to the city eight months after the 'imperial army' of 12,000 bandits had withdrawn.

The advance guard passed through the crowd, looking to neither right nor left, ignoring the sullen silence, like hounds leashed in among game. Their presence here substantiated what had only been heard and half-believed, that the Pope had, in reality if not in name, abdicated and was returning as a puppet of the Emperor's. The strong escort was necessary because war had broken out again, lapping up to the walls of Rome, but this time it was war between Roman and Roman as the Orsini and Colonna families expressed their ancient mutual hatred in a new form. It was necessary to protect the Bishop of Rome from the leading families of Rome and it seemed drably appropriate that the only force available to protect him should be wearing the imperial trappings of the arch-enemy of Rome.

But the sullen silence became a cry of heartfelt welcome as Clement approached, and he responded with sudden tears in his eyes, making the graceful gesture of benediction. He had specifically forbidden any formal welcoming committee of dignitaries, for there was little to rejoice about in the manner of his home-coming, but the spontaneous gesture touched him deeply. The Romans themselves might have been hard put to it to explain just why they gave that welcome to the man who had brought the catastrophe upon them. In fact, their presence at the Porta del Popolo, and the streets leading from it, was the clearest possible demonstration that the Bishop of Rome and the people of Rome were united, at a deeply instinctive level, in a manner that totally defied the rational analysis of outsiders.

The party rode on past the haunted tomb of Nero; on down the handsome new riverside road designed, in another age it seemed, to please Clement's so fortunate cousin Leo; on over the bridge, where the Tiber was flooding yellow-brown with early rains; on past the great bulk of Sant' Angelo soaring up into the gloom. The walkway, from which Clement had watched the crucifixion of his city and implored his God and whence Cellini had directed his murderous fire, was lost in darkness, but the graceful twin pillars of the loggia of Julius I were just visible, giving scale.

Beyond Sant' Angelo lay the forlorn, deserted Vatican. The marble halls and chapels no longer reeked of human and animal ordure, but this city within a city, that once controlled the spiritual and temporal destinies of millions, was virtually dead. Even eight months after the enemy had withdrawn the pulse of Rome beat feebly. Few of those who had fled had yet returned, for armed men were trampling back and forth over the peninsula and Rome had lost, for ever, its sacrosanct nature, its only protection now being its poverty. 'Rome is finished, four-fifths of it quite uninhabited', Francesco Gonzaga recorded in a despatch on the day after Clement's arrival. It was a snap judgement, but probably did not exaggerate greatly, for another report put the total number of houses destroyed at 13,600, perhaps half the total stock. Many of the major streets were still blocked with the debris of destroyed houses and would be for months yet, since there was no labour force to clear them. From the heaps of rubble and from the cellars came again and again the sickly sweet stench of decay from the hundreds of corpses still lying under collapsed walls or hastily interred in shallow graves during the height of the plague. Most of the living were supported by charity, and struggled every day for places in the soup kitchens that had been set up.

No city dies until its last citizen dies or flees. The pulse of Rome had beaten even more feebly than this in the past and had yet recovered. It would recover again, but in a new form. The Florentine Michelangelo sensed this more clearly than any Roman when, six years later, he climbed up his scaffolding set against the bare eastern wall of the Sistine Chapel and began to outline upon it the terrible *Last Judgement*. Above his head was the luminous glory of his Ceiling, that confident product of the years before the Sack when the city had been a treasure house of talent: the arrogant confidence of its people and its rulers then were reflected in those stupendous human figures, mankind raised to its zenith and scarcely to be distinguished from the divine. And from that he turned to the Judgement, where the dominant figure is the cursing Christ flanked by his avenging saints, and mankind is strangled by devils or dragged rotting from graves by indifferent angels.

The century before the Sack saw Rome become a powerhouse of culture. Unable, herself, to create, it had always been Rome's supreme skill to attract creators towards her and use them as instruments of expression. From the time when the energetic little Pope Nicholas V had ascended the throne to that moment when, eighty years later, Bourbon gave the signal for the attack on the walls, the city had been the proxy home for an astonishing range of talents. 'What man, coming to this city, was not tenderly welcomed and cherished on her gentle lap?' demanded Erasmus. 'What stranger from the far ends of earth was not received by her as an honoured guest? To how many was she not dearer, sweeter and more precious than her own native land? And was there anyone who lived in Rome, for however short a time, who did not leave her walls unwillingly, and joyfully embrace the first opportunity of returning there? Who, indeed, is there who does not share our grief, for we have seen Rome taken by a more cruel foe than the Gauls of old and exposed to barbarities unknown in the days of Scythians, and Huns, Goths and Vandals.'

The painters and the scholars, the goldsmiths, sculptors, philosophers, poets and novelists who had delightedly hastened into the city over decades, taking much but giving more, were scattered as though by the force of an explosion. The painter Peruzzi had been first tortured, then forced to paint the portrait of the dead Bourbon, then released only to be captured, again tortured and robbed of what little he had. Giovanni da Udine, tortured and robbed, fled; Caravaggio fled; Maturino was dead of the plague; Sansovino, robbed, fled; Marcantonio Raimondo, the engraver who had earned the wrath of Giberti by illustrating Aretino's pornography, was one of the few able to purchase his immunity and sensibly shook the dust of Rome from his heels for ever. Parmigiano, too, owed his survival to the vanity of a group of landsknechts: he hastily painted their portraits and was allowed to escape.

The writers suffered worse, for they were rarely rich enough to buy freedom with a ransome, nor did they possess a skill which would appeal to illiterate foreign soldiers. The poet Casanova was last seen begging for food before he disappeared, probably falling victim to the plague. The German scholar Göritz benefited not at all by his nationality: he fell into the hands of landsknechts, paid every ducat he possessed in ransome and fled quite penniless to Verona where he died. The humanist scholar Angelo Colocci was twice taken prisoner, twice scraped a ransome together, and watched in anguish as his precious collection of manuscripts was burnt. Angelo Cesi, the lawyer, was dragged from his sickbed by Spaniards and died from his ill-treatment. The Grammarian Julianus Camers committed suicide. Venice was one of the cities which benefited from the mass exodus: Francesco Cherea, one of the favourite comedians of Leo X, fled there and, seeking a livelihood, founded the *Commedia dell' Arte* . . .

So the tale went. Clement was not the brilliant, prodigal patron that his cousin had been; but he was a deeply cultured man and knew as well as any other that something irreplaceable had been destroyed, its components dispersed for ever. Cheer up, was the robust advice sent to him by the swashbuckling Pietro Aretino: 'You should console yourself for all your afflictions, seeing that it is because of the will of God that you find yourself at the mercy of the Emperor, and therefore in a position to experience both divine mercy and imperial clemency.' Clement was scarcely in a position to relish puns upon his name, even though Aretino meant well – he had just written a letter to the Emperor, urging him to succour the fallen Pope.

More effective than the exhortations of this bibulous blackmailer was the gentle remonstrance of the Venetian ambassador Contarini. He had arrived at the Vatican Palace in January 1529 and, according to his lengthy report to his government, he and the Pope had been reviewing the events of the past two years. Clement had referred disconsolately to the total collapse of his papal states and the fact that he was now little more than the Bishop of Rome. 'Your Holiness must not imagine that the welfare of the Church of Christ rests in this little state of the Church', Contarini said respectfully but reproachfully. 'On the contrary, the Church existed before she possessed the State and was indeed the better Church. The Church is the community of all Christians – while the temporal state is only like any other province of Italy and consequently must promote the welfare of the true Church, which consists in the peace of Christendom.'

Clement heard him out patiently enough. Although Contarini did not know it, Clement was about to 'promote the peace of Christendom' by conspiring with the Emperor to attack Florence in order to bring it back under the Medici sceptre. As Guicciardini was to remark scornfully years later, Clement's misfortunes had done nothing to curb his appetite for double-dealing. This man who had been as excellent as lieutenant as he had been hopeless as a leader, whose true skills were those of lawyer, but who fancied himself as prince, now opened his soul to Contarini, displaying the threadbare philosophy for whose sake the great city outside now lay almost mortally wounded: 'I know that you speak the truth', he said at length.

> As a conscientious man I ought to act as you tell me. But I see the world reduced to such conditions that the most cunning is revered as the most worthy of honour, and people say of him who acts otherwise that he is a good-natured fellow but worth nothing, and so he is left alone. The imperialists will first establish themselves in Naples, then in Lombardy and Tuscany; they will make terms with Florence and Ferrara and with you, the Venetians, also, while I shall remain a good-natured man, but plundered to the last farthing and unable to recover anything of my own. I repeat. I see perfectly that the way you point out ought to be the right way, but I tell you also that in this world the idea does not correspond with reality and he who acts from amiable motives is nothing but a fool.

The ghost of Clement's fellow Florentine, Machiavelli, must have smiled sardonically, for here at least was one man who had read and digested *The Prince*. But the Venetian Contarini said nothing and shortly afterwards left the cheerless palace for his cheerless lodgings and took up his pen to write his daily report.

Bibliography

Albèri, E., *Le relazioni degli ambasciatori Veneti al Senato durante il secolo decimosesto*, Florence, 1839–55.

Alberini, Marcello, *I Ricordi* in D. Orano *Il Sacco di Roma Studi documenti* (Vol 1), Rome, 1911.

Aretino, Pietro, *Selected letters* translated by George Bull, London, 1976.

Balan, P., *Clemente VII e l'Italia dei suoi tempi*, Modena, 1887.

Bellay, *Mémoires de Martin et Guillaume du Bellay*, Paris, 1908.

Brandi, Karl, *The Emperor Charles V* translated by C.V. Wedgwood, London, 1939.

Brantôme, P. de Bourdeille de, *Oeuvres complètes . . .*, Paris, 1864–82.

Brown, Rawdon (ed.), *Calendar of state papers and manuscripts relating to English affairs . . .*, London, 1864.

Cartwright, Julia, *Isabella d'Este* (2 vols), London, 1903.

— —, *Baldassare Castiglione* (2 vols), London.

Castiglione, Baldassare, *Lettere de Conte Baldesar Castiglione*, Padua, 1769.

Cellini, Benvenuto, *The Life of Benvenuto Cellini:* translated by J.A. Symonds, London, 1889.

Comines, Philip de, *Historical Memoirs*, London, 1817.

Giovio, Paolo, *La vita di dicenove huomini illustri*, translated by L. Domenichi, Venice, 1561.

Gregorovius, Ferdinand, *History of the City of Rome in the Middle Ages* translated by Annie Hamilton (Vol VIII), London, 1912.

Guicciardini, Francesco, *The history of Italy* translated by Austin Park Goddard, London, 1763.

— —, *Scritti inediti sopra la politica de Clemente VII doppo la battaglia di Pavia* (ed. P. Guicciardini), Florence, 1940.

Guicciardini, Luigi, *Il sacco di Roma*, Cologne, 1758.

Hackett, Francis, *Henry the Eighth*, Lordon, 1946.

Hook, Judith, *The Sack of Rome*, London, 1972.

Louise de Savoy, *Journal*, Paris, 1838.

Luzio, A., *Isabella d'Este e il sacco di Roma*, Milan, 1908.

Machiavelli, Niccolo, *The Discourses* translated by L.J. Walker, London, 1950.

— —, *Opere*, Milan, 1804.

Marck, Robert de la, *Mémoires,* Paris, 1913.

Maurano, Silvio, *Il sacco di Roma,* Milan, 1967.

Mayer, Dorothy Moulton, *The Great Regent: Louise of Savoy 1476–1531,* London, 1966.

Milanesi, C. (ed.), *Il sacco di Roma del 1527: narrazioni di contemporanei,* Florence, 1867.

Pastor, Ludwig, *The history of the Popes from the close of the Middle Ages* (Vols VIII–IX), 1908–10.

Pecchiai, Pio, *Roma nel Cinquecento* (Vol XIII of *Storia di Roma*), Bologna, 1948.

Ridolfi, Roberto, *The Life of Niccoló Machiavelli* translated by Cecil Grayson, London, 1967.

— —, *The Life of Francesco Guicciardini* translated by Cecil Grayson, London, 1963.

Sanuto, Marino, *I Diarii,* Venice, 1879 seq.

Schertlin, Sebastian, *Lebensbeschreibung* (ed. by C.S. von Holzhuber), Nuremberg, 1977.

Seward, Desmond, *Prince of the Renaissance: the life of François I,* London, 1973.

Appendix

Genealogies

I The Claims to Milan
  (a) Visconti
  (b) Sforza

II Gonzaga/Bourbon: Este
  (a) Mantua (Gonzaga)
  (b) Ferrara (Este)

III Urbino (Montefeltre/della Rovere)

I The Claims to Milan

A city of the Empire, Milan was alienated when Giangaleazzo Visconti purchased the dukedom from the Emperor Wenceslas in 1395 for 100,000 florins.

(a) Visconti

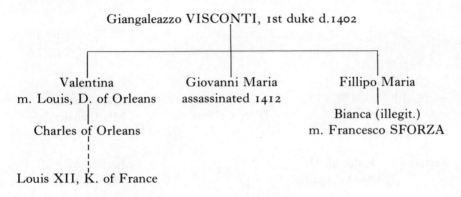

Giangaleazzo VISCONTI, 1st duke d.1402

Valentina
m. Louis, D. of Orleans

Giovanni Maria
assassinated 1412

Fillipo Maria

Charles of Orleans

Bianca (illegit.)
m. Francesco SFORZA

Louis XII, K. of France

(b) Sforza

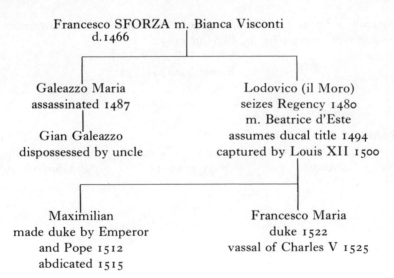

Francesco SFORZA m. Bianca Visconti
d.1466

Galeazzo Maria
assassinated 1487

Lodovico (il Moro)
seizes Regency 1480
m. Beatrice d'Este
assumes ducal title 1494
captured by Louis XII 1500

Gian Galeazzo
dispossessed by uncle

Maximilian
made duke by Emperor
and Pope 1512
abdicated 1515

Francesco Maria
duke 1522
vassal of Charles V 1525

II Gonzaga/Bourbon: Este

(a) Mantua (Gonzaga)

Luigi Gonzaga purchases office of Imperial Vicar from Ludwig the Bavarian in 1329 after he has killed the reigning lord, Bonaccolsi. In 1433 Gian Francesco is created Marquis by Emperor Sigismund.

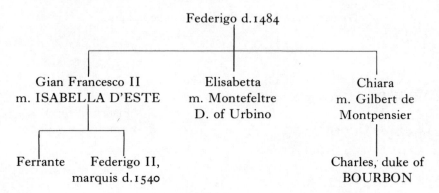

Federigo d.1484

Gian Francesco II
m. ISABELLA D'ESTE

Ferrante   Federigo II,
marquis d.1540

Elisabetta
m. Montefeltre
D. of Urbino

Chiara
m. Gilbert de
Montpensier

Charles, duke of
BOURBON

(b) Ferrara (Este)

Originally a Carolingian house, governors of Este in the Euganean hills. Invested with Ferrara by the Pope in 1329.

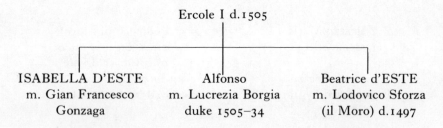

Ercole I d.1505

ISABELLA D'ESTE
m. Gian Francesco
Gonzaga

Alfonso
m. Lucrezia Borgia
duke 1505–34

Beatrice d'ESTE
m. Lodovico Sforza
(il Moro) d.1497

III Urbino (Montefeltre/della Rovere)

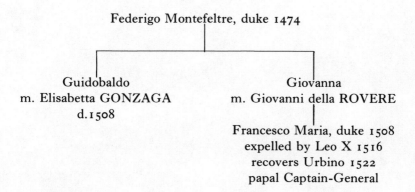

Federigo Montefeltre, duke 1474

Guidobaldo
m. Elisabetta GONZAGA
d. 1508

Giovanna
m. Giovanni della ROVERE

Francesco Maria, duke 1508
expelled by Leo X 1516
recovers Urbino 1522
papal Captain-General

Index